HANDBOOK OF MAMMALS
OF THE NORTH-CENTRAL STATES

The University of Minnesota Press
gratefully acknowledges the publication assistance
provided by Mr. and Mrs. Richard G. Gray, Sr.

Handbook of Mammals
of the
North-Central States

J. Knox Jones, Jr.,
and Elmer C. Birney

Photographs by Roger W. Barbour

Editorial and Organizational Assistance by
Marijane R. Davis

UNIVERSITY OF MINNESOTA PRESS □ MINNEAPOLIS

Published by the University of Minnesota Press,
2037 University Avenue Southeast, Minneapolis, MN 55414.
Published simultaneously in Canada
by Fitzhenry & Whiteside Limited, Markham.
Printed in the United States of America.
Designed by Gwen M. Willems.

Library of Congress Cataloging-in-Publication Data

Jones, J. Knox.
Handbook of mammals of the north-central states.
Bibliography: p.
Includes index.
1. Mammals – Middle West. 2. Mammals – Middle West –
Identification. I. Birney, Elmer C. II. Title.
QL719.M56J65 1988   599.0977   86-4302
ISBN 0-8166-1419-9
ISBN 0-8166-1420-2 (pbk.)

The University of Minnesota is
an equal-opportunity educator and employer.

Contents

HANDBOOK OF MAMMALS
OF THE NORTH-CENTRAL STATES

Introduction

The north-central states – Minnesota, Iowa, Wisconsin, Illinois, Michigan, Indiana, and Ohio – form a large and ecologically diverse area lying south of the western four Great Lakes and west of the Appalachian Mountains. Biologically, this region is characterized by relatively high rainfall and sharply defined seasons, which in presettlement times produced a mixture of coniferous and deciduous forest and grassland. The area was settled from east to west by annual waves of European immigrants and eastern seaboard settlers wishing to seek their fortunes in the fertile areas west of the mountains. Settlement and its associated habitat alteration were especially intense during the first half of the last century. By the time of the Civil War, all seven states had achieved statehood, and the region represented the western part of the Union. Today they retain commonality as the states of the Big Ten universities, and they continue to share political, economic, and social bonds.

With the exception of the northern parts of the three northernmost states – Minnesota, Wisconsin, and Michigan – the north-central region is relatively heavily populated (about 50 million people living on 388,640 square miles of land, a mean density of 130 people per square mile, with more than 50 percent of the population congregated in urban settings). Included in the several major metropolitan areas are Detroit, Cleveland, Cincinnati, Indianapolis, Chicago, Milwaukee, Des Moines, and Minneapolis-St. Paul. Perhaps of greater importance than large metropolitan areas to the mammals of this region is the relatively high human density in rural environments, especially in heavily agricultural areas such as Indiana, Illinois, Iowa, and western Minnesota. In such places, scarcely an acre can be found today that is not plowed, mowed, or grazed annually. Even the forested portions have felt the impact of human settlement through extensive logging, mining, and recreational use.

Despite the massive direct and indirect effect of European people on the

3

environments of the north-central states, the area continues to support a large mammalian fauna, including at least 88 native species that one can expect to find today. This number is in addition to the several species that existed there prior to settlement but since have disappeared, or at best occur only occasionally. Two species of free-tailed bats have been taken as distant wanderers from established populations well to the south or southwest. In some cases, species have managed to reestablish themselves (for example, the beaver), have been reintroduced with limited success (the wapiti), or seem to "hang on" just outside the area and occasionally wander in or near the periphery (the caribou). Some species (for example, the Virginia opossum) have significantly expanded their distribution in the region as habitats have been altered by humans. In addition to the impact that settlement has had on the native mammals, wild individuals of five non-native species have been taken in the region. Two of these (the Norway rat and the house mouse) are ubiquitously distributed, usually in close association with humans.

It is the purpose of this handbook to present a brief summary of the biology and current status of the 99 native and five introduced species that either occur in the north-central states today or are known to have lived there at the time of initial settlement. In addition to the written summary, each species account includes a photograph of the animal and, except for extirpated species, a distribution map showing where the species currently exists within the seven-state area and an inset of its historically documented distribution in all of North America. Keys to aid in identification are provided for all species covered.

This effort was planned from the beginning as a handbook for use by field personnel and others who need a basic introduction to mammals and means of identifying them. Introductory comments and accounts of species have been held to what we judge as a minimum to be meaningfully complete without allowing the handbook to become too large to be carried in the field or so expensive as to be beyond the budget of anyone interested in mammals.

Fortunately, although mostly of large size, frequently highly priced, and in some cases somewhat outdated, there are good summaries of varying scope of the mammalian faunas of each of the seven north-central states. We have used these references liberally in preparing accounts of species. The most recent publications dealing with each of these states are, for Illinois, Hoffmeister and Mohr (1957); for Indiana, Mumford and Whitaker (1982); for Iowa, Bowles (1975); for Michigan, Baker (1983); for Minnesota, Hazard (1982); for Ohio, Gottschang (1981); and for Wisconsin, Jackson (1961). Moreover, mammals occurring in the United States east of the Mississippi River were treated in a book by Hamilton and Whitaker (1979), and Burt's (1957) *Mammals of the*

Great Lakes Region covers much of the area of the north-central states and adjacent Canada.

We also took into account faunal works on mammals in states and provinces adjacent to the north-central region as follows: Banfield (1974)–Canada; Barbour and Davis (1974)–Kentucky; Doutt et al. (1966)–Pennsylvania; Jones et al. (1983)–Dakotas and Nebraska; Peterson (1966)–eastern Canada; and Schwartz and Schwartz (1981)–Missouri. For detailed information on the orders and families of living mammals, the reader is directed to Anderson and Jones (1984), and for data relating primarily to genera, to Nowak and Paradiso (1983). The two-volume work by Hall (1981) on mammals of North America as a whole is recommended for distributional records, systematics, and drawings of crania and lower jaws, as are Eisenberg (1981) for general mammalian evolution and Vaughan (1986) as a good mammalogy textbook. Scientific and vernacular names of species follow Jones et al. (1986).

Organization

In preparing this handbook, it was our goal to provide a concise yet authoritative reference to mammals and the environments in which they live in a seven-state region of the north-central United States. The environmental setting and zoogeographic patterns are discussed as an introduction to accounts of individual species of mammals occurring (or that occurred in historical times) within the north-central region. A typical species account is limited to one page of text; thus, it was necessary to select carefully the information presented for each taxon and yet to be as complete and accurate as possible. With this in mind, readers are urged to peruse accounts of related species–all bats of the genus *Myotis*, for example, or all shrews or voles or mustelids–because basic information applicable to all species of a group may be found in only one such account. This arrangement was necessitated by space limitations, and we hope that knowledgeable readers will sympathize with us in our decisions of what to include and what to exclude from accounts, particularly those of well-known species.

The introductory sections of the handbook are followed by a checklist of mammals of the north-central region, arranged in currently accepted phylogenetic sequence by order, family, and genus; species names are entered alphabetically in each genus. Species are treated in text in the same order as in the checklist except for *Rangifer tarandus*, which is slightly misplaced because of space considerations, and introduced taxa, which are listed in a separate section. Also, accounts are restricted to the species level except for the two noninterbreeding subspecies of *Peromyscus maniculatus*, which are entered separately. The checklist is followed by a key to mammalian orders.

The following chapters are grouped by mammalian order, with brief introductory remarks and keys preceding the accounts of species. In two instances (Rodentia and Carnivora), keys are broken down by family because of the large number of included kinds of mammals. Technical terms used in keys and text are described in a terminal glossary. In constructing the keys, we tried whenever possible to include both external and cranial or dental characters. Users of keys should be aware, however, that characteristics, especially those relating to measurements, weights, and pelage, are of typical adults and may not apply to young animals. Furthermore, it may be necessary to have a cleaned skull, sometimes under magnification, to appreciate characters of the skull and teeth. It is important to use keys, descriptions of species, distribution maps, and photographs of mammals together in the identification process.

One mammalian species that is native to our region is not admitted to the checklist nor covered in an account, even though it has resided in the seven states for perhaps 13,000 years, and especially in the past 200 years has substantially modified environments and, directly or indirectly, impacted the distribution, abundance, and patterns of gene flow of every other mammal found there. *Homo sapiens*, the only native primate, is mentioned often in our discussion of environments and in some species accounts, particularly those of larger mammals. We thought it futile, even nonsensical, to attempt to write a one-page account of modern man, our own complex species.

For each native species treated – except for those extirpated from the region within historical times, the two species of *Tadarida*, and two of the three species of *Blarina* – the summarized information is divided into the four categories of Distribution, Description, Natural History, and Selected References.

Distribution. Here is provided a statement of the general (including former) distribution of the species and an indication of its range or status in the north-central states. The facing map (except for extirpated species) depicts current distribution in the region; an inset map shows the historically documented range in North America.

In preparing maps, we consulted the authorities cited earlier in introductory remarks. Inset maps generally follow those of Hall (1981).

Description. An indication, in telegraphic style, is given of the general characters of each species, such as size and color, with special reference to those that distinguish it from closely related taxa. Ranges of measurements given are those typical of adults in the north-central states (thus not necessarily absolute extremes) and are in millimeters in the usual sequence (total length, length of tail, length of hind foot, and length of ear from notch). Weights are in grams or, for larger mammals, in kilograms. Length of ear is excluded for insectivores, because their ears are small and inconspicuous, and length of forearm is included for bats. A photograph of each species appears on the page facing the account.

Natural History. This section provides information relative to habitats preferred or tolerated by a species, activity patterns, population densities, retreats, food habits, reproduction, and the like. Because of space limitations, some aspects of biology—molt, predators, parasites, longevity, and so forth—may be given for only one or a few related species by way of example.

Selected References. In this section, one to five citations to important publications relating to each species are given, with special reference to the north-central region. If a current Mammalian Species account (published by the American Society of Mammalogists and intended to be a concise summary of the biology of an individual species, complete with literature citations) is available, it frequently is the only reference entered. In any event, the citations should guide the interested student to much of the pertinent literature dealing with the species in question.

In canvassing publications for compilation of this handbook, we tried to take into account all relevant work that appeared through the end of 1984. A few citations dated 1985 and later also will be found.

Following the accounts of native mammals, there is a short chapter on introduced species and those of possible occurrence in the region, a glossary of terms used in mammalogy, a listing of the references cited in text, and an index to vernacular and scientific names of mammals.

Acknowledgments

As noted on the title page, Roger W. Barbour of the University of Kentucky arranged for most of the photographs used herein and Marijane R. Davis of Texas Tech University provided valuable organizational and editorial assistance. Most of the photographs were taken personally by Dr. Barbour; credits to other photographers are in the legends to individual figures and we thank them collectively here.

Many colleagues and co-workers contributed in one way or another to the completion of this manuscript, and we are mindful of their assistance. We should mention especially Robert C. Bright of the University of Minnesota for his helpful suggestions on introductory sections and Gerda Nordquist of the University of Minnesota and Elizabeth M. Jones of Texas Tech University for reading and commenting on species accounts. Charles A. Long of Wisconsin State University at Stevens Point kindly checked a number of distribution maps for us.

Clerical assistance was provided by Dorothy Bromenshenkel, Diane Conde, Caroline Franke, and Susan Walz of the University of Minnesota and Patricia Propst, Mary Ann Seaman, and especially Shirley Burgeson of Texas Tech University. Don Luce and Carlyn Iverson of the University of Minnesota and Diane Tucker of Texas Tech University assisted with the preparation of illustrations. Nicky L. Olson of Texas Tech University was helpful in reproduction of photographs for use in the text.

ENVIRONMENTS OF
THE NORTH-CENTRAL STATES

Environments of the North-Central States

Environmental-Evolutionary Perspective

The environment of a mammal (or any other organism) typically is highly dynamic and all inclusive. The physical environment includes everything from the temperature and the soil to the presence or absence of food species, predators, places for retreat, and the like. The social environment of a mammal may be equally important. For example, if a male black bear in July crosses the track of a female in estrus, he will follow that trail, but his probability of ultimate success depends on whether he finds the female alone or accompanied by one or more other adult males. Similarly, a two- or three-year-old lone male wolf will search for an area where he can take up residence, perhaps the little-used area between two resident packs. If wolf density is high and pack territories small, with peripheries frequently visited, the lone wolf must keep moving, and his life is in serious danger if he is detected by a resident pack. That is one social environment, but now consider an area of low density where packs are small, territories are large, and territorial peripheries are infrequently visited. This is quite a different social setting, and the chances of the male attracting a female and together scent-marking and defending a new territory between the original two territories are good. In areas of low density, nearly every wolf two years of age or older is an alpha animal in its own pack and thus has breeding status (Fritts and Mech, 1981). Conversely, wolves of three or even four years of age in an area of high density must either endure a lower social rank and not breed or they must disperse long distances, often to the margin of the habitable range of the species, to establish a territory and attract a mate. Here, of course, they often come into direct conflict with humans and have little chance to survive, let alone to reproduce. The point is that, although the physical environment is of fundamental importance, the so-

11

cial environment may be equally important to the individual mammal, determining what it does, where it moves, and whether it is able to breed. With only these two examples, we leave the topic of the social environment – not because it is uninteresting or unimportant, for obviously it is neither. The social environment affects individuals within populations, however, and our focus is that of the entire species and the distribution and natural history of populations that make up each species.

Our particular scope notwithstanding, we hope it never leaves the mind of the reader that each and every population is in fact made up of individuals. Furthermore, each individual attempts to secure more than its "fair" share of resources, to live longer than its conspecifics, and to convert resources acquired from its environment into progeny. The result is the perpetuation of genetic material of those individuals that are successful in their physical and social environments and the loss of genetic combinations that are unsuccessful. That message, stated here in its simplest possible form, was Charles Darwin's great insight, and none more powerful exists in all of biology. Darwin and his contemporary, Alfred Russel Wallace, were the first to realize that all organisms, from bacteria to humans, are playing the same game – garner resources and convert them through reproduction into offspring that perpetuate successful genetic material (the nucleic acids) on to the next and subsequent generations.

Equally important, of course, is the fact that a given combination of genetic material only can be successful (that is, result in reproduction and hence perpetuation) within a certain environmental range. Extinction or local extirpation results when the environment changes so rapidly or so greatly that individuals of a species or local population are unable to continue this cycle of life. Such an environmental change may take any of a number of forms, from something as insidious as the introduction of a toxin like DDT that slows or stops reproduction, or the activities of hunters or trappers with no concept of wildlife management (as probably happened to several large mammals late in the Pleistocene and again when Europeans settled this country), to well-intentioned farmers plowing native prairie, draining a wetland, or grazing a woodlot and thus modifying the environment so that other species find no food or are exposed to predators. Some environmental perturbations may make it possible for a species to expand its distribution, perhaps into the range of a prey species, a predator, or a competitor. This, in turn, is an environmental change for each affected resident species, and the results may be varied.

If environmental changes are gradual enough, some species can modify their way of life by, for example, shifting food habits, feeding times, or selection of nest sites, and thus persisting. In the newly changed environment, a slightly modified combination of genetic material (acquired by mutation, gene flow, and the natural shuffling of gene combinations that takes place every generation in sexually reproducing organisms) may produce individuals that are relatively more successful, more *fit* (as measured by reproductive performance), than those produced by previously successful genetic combinations. If so, the genetic material that is passed on will be different, on average, from generation to generation. Any such change in the genetic constitution of organisms through time is biological evolution. The evolutionary process has been going on continuously on earth since the inception of life, and it has resulted in the present flora and fauna of the world. The fundamental relationship between environment and evolution is elegantly articulated in a brief essay entitled *The Ecological Theater and the Evolutionary Play* by the renowned ecologist G. Evelyn Hutchinson (1965).

For mammals, the evolutionary continuum of genetic material passed through invertebrates, fish, amphibians, reptiles, and finally to the Mammalia. The fossil record of mammals dates back about 200 million years. Early mammalian evolution is discussed in several of the references cited previously, especially Vaughan (1986) and Eisenberg (1981). Excellent coverage of mammalian evolution up to the Paleocene (65 million years before the present) is presented by Lillegraven et al. (1979). Since the early Paleocene, both marsupial and placental mammals have radiated greatly; some lineages became extinct, whereas others held their own or diminished slowly, and yet others met with great success and radiated repeatedly (see Dawson and Krishtalka, 1984). The result of millions of years of environmental change–the ever-dynamic and worldwide environmental theater–has been the evolutionary play acted out by every individual mammal of every species that existed during that period, right up to present time. One portion of the theater–the environment of the seven north-central states–is discussed below in historical perspective. The play itself is most difficult to observe at any given time, although we often see and study the actors, which of course are represented by the mammals discussed in the accounts beyond.

Ecosystem Approach

Ecosystems are the total of all of the physical and biological attributes of a given area. They are driven by an energy source, which for nearly all ecosystems is the sun. Light energy from the sun is utilized by green plants to convert simple, low-energy molecules, such as water and carbon dioxide, into high-energy molecules, such as sugar and cellulose. Plants, being autotrophic, are the primary producers of an ecosystem. Their parts (seeds, leaves, stems, and even roots) may be viewed as concentrations of energy and nutrients essential to the maintenance of life through respiration, successful reproduction, and growth of animals. Herbivores, be they insects, birds, or mammals, feed on plants as a means of making energy and nutrients available to themselves and their offspring. Organisms of this second trophic level of the ecosystem are referred to as primary consumers, and it is this level that includes many of the mammals we cover herein. Feeding on primary consumers are secondary consumers, feeding on them are tertiary consumers, and so on. But, in actuality, ecosystems are more complicated than these terms imply because few if any carnivores feed on animals of a single trophic level; in fact, most mammals feed at more than one trophic level.

The ecosystem approach is valuable because it leads to many predictions and insights for the amateur naturalist, the professional field biologist, and the theoretical ecologist alike. We know that through respiration, for example, energy is used by every individual through which it passes, and thus relatively little energy is left for secondary and tertiary consumers. Thus we might predict that the number of species or of individuals, or both, of higher level consumers in an ecosystem would be low. Field studies of mammals mostly support this prediction. But suppose we predicted that because there is little available energy at higher trophic levels, organisms of these levels would tend to be small? Then we must go to the field and determine whether or not nature supports our prediction. For mammals, this hypothesis seems not to be supported, as we find the tiny least weasel at one extreme and the wolf and mountain lion at the other. Perhaps an alternative hypothesis would predict that instead of being correlated to trophic level per se, body size of mammals at higher trophic levels is related to the body size of their prey. And so it goes, the mammalian ecologist looking at nature, at theory, developing hypotheses or predictions, and then going back to nature for the empirical data to conduct the test. This has been a highly productive approach for mammalogists and ecologists, and it has led to our current level of understanding of both ecosystem function and mammalian biology.

In an ecosystem, energy and nutrients flow from one trophic level to the next, and eventually what remains becomes available in the form of feces or carcasses to the decomposers—that is, the bacteria and fungi that use the last of the available energy for their own respiration and reproduction. Decomposition makes the original nutrient molecules available once again to primary producers. Nutrients thus cycle through the system and may be part of the living or the nonliving component of an ecosystem at any point in time. Energy, however, is eventually used and lost from the system, and thus instead of a cycle we refer to its movement through an ecosystem as energy flow.

All of the living organisms of an ecosystem may be referred to as the biological community, or simply the community. Mammals are a part of most communities of the north-central states. Beaver, otter, and muskrats are a part of most aquatic ecosystems, and all natural terrestrial communities include at least three or four kinds of mammals. Even regularly tilled agricultural fields can and do support a mammalian community at certain times of the year, primarily from the time after the crop provides cover and food, or both, until after the residue has been plowed under in preparation for the subsequent crop. Cropland farmed by modern no-till methods may support a mammalian community year-round. For an excellent discussion of mammalian habitats and community composition of mammals in one of the north-central states, Indiana, the reader is referred to pages 29–47 in the book by Mumford and Whitaker (1982).

What determines the composition of mammalian communities? The answer, of course, is far too complex to address here or even in a full-length book just on that question, but some generalizations can be made. For example, there undoubtedly are some mammals in Europe today that would be successful in the north-central region if they could get there, but an ocean and considerable continental mass deny them that opportunity. Assuming opportunity, our hypothetical species still must have access to usable resources such as food and cover. Not even access is sufficient, because the species must be able to compete with others in the community to get an adequate share of available resources and thus maintain a viable population. Furthermore, the community must not contain some intolerable chemical that causes death or inhibits reproduction and no predator or parasite that is so efficient at getting its own energy from the species that it cannot reproduce rapidly enough to persist. In temporally variable ecosystems, such as those of the temperate north-central states, our species must be capable of either surviving the lean times or going elsewhere. For example, some bats and rodents hibernate and some bats migrate south for the winter. In sum, the answer to our question probably involves opportunity, chance, and a whole series of adaptations for dealing with the complexities of each specific environment.

Ecosystems by definition have biotic and abiotic components, and each also has its own unique history. In the following paragraphs, we have attempted to describe the north-central region, with emphases on how the area came to be as it now is and how its present mammalian fauna lives and is organized today.

Geologic Past

The physical environments within the north-central states may be likened to a single frame of a long film focused on the ever-dynamic ecological theater. What of the long history of this region? How did the array of environments encountered by our current mammalian fauna come into being? Geologists, physiographers, paleoecologists, and scientists of many other specialties have searched for the answers to these and related questions with remarkable success during the past century. Despite their successes, many questions remain unanswered, and some of what appears as truth today undoubtedly will be called into question tomorrow. What follows is an overview of the total information available in the references cited and elsewhere in the pertinent literature.

Estimates of the age of the earth range from less than five billion years to about 20 billion years. Most estimates place the age of first life on earth at about 3.5 billion years. Some of the oldest crustal material on the planet can be found exposed in western Minnesota. About 3.6 billion years old, the Montevideo Gneiss is a metamorphic rock that originated as granite (Ojakangas and Matsch, 1982). Some of the rocks exposed near Lake Superior are of similar age. These, however, are part of the continental shield. Every continent has a nucleus of ancient Precambrian rocks referred to by geologists as a *shield*. For North America, this is the Canadian Shield, which covers most of northeastern Canada and extends south well into both Minnesota and Wisconsin. Much of North American history from 3.6 billion until 600 million years ago is documented within the shield. For example, portions of the north-central states experienced extensive mountain building about 2.7 billion years ago and again at 1.8 billion years, and volcanism was commonplace 1.1 billion years ago. The most recent episode of mountain building in the area was approximately 225 million years ago, when the Appalachians were formed. The present rugged terrain in the unglaciated portions of eastern Ohio owes its origin to this ancient geologic activity. But what became of the earlier mountains? In a word, the answer is erosion, especially that by the never-ending action of running water. Furthermore, deposits of rocks dated at 2.1–2.4 billion years from southeastern Wyoming, the Upper Peninsula of Michigan, and at least three locations in Canada appear to document the earth's oldest glaciation, which undoubtedly helped to level the landscape at that time (Ojakangas and Matsch, 1982).

About two billion years ago, a unique event took place at a few widely separated places in Australia, South America, Russia, Africa, and in three states of the north-central region: the world's major iron deposits were formed. Just why this event was synchronous but limited to a single period worldwide is not known, but it may well have involved the shift from high levels of atmospheric carbon dioxide to high levels of oxygen that resulted from the early evolution and radiation of green plants. However they formed, it was of immense importance to the industrial and agricultural revolutions and thus to nearly every aspect of life as we now know it. Furthermore, little-used and abandoned iron mines today serve as important hibernation sites for some bat species, including several species of *Myotis* and *Eptesicus fuscus*. In the north-central states, major iron ranges are the Gunflint, Vermilion, Mesabi, and Cuyuna ranges in Minnesota, the Gogebic Range in Wisconsin and Michigan's Upper Peninsula, and the Marquette and Menominee ranges and the Crystal Falls-Iron River district of the Upper Peninsula of Michigan. According to Ojakangas and Matsch (1982), all of these deposits appear to have been laid down near the shore in shallow waters of a large, ancient marine basin.

Plate tectonics and seafloor spreading are well known today, at least in a general way, to geologists and biogeographers the world over. Such names as Gondwanaland, Laurasia, and Mid-Atlantic Ridge are readily recognized, their mere mention conjuring images of the gradual breakup of Pangaea some 200 million years ago. Perhaps not so well known is an episode powered by the same forces some 1.1–1.2 billion years ago that nearly subdivided North America. At that time a rift formed that extended from about what is now eastern Lake Superior to what is now Kansas. For several million years fluid basaltic lava welled up in this zone, pouring copious quantities of lava onto the land. The result was not an ocean, as it would have been had the activity continued. If North America had been divided by this rift, however, the present mammalian fauna of Wisconsin and eastern Iowa might bear no greater resemblance to that of western Minnesota and northwestern Iowa than we see between the faunas of Europe and North America.

North America can be divided into five great physiographic provinces (Judson et al., 1976). One of these, the Laurentian Upland, encompasses almost the exact area of the Canadian Shield. In the north-central states, the Laurentian Upland includes roughly the northern two-thirds of Minnesota, the northern third of Wisconsin, and the Upper Peninsula of Michigan. The westernmost North American physiographic province, the Western Mountains, lies far to the west of the north-central region, but all three of the remaining provinces are present. The Appalachian province, which includes the eastern two-thirds of Ohio, originated with the uplift of the Appalachian mountain range. The Coastal Plains lie mostly to the south of the north-central states, barely extending into the southern part of Illinois. The Interior Plains and Lowlands cover the remaining part of the north-central region. It is the formation and history of this great expanse, which encompasses the vast majority of our area, that we turn to next.

Sedimentary rocks of the Interior Plains and Lowlands were deposited during the Paleozoic Era. They are much younger than the ancient igneous, metamorphic, and sedimentary rocks of the Laurentian Upland. Much of the North American continent underwent a slow subsidence during the early Paleozoic, when the oceans advanced and the continental interior, which previously had been above sea level, gradually became part of the seafloor (Ojakangas and Matsch, 1982). Although this was by no means the first time that seas had covered this region, nor the last, it was the first time that they contained a rich assemblage of organisms.

The subject of origin of these "suddenly complex" organisms is beyond the scope of this book, so let us simply point out that radiation of complex life forms almost certainly was made possible, perhaps even inevitable, by the initial evolution of chlorophyll and thus the origin of green plants. These organisms were capable of converting light energy into biologically usable energy in the form of organic molecules. At the same time, they gradually shifted the equilibrium of carbon dioxide and oxygen in the atmosphere. Either of these events would represent an environmental change of staggering potential. Together they created a multitude of ecological niches when oxygen-intolerant organisms either became extinct or gradually evolved oxygen tolerance and when both the amount of biologically usable energy and the size of energy-rich molecules increased dramatically as more complex plant species evolved. Given the new availability of organic molecules formed by these early autotrophs, it was possible for heterotrophs to become more abundant and more diverse as they took advantage of these new resources, still about 300 million years before the first mammals appeared.

Throughout the Paleozoic and Mesozoic eras, the interior of North America was subjected to broad, gentle subsidence and uplift. The seas withdrew as the region uplifted, terrestrial communities formed, and erosion by running water carried some of the surface into the existing seas. Each uplift was in turn followed by a period of subsidence and a return of the sea. Each return of the sea brought a somewhat different floral and faunal assemblage than the previous inundations. The last transgression of the sea into the continental interior occurred about 100 million years ago in the mid-Cretaceous. The eastern shore was highly irregular and of gradual slope, passing from what is now northern Minnesota through Iowa and on into Texas. Late in the Cretaceous, this final great epicontinental sea withdrew, and all of the north-central region has subsequently remained above sea level (Ojakangas and Matsch, 1982).

During the early Paleozoic, North America was situated in such a way that the north-central region was tropical, even partially or wholly in the Southern Hemisphere with the equator just north of, or passing through, the region at any given time (Ojakangas and Matsch, 1982). Late in the Paleozoic, however, North America began to move northward; by the end of the Cretaceous (65 million years ago), the equator passed through northern South America and the north-central states, now with a rich terrestrial mammalian fauna, were far to the north. At this time, the vegetation of the north-central region included a variety of plant groups, including ferns, conifers, and deciduous trees.

As the last Cretaceous sea withdrew toward the present North American coastlines, the Rocky Mountains were in the process of a spectacular uplift. The effect of this formation was only indirect in the north-central states; the great fans of river sediments carried eastward from the mountains were deposited as the Great Plains and did not reach our area. What did reach the western portion of the north-central region, as far east as northern Indiana, was the grassland that developed during the Tertiary in the great rain shadow of the Rockies. Several species of native mammals occur in the region today only in grassy habitats.

Fossil beds laid down in such areas as the Badlands of South Dakota document the mid-Tertiary existence of such mammals as oreodonts, titanotheres, and other species of both large and small size. By this time, mammals clearly had radiated around the world to fill many of the ecological niches that had been occupied by reptiles during the late Paleozoic and most of the Mesozoic. Kurtén (1972) provided an excellent epoch-by-epoch account of the environments and mammals of the Tertiary. Geologically, this was a period of moderate erosion in the north-central states that was associated with average cooling as some modern-day elements of both flora and fauna replaced more archaic elements. The Tertiary was a period of serenity in the north-central region compared with what was to follow during the Quaternary. The Quaternary, the two-million-year period leading immediately to the present, was a time of cyclic variation between warm and cold. During the four or more major cold periods, large masses of ice built up to form the great continental glaciers.

Changing climates that marked the beginning of the Quaternary had pervasive effects in the north-central region and throughout the world. Not only did changing temperatures result in changes in the distribution of plant communities and, therefore, of all the consumer communities dependent upon them; even the continents expanded into the seas as the volume of ocean water was reduced by so much water being frozen into glaciers and thus unable to return to the seas. Finally, there were the glaciers themselves, which were not stationary, but instead moved along powered by their own sheer weight. Only a few places within the north-central states escaped the immediate effects of glaciation, and even these areas were subject to cold summers near glacial ice, perhaps including permafrost for periods of hundreds of years at a time (see Pewe, 1983).

As important as the climatic and environmental changes were at the time, so too did the glaciers rearrange the topography of the areas affected, often covering bedrock or other surface features with from a few inches to many yards of new surface material. Lakes, even those as large as the Great Lakes (Hough, 1958), were formed by glacial processes. Sea level rose as newly formed streams and rivers carried meltwater from the glaciers to the oceans, causing the continents to shrink from the inundation.

Ojakangas and Matsch (1982), from which source the following descriptions and terms are taken, provided a summary of glaciation and its effect on the environment. Glaciers form over a period of time whenever snow accumulates faster than it melts. Snowflakes first are compacted, then partially melted, and finally refrozen to form aggregates of small granular ice crystals. Depending on temperature and snowfall, these may form in a single season. Eventually, usually after many seasons of continued net accumulation, these crystals gradually are modified to form larger crystals. As the ice mass grows it begins to deform under the force of its own weight, and thus a glacier is born. Gravity controls the rate of its movement. The glacier, of course, moves with immense force because of its great mass. Once formed, it moves as long as it continues to grow, sits still if deposition and melting are equal, and shrinks back or retreats if melting and sublimation are not adequately compensated for by new snow.

As agents of geologic change, glaciers shape the landscape by both erosion and deposition. The sculpting of a topographic surface by abrasion, quarrying, and deposition is the indelible mark of glacial activity. The eroded rock debris is invariably transported either by the glacier itself, the meltwater, or both and eventually deposited elsewhere to create new landforms. The nature of landforms altered by glaciers is dependent on the complex interactions of the geometry and physical state of the glacier, the nature of the rock and soil over which it passes, and the duration of the event.

Glacial abrasion takes place only if the base of the glacier is not frozen to the underlying surface. Even when basal sliding occurs, clean ice is not hard enough to scratch most rocks. When impregnated with rock and mineral fragments, especially quartzite, granite, and basalt, the glacier base becomes an effective abrasive, causing parallel linear striations or grooves. Quarrying occurs when large fragments of fractured bedrock are pulled away. These may be further broken up or deposited as small hills, and the excavation basins may eventually fill with water to become lakes.

The material (till) deposited by the glacier may range widely in size from boulders to fine rock powder. Much of the soil of glaciated portions of the north-central states is formed from till and outwash (redeposited sand and gravel carried away from the glacier by meltwater). Glacier margins are sites of especially heavy till deposition, left there during periods of melting. These long, narrow bands of till, termed *moraines*, tend to mark the configuration of the margin of the ice. Till dropped during a glacial advance or deposited by a retreating glacier in the form of low hills and swales results in ground moraines. In addition to the lakes created by quarrying, many others are formed either as kettles (pits formed by a mass of buried ice that eventually melts) or dams formed when moraines block natural drainage lines. For example, Mille Lacs, the largest lake in the north-central states excluding the Great Lakes, was created when the Lake Superior lobe of the most recent glacier retreated and left an end moraine that has since served as a natural dam. Belts of lakes typically mark the path and extent of former glaciers.

The Great Ice Age of the Quaternary represents the epoch known as the Pleistocene. The present time period, the Holocene or Recent, began only about 10,000 years ago, and it well may be no more than an interglacial period to be followed in the next few thousand years by another glaciation. The previous four major glaciations all extended to similar latitudes (map 1), then retreated as each episode of glaciation was followed by a warmer interglacial period.

Because landscapes are restructured by each new glacial advance, as existing surfaces are disturbed and new layers of till and outwash are deposited, the most recent advance invariably leaves the most obvious surface characteristics of the landscape. Of the major glaciations in this region, the most recent was the Wisconsin, the sculptor of our present landforms. Because its deposits have not yet been disturbed by a new advance, its effects are easier to study and much better known than are those of its predecessors. From oldest to youngest, the four major advances and the interglacial periods that followed are summarized below.

Nebraskan Glaciation

The exact dates of the Nebraskan glaciation are disputed. Although it previously was thought to be the first major Pleistocene advance, Ojakangas and Matsch (1982) discussed the complicating factor that Nebraskan till can be found above a layer of volcanic ash only 700,000 years old in Iowa, South

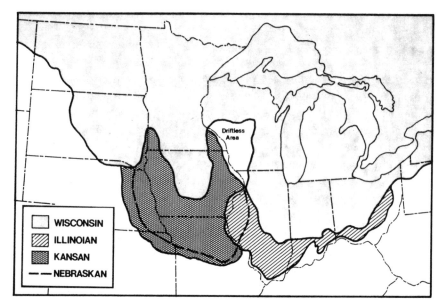

Map 1. Approximate boundaries of major glacial advances in the north-central region during the Pleistocene. After Ojakangas and Matsch (1982), with permission of University of Minnesota Press.

Dakota, and Nebraska. Older till lies below this layer of ash. In any event, the Nebraskan apparently extended only into Minnesota, Iowa, Illinois, and Wisconsin among north-central states. At no place do deposits known definitely to be of this event remain on the surface. In southern Iowa, the average thickness of Nebraskan deposits is about 100–150 feet (Wright and Ruhe, 1965).

Aftonian Interglacial

During interglacial periods, those communities previously compressed southward into suitably warm habitats were able to extend gradually back to the north as the glaciated regions warmed, land surfaces were uncovered, and permafrost left the ground. Thus, these were periods of "healing" of the landscape, ecological succession, and soil formation. Drainage patterns became established after previously used systems had been filled or dammed by till or perhaps flooded away as new routes were cut by the heavy flow of meltwater. Aftonian soils are known from a few localities in Iowa (Wright and Ruhe, 1965), Illinois (Frye et al., 1965), and as buried alluvial materials in Indiana (Wayne and Zumberge, 1965).

Kansan Glaciation

Till of the Kansan glacier is much like, or even indistinguishable from, that of the Nebraskan. Its average thickness in Iowa has been estimated at about 60 feet, but it is exposed there only along the eroded walls of some valleys in the south-central part of the state (Wright and Ruhe, 1965). In Illinois, no surface Kansan till of an eastern source is known, but some surface deposits and many subsurface deposits of this age are found in the west (Frye et al., 1965). Kansan till in Indiana was not discovered until 1954, but it has since been found in several areas. It is now known that the Kansan consisted of at least two distinct pulsations there, separated by a brief ice-free time. No Kansan drift has been recognized in Michigan (Wayne and Zumberge, 1965), and in Ohio it is known only from the southwestern corner (Goldthwait et al., 1965).

Yarmouth Interglacial

Yarmouth paleosols of an average thickness of 10 feet have been discovered beneath subsequently deposited drift in southeasternmost Iowa, and it is commonly known in thinner layers elsewhere in that state (Wright and Ruhe, 1965). Yarmouth soils are not known from Wisconsin, but they have been detected in Illinois as covered material in the extreme west (Frye et al., 1965). Though not reported from Michigan, Yarmouth soils are exposed at some localities in western Indiana and occur elsewhere in the state as buried alluvial deposits. Pollen from these deposits has been identified as pine, spruce, and oak, indicating that the Yarmouth may have been somewhat cooler than the supposed interglacial period in which we now live.

Illinoian Glaciation

This glacial event was marked by the most southerly penetration of ice in the North American Quaternary. The Illinoian advance was the last to rearrange the landscape in much of the southern portion of the north-central region. Specifically, those areas not subsequently overridden by Wisconsin ice are western and southern Illinois, the glaciated parts of southern Indiana, and a band in east-central Ohio east of maximum Wisconsin penetration (map 1).

Drift from Minnesota and Wisconsin has been reported as Illinoian, but these deposits are probably early Wisconsin (Frye et al., 1965). Deposits of this age in Michigan are known from only a few exposures (Wayne and Zumberge, 1965), but in the southern four states of our region this glaciation left its mark over large areas. In the north, Illinoian deposits are usually covered by deposits of Wisconsin age; but farther south they remain exposed, especially in Illinois, Indiana, and Ohio. In Iowa, Illinoian till is found only near the Mississippi River in the east. An early loess of Illinoian age is a widespread and important element of the soils of a band 30–100 miles wide east of the Missouri River in Iowa and extending also into northern Missouri and Illinois.

Three separate substages of Illinoian ice are known in Illinois, all of which are described and discussed by Frye et al. (1965). Similarly, tills of the three advances are known from southwestern Indiana, where they are mixed both with soils formed between their respective advances and with layers of Illinoian loess (Wayne and Zumberge, 1965). In Ohio, much of the till of this age is covered by several feet of loess. In the easternmost areas of Ohio affected by Illinoian ice, a ground moraine is deposited over highly irregular, partially buried bedrock hills, and the area retains much more relief than is seen in most north-central glaciated areas (Goldthwait et al., 1965).

Sangamon Interglacial

Overlying till and loess deposited during the Illinoian is the widespread soil of the Sangamon. In Iowa, much of this is actually a combined Yarmouth-Sangamon paleosol because Illinoian ice did not extend westward far beyond the Mississippi. In northern Iowa and other areas covered by Wisconsin till or loess, Sangamon soil is now buried. Follmer (1983) provided a detailed account of Sangamon and Wisconsin pedogenesis.

Wisconsin Glaciation

Although perhaps less spectacular than some previous glaciations, the Wisconsin is much better known because its deposits remain on or near the surface. About 75,000 years ago, after the long, warm Sangamon, the climate again began to cool. The Laurentide Ice Sheet formed across Canada as a result of the lower temperatures, and until only about 9,500 years ago the north-central region was under the powerful influence of Wisconsin glaciation.

Much of the early history of Wisconsin ice is speculative because deposits of early advances often were obscured by those that occurred later. The possibility of five separate Wisconsin glacial advances was discussed by Frye et al. (1965) for Wisconsin and Illinois: Altonian at roughly 38,000 years ago, Farmdalian at 25,000, Woodfordian at 20,000, Twocreekan at 11,850, and Valderan at as late as 6,000 years ago. A later summary of the activities of the lobes of the Laurentide Ice Sheet (Mickelson et al., 1983) avoided the use of specifically named advances. Instead, these authors presented a picture of continual waxing and waning of the various lobes that penetrated the north-central region. They suggested that Wisconsin ice was at its maximum about 21,000 years ago, with major subsequent readvances in the southern Great Lakes region at 20,000, 19,000, 18,100, 17,200, 16,700, 15,500, and 14,800 years before the present. In the northern Great Lakes region, ice had retreated back into the basins of the newly formed Great Lakes by 14,500 years ago, only to advance farther southward in the region at about 12,900, 12,300, 11,700, and 9,900 years before the present. By about 9,500 years ago, the last glacial ice in the north-central states had melted.

Mickelson et al. (1983) divided the United States extension of the Laurentide Ice Sheet into four major regions, three of which extended one or more lobes into our area: (1) Western Region, which included the western two-thirds of Minnesota and all the glaciated portion of Iowa. Major lobes were Red River, Rainy, Wadena, and Des Moines, which takes its name from the city near its point of southernmost advance. (2) Northern Great Lakes Region, which extended southward to near the southern edges of the present Lakes Michigan and Erie. Major lobes were the huge Lake Superior lobe in the west; the Green Bay, Lake Michigan, and Saginaw lobes over what is now eastern Wisconsin, Lake Michigan, and most of the Lower Peninsula of Michigan, respectively; the Georgian Bay and Lake Huron lobes over Lake Huron; and the Lake Erie lobe over that lake, with sublobes extending into Ohio. (3) Southern Great Lakes Region, which included northeastern Illinois, the glaciated portion of Indiana, and the western portion of the glaciated area of Ohio. This region was affected by southern sublobes of the Lake Michigan and Lake Huron lobes. The general direction of ice flow was southward and toward the edges of each lobe, or both. A major exception was the Grantsberg sublobe of the Des Moines lobe, which flowed northeastward from east-central Minnesota into the path of the Lake Superior lobe.

Associated with each lobe and sublobe of this great ice mass are the moraines, eskers, and other structures that remain as records of the past and as the present elements of the landscape of the north-central states.

Physiography and Drainage Patterns

Although the seven north-central states are large in area and diverse in terms of geologic history, the area is remarkably homogeneous in many ways. For the most part it is relatively low and flat, with often no more relief than gently rolling hills or the abundant streams and rivers that drain the area. Exceptions are the steep hills and river systems of the Allegheny Plateau of eastern Ohio, the hills of the unglaciated portion of southern Indiana (about one-sixth of the total area of that state), and the relatively rugged areas of Lake Superior's north shore, northeastern Wisconsin, and the western part of the

Upper Peninsula of Michigan. The latter three all are derived from the old Canadian Shield and today are part of the physiographic province known as the Laurentian Upland. There is found the highest point of elevation in the north-central states, Eagle Mountain, at 2,300 feet above sea level in extreme northeastern Minnesota, just north of Lake Superior. Although altitudes remain below 1,500 feet, the steepest slopes and roughest terrain in the north-central states are found on the Allegheny Plateau of Ohio. The lowest point in the seven-state region is 314 feet, where the Ohio and Mississippi rivers converge at the southern tip of Illinois.

The north-central states are characterized by many lakes and islands. Minnesota alone has more than 10,000 lakes of at least 40 acres of surface area, as well as several thousand of lesser extent. Northern Wisconsin is also a lake district, and lakes are common throughout the remainder of both Wisconsin and Michigan. That portion of northern Iowa covered by the great Des Moines ice lobe contains the greatest concentration of lakes in that state. Both Illinois and Indiana have many lakes, none of which is as large as, say, Lake of the Woods, Mille Lacs, or the Red Lakes of Minnesota or Lake Winnebago in Wisconsin; but several are substantive and important features of the landscape and local environment. Ohio has many lakes, especially in the eastern Allegheny area, but Grand Lake in the west is the largest.

Islands are an important element of the north-central states, occurring in all of the Great Lakes, some of the other larger lakes, and in several rivers. Of these, the best known and most studied is Isle Royale, in Lake Superior. As is the case for most islands, many fewer species of mammals are found on Isle Royale than in comparable habitats of the adjacent mainland. The island does support populations of moose and wolves, in addition to a few other kinds of mammals, but these two species have received by far the most study (Allen, 1979). The Apostle Islands of Wisconsin, in southwestern Lake Superior, represent one of the larger island groups of the region.

Runoff water in the north-central states may flow in any direction and eventually may empty into Hudson Bay, the Atlantic Ocean via the St. Lawrence River, or the Gulf of Mexico via the Mississippi drainage system. Minnesota is the only state that straddles all three of these continental watersheds. The Red River of the North flows northward along the North Dakota-Minnesota border and together with the Rainey River drains the basin of glacial Lake Agassiz into Lake of the Woods and eventually into Hudson Bay. It has been said that when the Treaty of Paris was signed, the French had an inaccurate map showing that this area drained via the Pigeon River into Lake Superior, and therefore agreed to turn it over to British control. (At the same meeting, Benjamin Franklin is alleged to have secured Michigan's Upper Peninsula by a deft but little-known sweep of his pen from Lake Huron into Lake Superior, instead of through the Straits of Mackinac as had been earlier agreed.) The Pigeon River is actually relatively small and along with several others helps to drain that part of northeastern Minnesota near Lake Superior into the lake.

Water that drains into the Great Lakes flows eventually into the St. Lawrence River, which empties into the Atlantic. From Duluth, at the western tip of Lake Superior, this is a trip of about 2,000 miles. A small portion of Lake Superior's south shore area in Wisconsin drains northward into the lake via small rivers such as the Brule. Not far south of the lake, however, the pattern of flow is to the south as major rivers such as the St. Croix and Wisconsin flow toward the Mississippi. Northeastern and eastern areas in Wisconsin also drain into the St. Lawrence system, through Lake Michigan. Lake Winnebago, Wisconsin's largest of many lakes, empties into Lake Michigan via Green Bay.

Michigan is a state of many streams and rivers, most of which are relatively small and nearly all of which drain into the St. Lawrence system. (The only exception is a tiny portion of the Upper Peninsula that drains southward through Wisconsin to the Mississippi.) Depending on point of origin within Michigan, however, water may pass first into any one of four of the Great Lakes—Superior, Michigan, Huron, or Erie.

Only a few of 500 or so streams and rivers in Illinois drain into Lake Michigan, those all in the extreme northeastern corner of the state. (The direction of flow of the Chicago River has been intentionally reversed so that water now flows from the lake and feeds into the Mississippi drainage system.) Northern Indiana is characterized by an almost imperceptible groundswell in the northeast. On the north side, rivers such as the St. Joseph flow into Lake Michigan and others such as the Maumee empty into Lake Erie. About 30 percent of Ohio drains northward into Lake Erie, via such rivers as the Maumee and Cuyahoga (see Hough, 1958, for a map of the Great Lakes drainage basin).

Streams and rivers throughout the remainder of the north-central region all flow more or less southward and eventually reach the Mississippi and the Gulf of Mexico. The Mississippi itself heads in our region. It flows out of Lake Itasca, in northern Minnesota, northwestward toward the Lake Agassiz basin, and it probably would be no more than a little-known tributary of the Red River except that it turned northward, then northeastward, and eventually southeastward as it failed to find a path through the glacial till that formed the eastern shore of that ancient lake. Thus the Mississippi was born, and it grows ever larger as it receives the Minnesota and the St. Croix, along with a host of smaller tributaries, before leaving Minnesota. It is further fed substantially by the Wisconsin River and from Illinois the Rock, the Illinois, and eventually the Ohio rivers. The Ohio, of course, has already drained the southern and eastern 70 percent of Ohio and most of Indiana, including that portion drained by the Wabash and its tributaries, all of which flow into the Ohio as it leaves Indiana.

All of Iowa drains directly or indirectly into the Mississippi. The eastern three-fourths of northern Iowa and the eastern half of southern Iowa drain more or less directly into it by way of the Des Moines and a number of smaller rivers that empty into the Mississippi farther north. Runoff water in the rest of Iowa and that from the southwestern corner of Minnesota flow south or southwest into the Big Sioux River or directly into the Missouri. The Missouri, which receives the Big Sioux at Sioux City, forms the remaining western border of Iowa. This river eventually turns eastward across the state of Missouri and, like all the others, empties into the Mississippi.

Soils

Soil is the natural substrate of most terrestrial plants. The plant community that grows in a given area is dependent on many environmental factors – including temperature, angle of incidence and amount of sunlight, and moisture – but also of major importance is the nature of the soil. The soils of a given area form from the parent material that is present. As we have discussed previously, for the glaciated portions of the north-central states the surface material was repeatedly rearranged throughout the Quaternary. Most of the soils there now have reformed and matured under a variety of successional plant communities since the final retreat of the Laurentide Ice Sheet some 9,000–12,000 years ago. Unglaciated areas have had a longer time to develop a mature soil profile, but even some of the unglaciated areas were covered by loess in amounts ranging from a few inches to several feet. Other unglaciated areas, such as eastern Ohio and southern Indiana, have undergone continuous water erosion or have been forming from rocky parent material. Thus, even though they have had more time to form, they are not nearly as deep and rich as some of those soils that have formed under prairies and deciduous forests in glaciated areas. Ten thousand years under good conditions of moisture, sunshine, and heavy plant growth is more than adequate for the development of a rich soil. This is especially true when the new soil is forming on a mineral-rich mixture of sand, silt, and clay, which characterized the loess and much of the glacial drift deposited in association with Wisconsin glaciation.

Our information on soils of the north-central states is taken from Brady (1984) unless otherwise noted. Soil types discussed follow the new comprehensive soil classification system, with older, more commonly used names provided in parentheses for convenience. Brady presented a soil map of the United States that shows the dominant orders and suborders of soils. The area of greatest soil complexity in the north-central region is northern Minnesota, where soils of five separate orders may be found in relatively close proximity. Iowa and Ohio show the least soil complexity, with only two soil orders represented in each state. In total, seven dominant soil orders and 12 suborders are found in the seven-state region.

Alfisols (Gray-Brown Podzolic Soils of Older Classification Systems)

Alfisols are widespread in the north-central states, occurring in each of the seven states. They are the most common soils over much of Wisconsin, Indiana, Ohio, and southern Michigan. In general, Alfisols have gray to brown surface horizons and subsurface horizons with clay accumulation. They usually remain moist but may be dry during summer. These soils were formed in humid areas under deciduous forest, and sometimes under tall grasses. Some of the best agricultural soils are of this order, and most areas in the north-central states characterized by Alfisols are presently in heavy farm production.

Subtypes found in the north-central states are the Aqualfs, Boralfs, and Udalfs. Aqualfs (Low-Humic Gley soils and Planosols) are found near the western end of Lake Erie in southeastern Michigan and adjacent northwestern Ohio, and again in south-central Ohio. As the name implies, these are by nature seasonally saturated. In our area, however, most have been drained and now are used for growing crops. Boralfs (Gray Wooded soils) occur in the north-central states only in parts of northern Minnesota and along the south near-shore areas of Wisconsin and Michigan. These are cool- or cold-climate soils of some northern forests. Udalfs (Gray-Brown Podzolic soils) are soils of warm or temperate regions that formed in moist but well-drained, often gently or moderately sloping areas. They are of widespread agricultural importance today in east-central Minnesota, much of southern Wisconsin, eastern Indiana, and northern and western Ohio. Although now farmed or at least used as pastureland, in presettlement times these were the soils that supported the rich deciduous forests of the north-central states.

Entisols (Some Azonal Low-Humic Gley Soils)

These are recently formed mineral soils with no horizons below the plow layer. The only Entisols found in our region are subclassified as Psamments (sand or loamy sand). Psamment soils are found in the north-central states only in three small areas, one in north-central Minnesota, one in central Wisconsin, and one in northwestern Indiana.

Histosols (Organic Soils)

These soils have developed in a water-saturated environment. In our region, the only Histosols are the Fibrists (peats), found primarily in northern Minnesota. The largest peat deposits in the United States, these form the Big Bog that covers several hundred square miles south of Lake of the Woods. Other, smaller peat bogs are found elsewhere in Minnesota, northern Wisconsin, and northern Michigan, but many of these have been drained and farmed. With farming, the original peat particles tend to decompose after they are exposed to oxygen. Minnesota's great peat deposits have mostly formed during the past 5,000 years. An excellent account of their formation is provided by Ojakangas and Matsch (1982). During the energy crisis in the 1970s, there was considerable interest and political pressure to harvest peat as an energy source. Although this pressure has presently subsided, it is certain to reemerge when the demand for fossil fuels again exceeds the supply. Highly acidic peatlands are referred to as bogs, and they have a low species diversity of plants and animals, including mammals. Fens, on the other hand, which tend to be less acidic as a result of some movement of water through them, support a somewhat richer flora and fauna.

Inceptisols (Ando, Sol Brun Acide, Some Brown Forest, Low-Humic Gley, and Humic Gley Soils)

These are young soils the horizons of which have formed rather quickly. Inceptisols are more advanced than Entisols, but less so than any of the other soil types. In our region, Inceptisols include the Aquepts (some Low-Humic Gley and alluvial soils), which are found here only in east-central Michigan west of Lake Huron. Although seasonally saturated in presettlement days, they now are mostly drained and used for farming. The Allegheny Plateau of eastern Ohio is characterized by Ochrepts, which are thin, low-organic soils on sloping or steep hillsides. Originally they supported deciduous forest, but most of the forest was logged, which, together with some attempts at grain farming, resulted in much erosion. Now this area tends to be used as pastureland and in some places has been reforested (see Noble and Korsok, 1975).

Mollisols (Chestnut, Chernozem, Brunizem, Redzinas, Brown, Brown Forest, Solonetz, and Humic Gley Soils)

This order includes some of the most important agricultural soil of the world. Mollisols are characterized by thick, dark, surface horizons, which have granular or crumb structures. Most developed under prairie vegetation, though a few developed under forest. The distribution of Mollisols corresponds closely with the presettlement grasslands that extended into the north-central states from the west. This, of course, includes the soils of the so-termed Prairie Peninsula (see Transeau, 1935).

Aguolls (Humic Gley soils) are limited in our region to the floodplains of the Red, Missouri, southern Mississippi, Illinois, southern Wabash, and western Ohio rivers. Although these soils often are saturated in spring, they are among the richest soils of the seven-state region. Within our area, Borolls (some Chernozems) are found only in western Minnesota. Prairie soils of well-drained but cool or cold areas, these now are essentially under the influence of the plow, used primarily for grain production. Udolls (some Brunizems) are the predominant soil of Iowa and Illinois, occurring also in south-central Minnesota, south-central Wisconsin, and northeastern Indiana. These rich soils developed under mixed tallgrass prairie and deciduous forest in warm, moist temperate areas. Nearly all are plowed and used for raising corn, soybeans, and small grains.

Spodosols (Podzols, Brown Podzolic Soils, and Groundwater Podzols)

These mineral soils develop from coarse-textured, acidic parent materials subject to leaching. They typically develop under coniferous forest. They tend not to be naturally fertile and today mostly remain covered with forests, especially the coniferous trees that help to maintain their acidity. Spodosols of our region are the Orthods (Brown Podzolic soils) of the northern half of Michigan, including all of the Upper Peninsula, the northern fourth of Wisconsin, and the extreme northeastern border region of Minnesota. In Michigan and Wisconsin, some of these soils are used for truck farming.

Ultisols (Red-Yellow Podzolic Soils, Reddish-Brown Lateritic Soils)

These usually moist soils develop in warm climates. They tend to be highly weathered and acidic, though less acidic than Spodosols. Ultisols are found on old land surfaces, generally under forest vegetation. This soil order includes most of the soils of the southeastern United States and extends into our region only in the unglaciated portion of south-central Indiana. The Indiana representative of this soil is more specifically one of the Udults (Red-Yellow Podzolic soils). Not surprisingly, given that they were never "planed" by glaciation, Udults form the soil of the most rugged portion of Indiana.

Climate

Over the long-term course of events, no single factor exerts greater influence on biological communities than does climate. Anyone who has had the opportunity to experience two or more of the world's biomes can appreciate the interactive role of moisture and temperature in establishing broad limits in which plant communities can exist in a given area. Certain kinds of plant and animal species are readily associated with tundra, coniferous forest, deciduous forest, grassland, or desert. Even the soils that form from local parent materials are mostly dependent on the type of vegetation they support, which in turn is mostly a function of climate.

To be sure, local plant and animal communities can and do differ greatly on a scale much finer than dictated by broad climatic patterns. For example, few have not observed a cattail marsh in shallow water give way to a canary grass lowland growing on seasonally saturated soil, which in turn is replaced sharply by upland grasses where the ground emerges far enough for at least the few surface inches to be well drained. Or, similarly, who has not driven through an area where natural grassland and forest come together (the grassland-forest ecotone) and observed the grassy, south-facing slopes of hillsides contrasting sharply with the woody vegetation, usually trees, growing on the cooler, north-facing slopes. Clearly, soil type, drainage pattern, angle of incidence of sunlight, the number and size of primary consumers, and history of local land-use practice all interact with climate to determine the composition of local biotic communities. But again, the broad limits of what types of communities are possible are dictated by climate.

Although climate may be defined as the sum of local weather, even average climatic parameters are not constant over long periods of time. For example, it is known from a variety of data sets that during the late Pleistocene northern North America was much colder than at present. Farther south, temperatures then probably were not much different than now, perhaps no more than 3°–4°F cooler in the American tropics (Bryson and Hare, 1974). As the Pleistocene ended, it appears that mean annual temperatures increased more or less abruptly in geologic terms (1,000–2,000 years). Causes of such abrupt change are not well known. They may or may not result from common underlying causes of less drastic, short-term climatic differences. For example, historical records show that most of the areas within the seven-state region averaged 2°–4°F colder and as much as 10 percent wetter (especially in winter) during the 1850s and 1860s as compared with the 1931–60 "climatic normals" (Bryson and Hare, 1974).

According to Bryson and Hare, the north-south cordillera of western North America and the vast, low-relief plains region that extends from the Gulf Coast through the Canadian tundra are the two fundamental factors that dominate the character of climatic patterns in the north-central states. The cordillera plays its role as a significant obstacle to both the zonal westerlies and the trade winds, whereas the plains provide an unobstructed corridor for the north-south movement of both arctic and tropical air masses.

On average, wind-flow direction in the north-central region tends to be west to east. In the northern part of the region, winds also have a strong north-to-south character from September until May. The period during which northern winds predominate is shorter farther south, and there is much more mixing there of air masses from the two directions at all seasons. Throughout the north-central region, the result of these patterns of flow and the associated mixing of warm and cool air masses tends to be relatively high humidity and moisture. These wind patterns, together with the seasonally changing angle of incidence and duration of sunlight, result in a strongly seasonal environment of cold to cool winters alternating with warm to hot and generally humid summers.

Severity and duration of winter generally follow the predictable north-to-south latitudinal gradient. This may be disrupted locally by factors such as the Great Lakes. Furthermore, from the standpoint of a small mammal, such factors as snow cover can so alter the microhabitat that what may seem like harsh conditions to a human walking on the surface of the snow actually may be quite comfortable for a mouse or shrew in the subnivean space below. Even a deer that is protected from wind by a stand of balsam fir experiences quite a different environment than a deer hunter in a nearby open stand.

Court (1974:193) introduced the subject of the climate of our region with the following quotation:

Air from the south, warm and moist, and air from the north, cold and dry, meet over most of the conterminous United States in constantly varying patterns. Air from the Pacific Ocean pushes the conflict between the southern and northern flows to the eastern seaboard and out into the Atlantic Ocean. The result is a wide gamut of weather events: blizzards, droughts, hurricanes, ice storms, tornadoes, chinooks, hail, fog, downpours. These alternate with calm, clear periods with bright sunshine. . . .

The following specific climatic data are taken from this work.

Total mean annual precipitation is shown in map 2A. The general trend is

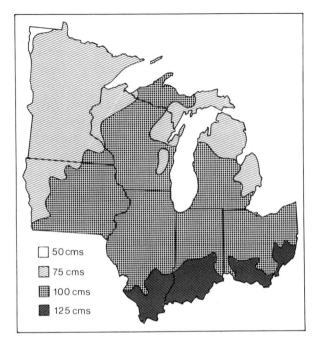

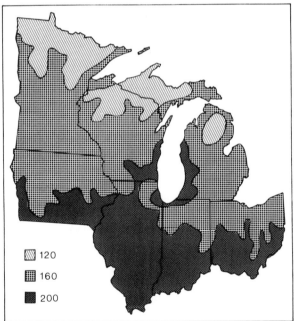

Map 2. Two climatic factors that affect the flora and fauna of the north-central region: (*A*, top) mean annual precipitation; (*B*, bottom) mean duration in days of frost-free period (growing season). Modified from Watts (1983), with permission of University of Minnesota Press.

from lowest precipitation in the northwest (50 cm, about 20 inches, in extreme northwestern Minnesota) to highest in southern parts of the region (100–120 cm in southern parts of Illinois, Indiana, and Ohio). Year-to-year variation in precipitation follows an east-west pattern, with up to 25 percent variation in the west to only about 15 percent variation in the east. June tends to be the month of greatest precipitation for most of the region, but one need not go far south of the north-central states until the months of greatest precipitation are in the winter. The southern part of the seven-state region often is affected by these winter storms, and consequently receives a relatively high percentage of its moisture in that season. Also, average annual evaporation (open pan) is somewhat greater in the southern states, averaging between 80 and 90 cm per year compared with 60–70 cm in the extreme northeast. The area of greatest evaporation in the seven-state region is extreme southwestern Iowa, where it exceeds 100 cm per year.

A final point regarding precipitation includes its physical form, and the environmental ramifications thereof. In northern Minnesota, northern Wisconsin, and the Upper Peninsula of Michigan, most precipitation from early November until late March or early April comes as snowfall. First and last snowfall dates from southern Illinois and Indiana are about one month later and earlier, respectively. Of great significance to mammals is the fate of the snow after it falls. In the northern areas, there is little melting until usually March or April; thus, for an average of about 150 days each year, the ground lies under a continuous cover of snow. Conversely, in the southern part of our region continuous snow cover for more than 10 days is the exception.

Temperatures in the north-central states vary within seasons in a north-south pattern. The latitudinal difference is much greater in winter than in summer. For example, mean daily temperature in January in northern Minnesota is only 5°F, whereas it is near 35°F in southern parts of Illinois, Indiana, and Ohio. In July, comparable temperatures for the two geographic extremes are about 68°F and 80°F. This is approximately a 30°F difference in winter and only about a 12°F difference in summer. Two factors contribute to this greater winter difference. First, snow cover in the northern latitudes results in reflection of much of the limited solar radiation available, which is rarely a problem in the south. Second, air movement patterns are such that in January the northern part of our region receives almost exclusively cold air from the north or west. In the southern part, a combination of Arctic and Gulf Coast air is received during the winter months.

Of great importance to the vegetation of an area is the duration of the frost-free summer period, often referred to as the growing season. This important parameter of temperature is shown in map 2B. Within the north-central region, this average value varies from as few as 90 days in parts of northern Wisconsin and Michigan (where late spring frosts result from cold winds blowing across the ice on Lakes Superior and Michigan) to as much as 210 days in extreme southern Illinois. Growing seasons of 120–180 days characterize most of our area. The life history strategies of all mammals within the north-central states track this seasonality, as new resources become available with the spring growth of vegetation.

Vegetation

With the climatic changes of the Pleistocene came the glacial advances and retreats discussed earlier. Both the temperature changes and the direct disruption of the landscape caused by the movement of ice resulted in wholesale changes in the vegetation of the north-central states. The vegetation of all glaciated and nearby areas was affected drastically. Cold-adapted plant communities repeatedly extended well south of the glaciers at the expense of warm-adapted species. However, the severity of the cold decreased rapidly to the south, so that biological communities were compressed in accordian fashion, with little effect on southern tropical areas. At glacial maximum, northern and southern floral and faunal elements were relatively more intermixed than is seen today, and the biota south of the ice was apparently more diverse than at present (see Guilday, 1984, and Guthire, 1984).

Vegetation changes in the north-central states and elsewhere in the eastern United States for the period 25,000 to 10,000 years before the present were described by Watts (1983) and are summarized herein from that source. At about the time of maximum southward extension of the Laurentide Ice Sheet, spruce-dominated forests occurred as far south as eastern Kansas and in the unglaciated portion of south-central Illinois. At the same time, pines were the dominant vegetation of the southeastern United States. Evidence for the vegetation of the unglaciated Allegheny Plateau of Ohio is sparse for this time period, but Watts (1983) suggested that tundra bordered the ice to the east in Pennsylvania, whereas spruce forest may have existed at or near the ice edge in Ohio. In the northern glaciated areas, the evidence suggests a tundra flora of dwarf shrubs and herbs growing on exposed soil between ice lobes. At maximum advance of the Des Moines Lobe, tundra would have extended at least into northern Iowa. The nearest forest known with certainty at the time was in southern Illinois and Missouri.

As the ice withdrew northward, the newly exposed sediment first supported a relatively brief phase of pioneer herbs and shrubs. This soon was replaced by a spruce-tamarack forest, which probably included some poplar, juniper, and possibly some ash and oak. Late glacial spruce forest of this type occurred generally throughout the Midwest with predominantly pine forests farther south. Spruce forest was even widespread farther west, in what is now northern prairie. In the heart of the prairie, it appears that grasses replaced the spruce more or less directly. In the prairie-forest boundary, deciduous trees (probably dominated by elm, but containing also ash, hickory, maple, hazel, and others – see Webb et al., 1983) apparently replaced spruce during brief periods as the grasses moved eastward.

In northern portions of the north-central region presently occupied by forest, this spruce-dominated forest probably lasted only until about 10,000 years ago. The spruce then declined rapidly, essentially disappearing from many areas over a period of possibly no more than 50 years. Soon thereafter, pine became an important element of northern forests, along with lesser amounts of fir and northern hardwoods. This transition period, documented by the rapid decline of spruce, marks the time boundary between Pleistocene and Holocene in the eastern United States.

Holocene vegetational changes leading to the presettlement flora of the north-central region are summarized by Webb et al. (1983), with additional coverage of eastern forest species by Davis (1983). During the early Holocene (to about 8,000 years before the present), many of the trends of the late Pleistocene continued – that is, eastern replacement of deciduous forest by grassland in eastern Minnesota, Iowa, and into the Prairie Peninsula. As indicated by detailed studies of local vegetation, soils, and pollen records (see Webb et al., 1983), fire almost certainly played a major role in this transition. In the absence of fire, the eastern boundary of the deciduous forest would have been somewhere west of its presettlement location. Komarek (1968) provided a summary of the effects of lightning and lightning fires as major forces in shaping plant communities.

Webb et al. (1983) summarized Holocene vegetational changes in the Midwest with the following main points. As the climate warmed, many changes took place in the distribution of plant species, some expanding and others contracting. Such groups as spruce and oak tended to move northward, whereas pine, hemlock, and beech expanded to the west and grasses moved eastward. Finally, these authors pointed out that the hemlock-northern hardwood forests of today did not become established in their present location until less than 6,000 years ago.

The presettlement vegetation of North America was mapped and described in considerable detail by Küchler (1964) and more generally by Watts (1983). Map 3 is modified primarily from the latter source. Webb et al. (1983) also presented a general map of presettlement vegetation in which they recog-

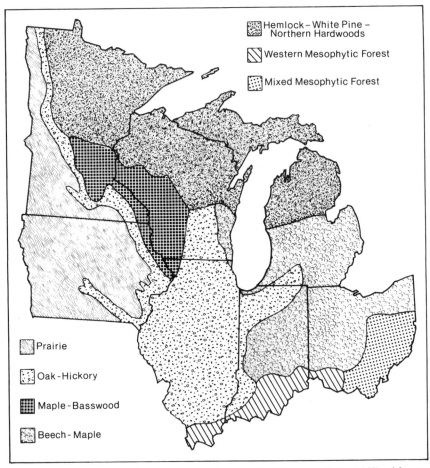

Map 3. Natural vegetation of the north-central region. Modified from Watts (1983), with permission of the University of Minnesota Press.

nized only four major vegetational regimes for the north-central states. In that scheme, a large Mixed Forest includes all of northeastern Minnesota east of the Mississippi River, the northern two-thirds of Wisconsin, and the Upper Peninsula and about the northern half of the Lower Peninsula of Michigan. Their Deciduous Forest includes all of Ohio, Indiana except the northwestern corner, the southern fourth of Illinois, and a long, narrow finger northwest across south-central Wisconsin and continuing along the Mississippi River to about where it receives the St. Croix and Minnesota rivers, then on in a north-westerly direction into Manitoba. In the classification of Webb et al., Prairie lies south and west of this finger in Minnesota and covers a little more than the western half of Iowa. Their fourth region is a Mosaic of Forest and Prairie, which covers eastern Iowa, northern Illinois and adjacent southern Wisconsin, and the northwestern corner of Indiana. In the following paragraphs, we have categorized the specific vegetation types described by Küchler (1964) into the four major vegetational regions mapped by Webb et al. (1983).

Mixed Forest

Five of Küchler's (1964) vegetation types constitute the northern mixed forest, which lies just south of the great spruce forest of eastern Canada. The Great Lakes Spruce-Fir Forest, dominated by balsam fir (*Abies balsamea*) and white spruce (*Picea glauca*), is widespread in northeastern Minnesota and adjacent northwestern Wisconsin. This is a dense evergreen forest. The Conifer Bog occupies the extensive peatlands of northern Minnesota and more restricted parts of northern Wisconsin and Michigan. Larch (*Larix laricina*), black spruce (*Picea mariana*), and white cedar (*Thuja occidentalis*) dominate this physiognomically variable habitat type. The Great Lakes Pine Forest is fairly widespread in the northern portions of Michigan's Lower Peninsula, and it occurs also in the northern parts of Wisconsin and Minnesota, where it forms a mosaic with the Great Lakes Spruce-Fir Forest. Dominants are jack pine (*Pinus banksiana*), red pine (*P. resinosa*), and white pine (*P. strobus*). This evergreen forest typically contains a variety of deciduous trees and shrubs. The Northern Hardwoods are found in northern Michigan, especially on the Lower Peninsula, are widespread in northern Wisconsin, and once occurred as a finger extending into northeastern Ohio south of Lake Erie. This is tall, deciduous forest with an admixture of evergreen trees. Dominants are sugar maple (*Acer saccharum*), yellow birch (*Betula allegheniensis*), beech (*Fagus grandifolia*), and hemlock (*Tsuga canadensis*). The Northern Hardwoods-Fir Forest is a dense, medium-height forest that includes both deciduous and evergreen trees. Dominants are balsam fir, sugar maple, paper birch (*Betula papyrifera*), and hemlock. This forest type is most common on the Upper Peninsula of Michigan, but it also occurs in adjacent Wisconsin and the northern Lower Peninsula.

Deciduous Forest

We have assigned seven of the forest types of Küchler (1964) to this vegetational region as drawn by Webb et al. (1983). The Maple-Basswood Forest, common within the long finger of deciduous forest that extends from southeast to northwest through Minnesota, is found also in northeastern Iowa and in western Wisconsin. Dominants of this medium-tall, broadleaf forest are sugar maple and basswood (*Tilia americana*). The Oak-Hickory Forest, widespread in the central United States, is the most common forest type in southern Michigan and is common also in Illinois, Indiana, and southeastern Ohio. Fingers of it extend into the prairie of Iowa along such rivers as the Des Moines and Missouri. Dominants are bitternut hickory (*Carya cordiformis*), shagbark hickory (*C. ovata*), white oak (*Quercus alba*), red oak (*Q. rubra*), and black oak (*Q. velutina*). The Elm-Ash Forest is a medium-tall to tall, deciduous forest found primarily in northern Ohio and eastern Michigan west of Lake Erie and near Saginaw Bay. It is dominated by white ash (*Fraxinus pennsylvanica*) and American elm (*Ulmus americana*). The Beech-Maple Forest, a tall, deciduous forest dominated by sugar maple and beech, is widespread in Indiana and Ohio and also is found commonly in southern Michigan. The Mixed Mesophytic Forest is widespread along the western face of the Appalachian Mountains, occurring in our region only in southeastern Ohio. Dominant species of this tall, deciduous forest are sugar maple, buckeye (*Aesculus octandra*), beech, tulip tree (*Liriodendron tulipifera*), white oak, red oak, and basswood. The Appalachian Oak Forest, which extends into our region only in east-central Ohio, is dominated by white oak and red oak. The Southern Floodplain Forest is found in the north-central states only in southern Illinois and Indiana, where it grows in association with such rivers as the Wabash, Ohio, and Mississippi. Dominant trees include several species of oak along with tupelo (*Nyssa aquatica*) and bald cypress (*Taxodium distichum*).

Prairie

Habitats of the prairie in the north-central region are assigned by Küchler (1964) to the Bluestem Prairie. This dense tallgrass habitat has, of course, mostly been plowed under for grain crops. In its more pristine form, it was dominated by big bluestem (*Andropogon gerardi*), little bluestem (*Schizachyrium scoparium*), switchgrass (*Panicum virgatum*), and Indian grass (*Sorghastrum nutans*). This vegetative type was widespread and homogeneously distributed over western and southwestern Minnesota and northwestern Iowa. It originally was found in more or less pure form in less extensive portions of northern Illinois, adjacent southern Wisconsin, and elsewhere as far east as central Ohio, but it never was found extensively in the latter state. Risser et al. (1981) provided a thorough treatment of this grassland type. Fingering into the Bluestem Prairie from the east is the Northern Floodplain Forest. It is limited in our region to the riparian areas associated with the Red, Minnesota, and the lower Mississippi rivers in Minnesota and along a short stretch of the Missouri River in northwestern Iowa. This vegetative type extends deep into the prairie farther west, where it serves as important habitat for several deciduous forest mammal species that cannot exist in uninterrupted open grasslands. Dominant trees are cottonwood (*Populus deltoides*), black willow (*Salix nigra*), and American elm. This is a low to tall deciduous forest that often contains many other deciduous species.

Mosaic of Forest and Prairie

This vast area of mixed deciduous forest and prairie contains extensive areas that are a mixture of Bluestem Prairie and Oak-Hickory Forest. The two types of vegetation are widely intermixed, with Prairie dominating more open, upland areas and south-facing slopes and woodland elements occupying more mesic areas, especially where natural evaporation is reduced. The only distinctly identified vegetative type described by Küchler (1964) for the mosaic region is the Oak Savanna, which is described as tallgrass prairie with deciduous trees scattered singly or in small groves. Dominants are big bluestem, little bluestem, and bur oak (*Quercus macrocarpa*). This vegetative type is widespread in southern Wisconsin and southeastern Minnesota, whereas the Bluestem Prairie-Oak Hickory Forest extends across southern Iowa, includes most of Illinois, and extends into western Indiana. It is this large area that Transeau (1935) and subsequent authors have termed the Prairie Peninsula. Smaller areas of this habitat once existed as far east as Ohio.

Human Influence

West (1983) summarized the extensive literature of the early history of humans in North America. Despite the several reports of evidence of humans on the continent from 150,000 to 16,000 years ago, West concluded that humans actually arrived only 12,000–13,000 years before the present. This first immigrant was the widespread Clovis man, who, West suggested, was an arctic-adapted hunter from eastern Siberia.

During the late Pleistocene, when sea levels were lowered by the temporary storage of water above sea level in the world's glaciers, the Bering land bridge was open. "Bridge" is perhaps a misleading name, as the region was actually quite wide and was not itself glaciated. Sometime between about 37,000 and 13,000 years ago, this corridor apparently became the home of the Beringian hunters. With the demise of the Great Ice Age, Beringia became permanently submerged as sea levels rose. It was probably at this time that North America became inhabited by humans.

The descendants of the displaced Beringians were the well-known Clovis hunters, who dispersed rapidly over both American continents, leaving their characteristic tools in southern South America by 11,000 years ago. West (1983) provided a list of Clovis-period sites in North America, with a range of radiocarbon dates in years before the present from 12,530 ± 370 (New York) to 8,940 ± 400 (Massachusetts). Mammal remains found at these sites include mammoth, bison, camel, musk-oxen, caribou, horse, four-horned pronghorn, sloth, tapir, and mastodon. The conclusion reached by West is that these people were nomadic big-game hunters throughout their early existence, primarily dependent upon late Pleistocene large mammals. They may have specialized on proboscideans, especially mammoth.

It long has been hotly debated whether these early hunters caused the late Pleistocene extinction of about 40 genera of mammals, mostly those of large body size, in North America. Most authors have pointed out that this obviously was a time of great environmental change and that extinctions, especially among larger species, occur at a relatively high rate when environments change drastically during a brief time period. Thus, Clovis man probably did not single-handedly cause all of the extinctions recorded (see Kurtén and Anderson, 1980, and Anderson, 1984, for summaries of North American Pleistocene mammals that became extinct during the late Pleistocene and early Holocene). For example, Webb (1984) has shown that during the past 10 million years there were six major extinction episodes that greatly reduced the terrestrial mammal fauna of North America. The late Pleistocene episode was the second largest, exceeded only by the 60 or so genera that became extinct nearly five million years ago. Similarly, Gingerich (1984) compared total rates of disappearance (extinction or emigration) with those of appearance (origination or immigration) for mammals of all sizes for the entire Pleistocene and concluded that more species appeared than disappeared during the epoch. Nevertheless, some 56 percent of the artiodactyls, perissodactyls, and proboscidians disappeared from North America during the period of Wisconsin glaciation. From evidence found in middens and hunting sites left by Clovis man, there is no doubt that these large mammals were killed extensively for food and other products.

The most current and thorough review of the interesting but highly complex question of causes of Pleistocene extinctions is that edited by Martin and Klein (1984). To us, it appears that, at least for some large, slow-reproducing species, the activities of Clovis people may have been important, at the very least expediting the extinction process.

West (1983) suggested that when the large-mammal food resource disappeared, Clovis populations declined, perhaps rapidly. This left a series of discontinuously distributed human populations over North America. These immediately post-Clovis groups probably became specialists at hunting smaller game species of more restricted distribution than had characterized the widespread Pleistocene megamammals. With the poorer hunting conditions of the period of 8,000–11,000 years ago, plants apparently became a more important component of the diet of humans in North America.

The activities of humans in eastern North America from about 8,000 years ago until about 1600 A.D., the time of initial settlement by Europeans, was summarized by Stoltman and Baerreis (1983). They recognized four *human ecosystem types*, which is the term they employed to include environment, subsistence, technology, population, and social organization. Note that this is somewhat of a departure from the common usage of the word *ecosystem* as typically employed by ecologists.

The pioneering ecosystem type, that of Clovis people in the late Pleistocene, persisted in some eastern forested regions into the Holocene. Stoltman and Baerreis (1983) suggested that big-game hunting was probably fundamental, with family groups of 25 or fewer people living as a band and moving freely to exploit new areas. Larger groups probably formed temporarily during certain seasons to hunt cooperatively.

In the Stoltman and Baerreis scheme, the foraging ecosystem type followed pioneering. Bands were less mobile and, therefore, interacted less with each other, resulting in part in greater variation of life-style during the foraging period than during pioneering. For example, in the forests of the Great Lakes region, large herds of caribou persisted until 5,000–6,000 years ago, and the pioneering life-style persisted as long as caribou were abundant. Elsewhere, the principal game species were moose and woodland caribou in northern coniferous forests and white-tailed deer in deciduous forests, all more or less solitary prey species. When these species were absent or scarce, other local resources such as small game, fish, and edible items of the local vegetation became important. This form of life probably prevailed in the eastern forests from about 7500 B.C. until 2500 B.C.

The cultivating ecosystem type replaced the foraging type in the eastern United States at about 2500 B.C., according to the scheme presented by Stoltman and Baerreis (1983). This stage involved a continuation of local hunting and foraging, but it also involved a certain amount of gardening activity. It almost certainly was characterized by a greater affinity to local areas where botanically diverse garden plots were tended. For the first time in North America, humans were now directly and intentionally altering plant communities and thus the natural habitats of the mammals of this region. However, the size of such plots was restricted, and the total impact on natural habitats and mammalian communities during the cultivating stage was undoubtedly minimal.

At some time between 400 A.D. and 900 A.D., the agricultural ecosystem type became established in the deciduous forest zone and the Prairie Peninsula. Beans and corn both became important crops. Local game, such as white-tailed deer, remained important, as were fish, nuts, and other native foods. Fields were managed by hand with the use of digging sticks, hoes, and other implements. Although the soil was being turned regularly, field plot size was much less extensive than with mechanized farming, and problems such as wind and water erosion were minimal. Stoltman and Baerreis (1983) recognized an upland subtype of the agricultural type for the vast area north of the Ohio River from the Mississippi River to the Atlantic seaboard.

Curtis (1959) listed five ways in which Indians influenced natural biotic communities: the use of fire; removal of large mammalian herbivores; harvesting seeds of native plants; tilling the soil for gardens and fields; and introducing new plant species, both accidentally and intentionally. Of these, fire was undoubtedly of greatest importance, as it could and did affect large areas. In mixed woodland-prairie habitats, such as most of the Prairie Peninsula and elsewhere in Wisconsin and Minnesota, fires clearly would have favored grasses at the expense of woody vegetation. Curtis (1959) estimated that nearly 50 percent of the plant communities of Wisconsin at the time of European settlement had been directly influenced by anthropogenic activity, especially fires that had been deliberately set.

Curtis (1959) pointed out a major difference in the effect of Indian culture on the environment compared with that which followed as the area was settled by Europeans. Although Indians exerted a significant retrogressive effect on plant communities, they had little or no effect on the long-term carrying capacity of the land itself. In fact, they probably increased annual productivity because their fires favored grasses over trees. Europeans, on the other hand, not only affected nearly 100 percent of the plant communities, they also affected basic soil and water resources as well, so that potential net productivity of plant communities was reduced.

The effect of Europeans on the natural biotic communities of the north-central states has been both intensive and extensive. Essentially all of the native forest, both deciduous and coniferous, has been cut. Extensive areas of second-growth forest are now found over much of northern Minnesota, Wisconsin, and Michigan, as well as in parts of eastern Ohio. Essentially all of the native prairie has been plowed, and that which had too much relief for plowing is used as pasture for domestic livestock. Habitats of prairie mammals, at least on average, have been disturbed and restricted more than elsewhere, mostly because of the high fertility of the Mollisols that formed under prairie vegetation.

Another important human activity in the north-central region since settlement is mining, including that for iron, copper, coal, and sand. Each type has its own effect on the environment. Surface mining temporarily disrupts terrestrial ecosystems, but plant succession on such areas often results in rich communities, including those of small mammals. Also, in areas lacking natural caves, bats use old mine shafts and tunnels for hibernation sites. As a result, bat populations in such areas as northern Minnesota may be much greater today than at the time of settlement. Also on the positive side, for some mammals at least, is the fact that such activities as timber harvest result in highly productive early seral stages of plant succession. These communities provide essential habitat for species such as moose and white-tailed deer, and they support a relatively high diversity of small mammals as well.

In a summary of the impact of Euro-Americans on the natural communities of the north-central states, one could emphasize the negative aspects: for example, plowing, grazing, erosion, urbanization, fertilizers, herbicides, insecticides, acid rain, and paved roads. Or, one could merely attempt to describe the highly altered landscape as it exists today. A thorough treatment of either approach would be a major volume in itself. In fact, all or most of the small mammals that occurred in the north-central region 400 years ago still can be found there today. Some have greatly expanded their distribution and numbers, whereas others have not fared so well. On the average, larger mammals, both artiodactyls and carnivores, have suffered the most. Most of the smaller terrestrial species remain relatively secure, at least for the present.

ZOOGEOGRAPHY

Zoogeography

The mammalian fauna of an area is best understood in historical perspective. As we have noted previously, plant and animal communities are ever dynamic. Changes are most dramatic during periods of rapid environmental change, such as those associated with glaciation or with an event such as occurred when Europeans settled North America. The preceding sections on past and present environments of the north-central states, including the geologic and vegetative history, are intended to provide a background on which past and present mammalian assemblages can be interpreted.

Historical mammalian faunas long have been the subject of study by mammalian paleontologists and zoogeographers. When faunas of the past are carefully analyzed together with data accumulated by geologists and paleoecologists, much can be learned about such diverse subjects as climatological trends, patterns of community change and stability, extinctions, rates of evolutionary change, and biogeographic affinities of present-day species. Kurtén (1972) provided an overview of mammalian evolution and environmental change during the Cenozoic Era, and the mammals of the Quaternary were summarized in encyclopedic form by Anderson (1984). Hoffmann and Jones (1970) conducted a thorough zoogeographical analysis of the mammals of the Central Great Plains. Similarly, Jones et al. (1983) presented an interesting analysis and discussion of the mammals of the Northern Great Plains and Bowles (1975) did the same for those mammals that occur today in Iowa.

Hibbard et al. (1965) illustrated historic changes in distribution of North American mammals during the Quaternary, and this work has been updated and expanded with special emphasis on mammals of the late Pleistocene and Holocene, respectively, by Lundelius et al. (1983) and Semken (1983). Origin, spread, and, in some cases, loss of the many living and now-extinct mammals of North America during the Quaternary were discussed by Hibbard et al.

49

(1965). Faunal movements involved those between temperate North America and the New World tropics, between North America and Eurasia, and distributional shifts within temperate North America. Many of the latter involved north-south shifts concurrent with the warming and cooling associated with glacial advances and retreats. Hibbard et al. concluded that the most extensive change in the mammalian fauna of North America during the Quaternary occurred after the Wisconsin ice began to retreat. In fact, the end of the Pleistocene in North America is recognized faunistically in part by the extinction of such mammals as elephants, mastodons, camels, large peccaries, the larger species of *Bison*, woodland musk-ox, giant beaver, ground sloths, and horses.

Lundelius et al. (1983) reiterated the comments of Hibbard et al. (1965) that the late Pleistocene, 25,000–10,000 years ago, was a time of great faunal change, which occurred in association with other substantial environmental changes of the time. Of special interest are the apparently disharmonious floral and faunal communities that existed during the late Pleistocene. These communities were composed of a mixture of northern and southern species that, based on distributions and habitats of living relatives, would appear to be ecologically incompatible. Certainly there are no modern analogues of these communities or the apparently more equable climates that supported them. Lundelius et al. (1983) suggested that the loss of species diversity in local plant communities at the end of the Pleistocene may in part explain the extinction of many late-Pleistocene mammals.

The badger (*Taxidea taxus*) is the only species of mammal living in the north-central states today that is known to have been there prior to the Quaternary, although species ancestral to modern species, such as *Zapus hudsonius*, undoubtedly were present. Fully half of the large-mammal immigrants from Eurasia have earliest-known North American records from the Wisconsin. For example, caribou and moose are species that persist in the north-central region since arriving from Eurasia at that time. Modern mammalian genera in our region that may have originated as late as the Pleistocene include *Sylvilagus*, *Lepus*, *Microtus*, *Rangifer*, *Alces*, *Antilocapra*, and *Bison* (Hibbard et al., 1965).

Graham (1976) studied the late Pleistocene and Recent mammals of the eastern United States and demonstrated that there were more species of shrews and moles in the deciduous forests of the Pleistocene than live there at present. He attributed this to more moderate environmental gradients late in the Pleistocene compared with today and suggested that the more equable climate of the past allowed greater integration of northern (boreal) and southern species in the eastern United States. A local mixing of northern and southern faunal elements during periods of glacial advance may be the rule and not the exception (also see Graham, 1979, and Graham and Lundelius, 1984).

By 11,000–10,000 years ago, the mammalian fauna of North America had taken on a "modern" character. The Holocene mammalian fauna of North America was described by Semken (1983:202) as "an impoverished residuum of the late-Pleistocene fauna." Semken continued, however, to note that modern mammalian distributions cannot be attributed wholly to climatic and environmental change associated with deglaciation. Other factors that have strongly influenced present distributions included Holocene climatic changes and the effects of both pre- and post-Columbian human activities, especially those associated with settlement by Europeans.

Table 1 provides both a taxonomic and zoogeographic overview of the mammals in each of the seven north-central states. Included in this tabulation are the 99 species assigned individually beyond to zoogeographic faunal units. Species of possible occurrence are not included. Mammals of the same seven orders are found in all states, with the number of species of each order in the states being remarkably similar. Only the numbers of bats (Chiroptera) and rodents (Rodentia) show marked differences. Number of bat species shows a clear trend from fewest in the northwestern part of the region, Minnesota (with seven), to most in the southeast, where Ohio (13) has nearly twice that number. In the case of rodents, the two westernmost states have the richest faunas, owing mostly to the presence of such grassland species as *Spermophilus richardsonii*, *Perognathus flavescens*, and *Onychomys leucogaster*. In addition, Minnesota alone has such northern rodents as *Thomomys talpoides*, *Phenacomys intermedius*, and *Synaptomys borealis*. Minnesota also is unique in having *Microtus chrotorrhinus*, an eastern species that does not quite extend westward into Ohio but does extend into the north-central region in rocky habitats north of the Great Lakes. Because of the combined grassland and northern forest mammals, Minnesota has 78 total species, several more than any other north-central state. The remaining six states form a tight cluster in number of species, ranging from a low of 65 (Michigan) to a high of 70 (Wisconsin and Illinois).

Carnivores comprise from 18 to 20 species, or between 25 and 30 percent of the mammals of each state. Iowa has the fewest species of insectivores, because northern shrews such as *Sorex arcticus* and *S. palustris* do not extend southward into any of the southern tier of north-central states and eastern species such as *S. longirostris* and *Condylura cristata* do not extend southwestward into Iowa. Similarly, Illinois has only seven insectivores, but that state's fauna does include *S. longirostris* and also *Blarina carolinensis* from the south. The two eastern states have nine insectivores, with *Parascalops breweri* occurring only in Ohio and *B. carolinensis* occurring in the southern tip of Illinois. Illinois, Indiana, and to some degree Ohio include several species that reach northern limits just within their state boundaries. In addition to *B. carolinensis*, examples include *Myotis austroriparius, M. grisescens, Plecotus rafinesquii, Sylvilagus aquaticus, Oryzomys palustris, Peromyscus gossypinus, Ochrotomys nuttalli, Neotoma floridana,* and, although now extirpated from the region, *Canis rufus.*

For all states, it is interesting to note that species of only two orders, Rodentia and Carnivora, include from 58 percent (Ohio) to 67 percent (Minnesota) of the total fauna. The number of artiodactyls is lowest in the three southeastern states, where only the white-tailed deer lives today and elk and bison have long since been extirpated. The northern tier of three states also includes moose and caribou, and the two western states add pronghorn and mule deer.

In an attempt to determine the geographic affinities of north-central mammals, we have conducted two analyses. First, we used many of the distribution maps presented with the species accounts beyond to make a single map showing all distributional margins that fall within the north-central region. Fifty-three species met the criteria to be included on the map. Species not included are those occurring throughout the seven states (20 species); those with distributions that have changed (either expanded or contracted) markedly in response to human activities (12 species); those known by only one or a few records, so that distribution within the region is not well defined (six species); and those not mapped for reasons discussed in the Introduction (eight species).

This map, which may be termed a *spaghetti diagram*, is presented as map 4. Although at first it looks like some not-to-be-cherished modern form of art, closer inspection does reveal some clear-cut trends. Three areas of the map seem worthy of special mention. Notice the many lines that coincide markedly with the unglaciated portions of southern Indiana and the adjacent southern hilly parts of Illinois and Ohio. There are found the northern distributional limits of the several southern species mentioned above, and interdigitating with them the southern margins of several northern species. Included in the northern group are *Sorex cinereus, Blarina brevicauda, Microtus pennsylvanicus, Mustela nivalis,* and *Taxidea taxus.*

The second area to catch the eye is south-central and west-central Wisconsin. Here, as we have seen in the previous environmental descriptions, the glacial history is complex, local soils are variable, and the vegetation is a complex mixture of grassland and forest, both coniferous and deciduous. Many species having boreomontane, eastern deciduous forest, and grassland affinities also

Table 1. Taxonomic and Zoogeographic Comparisons, Shown by Number (and Percentage), of the Mammals of the North-Central States

Order or Zoogeographic Affinity	Minnesota	Wisconsin	Michigan	Iowa	Illinois	Indiana	Ohio
Marsupialia	1 (1.3)	1 (1.4)	1 (1.5)	1 (1.4)	1 (1.4)	1 (1.5)	1 (1.5)
Insectivora	8 (10.3)	8 (11.4)	8 (12.3)	6 (8.7)	7 (10.0)	9 (13.6)	9 (13.3)
Chiroptera	7 (9.0)	9 (12.9)	9 (13.9)	10 (14.5)	13 (18.6)	12 (18.2)	13 (19.1)
Lagomorpha	3 (3.8)	3 (4.3)	2 (3.1)	2 (2.9)	3 (4.3)	2 (3.0)	2 (2.9)
Rodentia	31 (39.7)	24 (34.3)	21 (32.3)	25 (36.2)	24 (34.3)	21 (31.8)	20 (29.4)
Carnivora	21 (26.9)	20 (28.6)	19 (29.2)	20 (29.0)	19 (27.1)	18 (27.3)	20 (29.4)
Artiodactyla	7 (9.0)	5 (7.1)	5 (7.7)	5 (7.2)	3 (4.3)	3 (4.6)	3 (4.4)
Total	78	70	65	69	70	66	68
Widespread	26 (33.3)	25 (35.7)	25 (38.5)	26 (37.7)	25 (35.7)	25 (37.9)	26 (38.2)
Plains/Grassland	11 (14.1)	6 (8.6)	2 (3.1)	12 (17.4)	5 (7.1)	4 (6.1)	2 (2.9)
Eastern-Widespread	11 (14.1)	13 (18.6)	13 (20.0)	13 (18.9)	14 (20.0)	14 (21.2)	14 (20.6)
Eastern-New England	6 (7.7)	5 (7.1)	5 (7.7)	3 (4.3)	4 (5.7)	5 (7.6)	7 (10.3)
Eastern-Austral	0 (0.0)	0 (0.0)	0 (0.0)	0 (0.0)	9 (12.9)	7 (10.6)	5 (7.4)
Boreomontane	22 (28.2)	19 (27.2)	19 (29.2)	11 (15.9)	9 (12.9)	9 (13.6)	12 (17.7)
Neotropical	1 (1.3)	1 (1.4)	1 (1.5)	2 (2.9)	3 (4.3)	1 (1.5)	2 (2.9)
Southwestern	1 (1.3)	1 (1.4)	0 (0.0)	2 (2.9)	1 (1.4)	1 (1.5)	0 (0.0)
Total	78	70	65	69	70	66	68

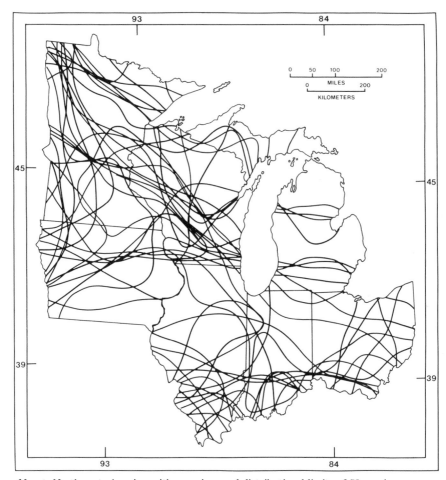

Map 4. North-central region with superimposed distributional limits of 53 species.

reach distributional limits here. We encourage the reader to compare this area of Wisconsin on our map with the similar maps prepared for the vegetation of Wisconsin by Curtis (1959). The similarities are striking, and they serve as a reminder of the dependence of animal species on plants and the dependence of plants on the complex interactions of soil and climate.

The third pattern worthy of mention appears in northwestern Minnesota between Lake of the Woods and the Red River. Here 13 species reach their distributional margins, again where coniferous forest, deciduous forest, and grassland give way to each other over a short distance. Some of the lines that originate in northwestern Minnesota extend southeastward into the middle of the aforementioned *tension zone* in Wisconsin, whereas others extend in a more southerly direction, often as far south as Iowa, and mark either the eastern limits of such grassland species as *Spermophilus richardsonii* and *Onychomys leucogaster* or the western limits of such eastern species as *Tamias striatus*, *Sciurus carolinensis*, *S. niger*, and *Synaptomys cooperi*.

Our second analysis involved study of the total species distribution (primarily from Hall, 1981), and, in cases such as *Didelphis*, *Sigmodon*, and *Reithrodontomys megalotis*, a knowledge of the distribution of closely related species. Thus armed, we assigned each species to a zoogeographic category that we think reflects the area of primary distribution and in some cases perhaps origin. These categories are often termed faunal units or elements, and our assignment of species to them is similar to assignments in other zoogeographic analyses, especially those by Hoffmann and Jones (1970), Bowles (1975), and Jones et al. (1983). Because much of our study area lies well to the east of those in the studies cited, however, we have treated several species not previously assigned, and we have a much higher percentage of species assignable to an *eastern* or *deciduous forest* unit. Accordingly, we have subdivided eastern species into three groups: Eastern Widespread are those species that occupy much or all of the eastern deciduous forest and occur throughout much or all of both the northeastern and the southeastern United States; Eastern Austral are those species that have distributions centering in the southeastern United States; and Eastern New England are those species having distributional clusters in the northeastern United States and southeastern Canada. Other faunal elements are: Widespread, for those species that occur over much or all of the United States and in some cases over most of North America, and thus their area of origin is obscure; Plains/Grassland for those taxa with clear-cut affinities to grassland habitats; Boreomontane for species having northern or montane, coniferous forest affinities; Neotropical for those southern mammals that have extended their distributions northward into our area from the New World tropics; and Southwestern, for two species with distributions that center in the arid southwestern United States and adjacent Mexico. Because a total of 99 species was considered, the number of species in each category closely approximates the percentage.

The Widespread faunal element includes 27 species, as follow:

> Small-footed myotis, *Myotis leibii*
> Little brown myotis, *Myotis lucifugus*
> Silver-haired bat, *Lasionycteris noctivagans*
> Big brown bat, *Eptesicus fuscus*

Red bat, *Lasiurus borealis*
Hoary bat, *Lasiurus cinereus*
Beaver, *Castor canadensis*
Deer mouse, *Peromyscus maniculatus*
Muskrat, *Ondatra zibethicus*
Porcupine, *Erethizon dorsatum*
Coyote, *Canis latrans*
Gray wolf, *Canis lupus*
Red fox, *Vulpes vulpes*
Gray fox, *Urocyon cinereoargenteus*
Black bear, *Ursus americanus*
Raccoon, *Procyon lotor*
Long-tailed weasel, *Mustela frenata*
Mink, *Mustela vison*
Badger, *Taxidea taxus*
Striped skunk, *Mephitis mephitis*
River otter, *Lutra canadensis*
Mountain lion, *Felis concolor*
Bobcat, *Felis rufus*
Wapiti, *Cervus elaphus*
Mule deer, *Odocoileus hemionus*
White-tailed deer, *Odocoileus virginianus*
Bison, *Bison bison*

Note that 13 species (48 percent) of this group are wide-ranging carnivores that are highly mobile and consume at an upper trophic level; they thus do not feed directly on the vegetation in which they live. Similarly, the six (22 percent) bat species in this category also have the potential to travel great distances (three are even strongly migratory) and as insectivores are freed of a dependence on specific kinds of vegetation. The red bat, assigned to this category by us with minor reservations, has been assigned to the Eastern faunal element by others; but given the distribution of this species into Mexico and the western United States, we have reassigned it despite its propensity for deciduous forests. Four (15 percent) of the rodents have widespread distributions: two, beaver and muskrat, are semiaquatic, and the presence of water, including rivers, streams, lakes, and even marshes, seems to be the habitat element of primary importance. The deer mouse is considered an extreme ecological generalist, and it may actually represent more than a single species. The last four species on the list are foliovorous artiodactyls. Two of these have been extirpated since Europeans arrived and two are deer, neither of which fits well into this category. The white-tailed deer is mostly a deciduous forest species and could have been assigned as Eastern Widespread. The mule deer is a western species that probably does not breed in the north-central states, and it certainly is not "widespread" in the same sense as most species in this category.

The Plains/Grassland faunal element, termed Campestrian by some authors, includes only 12 north-central species, as follow:

Elliot's short-tailed shrew, *Blarina hylophaga*
White-tailed jackrabbit, *Lepus townsendii*
Franklin's ground squirrel, *Spermophilus franklinii*
Richardson's ground squirrel, *Spermophilus richardsonii*
Thirteen-lined ground squirrel, *Spermophilus tridecemlineatus*
Plains pocket gopher, *Geomys bursarius*
Plains pocket mouse, *Perognathus flavescens*
Northern grasshopper mouse, *Onychomys leucogaster*
Prairie vole, *Microtus ochrogaster*
Eastern spotted skunk, *Spilogale putorius*
Swift fox, *Vulpes velox*
Pronghorn, *Antilocapra americana*

These species are found only in grassland habitats, though some extend well to the east in savannas and open areas maintained as grasslands by such disturbances as mowing and grazing. Five grassland species, *Spermophilus richardsonii*, *Perognathus flavescens*, *Onychomys leucogaster*, *Antilocapra americana*, and *Vulpes velox*, are (or were) limited to the grasslands of Minnesota and Iowa.

Eastern Widespread species are represented in the north-central states by 14 taxa, as follow:

Least shrew, *Cryptotis parva*
Eastern mole, *Scalopus aquaticus*
Social myotis, *Myotis sodalis*
Eastern pipistrelle, *Pipistrellus subflavus*
Evening bat, *Nycticeius humeralis*
Eastern cottontail, *Sylvilagus floridanus*
Eastern chipmunk, *Tamias striatus*
Woodchuck, *Marmota monax*
Gray squirrel, *Sciurus carolinensis*
Fox squirrel, *Sciurus niger*
Southern flying squirrel, *Glaucomys volans*

White-footed mouse, *Peromyscus leucopus*
Eastern woodrat, *Neotoma floridana*
Woodland vole, *Microtus pinetorum*

Species of this category occupy extensive distributions that tend to center in the eastern deciduous forest. Most occur over much of the north-central region, although the ranges of some either terminate where deciduous forest gives way to grassland (for example, the sciurids *Tamias striatus*, *Sciurus carolinesis*, and *Glaucomys volans*) or extend into the grassland mostly in association with the riparian woodlands that form long fingers westward beyond the contiguous forest (for example, *Sciurus niger* and *Peromyscus leucopus*). A few species in this faunal element are limited to southern parts of the north-central region and in that respect are similar to many Eastern Austral species (for example, *Myotis sodalis*, *Nycticeius humeralis*, and *Neotoma floridana*).

Eight eastern species have distributions that we have associated with New England and that tend to occur in mixed forest or even in moist grassy openings in mixed forests. Their distributions center in southeastern Canada and the adjacent northeastern United States and often extend southward in Appalachian forests and westward into the north-central region. These species are:

Smoky shrew, *Sorex fumeus*
Northern short-tailed shrew, *Blarina brevicauda*
Hairy-tailed mole, *Parascalops breweri*
Star-nosed mole, *Condylura cristata*
Northern myotis, *Myotis septentrionalis*
Rock vole, *Microtus chrotorrhinus*
Southern bog lemming, *Synaptomys cooperi*
Woodland jumping mouse, *Napaeozapus insignis*

Five species of this group occur broadly across at least the northern portion of our seven-state region, with *Microtus chrotorrhinus* being unique by penetrating the region only in the coniferous forest of northeastern Minnesota; two species, *Sorex fumeus* and *Parascalops breweri*, occupy limited ranges in the rugged parts of eastern Ohio and (in the case of *S. fumeus*) southern Indiana.

The third group of Eastern species, which we have termed the Austral faunal element, have distributions that center in the southeastern United States, and these taxa extend into the north-central states only in Illinois (nine species), Indiana (seven species), and Ohio (five species). The 10 species of this element are:

Southeastern shrew, *Sorex longirostris*
Southern short-tailed shrew, *Blarina carolinensis*
Southeastern myotis, *Myotis austroriparius*
Gray myotis, *Myotis grisescens*
Rafinesque's big-eared bat, *Plecotus rafinesquii*
Swamp rabbit, *Sylvilagus aquaticus*
Eastern harvest mouse, *Reithrodontomys humulis*
Cotton mouse, *Peromyscus gossypinus*
Golden mouse, *Ochrotomys nuttalli*
Red wolf, *Canis rufus*

This is a taxonomically and ecologically diverse group of species, but they have in common that all probably survived Pleistocene glaciation in the extreme southeastern United States. Today some of these species probably are either unable to survive the cold winters of more northerly areas (probably true for one or more of the three bats, *Sylvilagus aquaticus*, and *Ochrotomys nuttalli*) or perhaps are in a dynamic competitive interaction with ecologically similar, mostly allopatric congeners. Included here might be such species as *Blarina carolinensis* (see Jones et al., 1984), *Peromyscus gossypinus*, and, perhaps in presettlement days, the now-extirpated *Canis rufus*.

Extending into the north-central region from the north is a large Boreomontane faunal element. The 22 species of this unit are:

Arctic shrew, *Sorex arcticus*
Masked shrew, *Sorex cinereus*
Pygmy shrew, *Sorex hoyi*
Water shrew, *Sorex palustris*
Snowshoe hare, *Lepus americanus*
Least chipmunk, *Tamias minimus*
Red squirrel, *Tamiasciurus hudsonicus*
Northern flying squirrel, *Glaucomys sabrinus*
Northern pocket gopher, *Thomomys talpoides*
Southern red-backed vole, *Clethrionomys gapperi*
Heather vole, *Phenacomys intermedius*
Meadow vole, *Microtus pennsylvanicus*
Northern bog lemming, *Synaptomys borealis*
Meadow jumping mouse, *Zapus hudsonius*
Marten, *Martes americana*
Fisher, *Martes pennanti*
Ermine, *Mustela erminea*

Least weasel, *Mustela nivalis*
Wolverine, *Gulo gulo*
Lynx, *Felis lynx*
Moose, *Alces alces*
Caribou, *Rangifer tarandus*

Species of this group have relatively large distributional ranges, often occupying much or all of the coniferous forests of Alaska, Canada, the Rocky Mountains, and the Appalachian Mountains. Some, such as *Martes pennanti* and *Mustela erminea*, are also at home in mixed forest and even deciduous-grassland mosaics. Other zoogeographers, such as Jones et al. (1983), have recognized three distinct elements—Boreal, Montane, and Boreomontane—for this diverse group. This additional subdivision provides a finer-grained picture of the group. Their Boreal species (for example, *Sorex arcticus* and *Glaucomys sabrinus*) include those with ranges that center in central Canada; their Montane species are defined as having centers of distribution on the Rocky Mountains (none of our species falls into this element); and their Boreomontane element includes species that occur in both the boreal forests of Canada and in similar montane habitats farther south. For the north-central region, a single category is adequate because 16–18 of our 22 species necessarily would be assigned to the general category even if subdivided. Jones et al. (1983) included *Marmota monax* in their Boreal group because of its extensive distribution in Canada, but they acknowledged that it fits equally well into the Eastern category. Also, they included *Thomomys talpoides* in their Great Basin Element; because it would be the only species in such a group we have included it here, but we agree that it does not fit well into the Boreomontane category. No other Great Basin species extends into our region, and *Thomomys* only barely penetrates it in extreme northwestern Minnesota.

Four species recorded from the north-central states have neotropical affinities and make up the Neotropical faunal element. They are:

Virginia opossum, *Didelphis virginiana*
Brazilian free-tailed bat, *Tadarida brasiliensis*
Marsh rice rat, *Oryzomys palustris*
Hispid cotton rat, *Sigmodon hispidus*

Two of these species, *Didelphis virginiana* and *Sigmodon hispidus*, have extended their distributions far northward in the United States during recorded history; in fact, *Sigmodon* apparently has only recently reached extreme southeastern Iowa (see the account of this species beyond). *Oryzomys palustris* is a southern species that occurs in our area only in extreme southern Illinois; it could have been placed in the Eastern-Austral unit because it may occur no farther south than coastal Texas, Hall's extensive Mexican distribution actually being that of a related species, *O. couesi*. We have included it here primarily because of the neotropical affinity of the genus. *Tadarida brasiliensis* is known only from a few individuals that apparently wandered into the area, probably by accident. No breeding records of this species exist in or near the north-central region. Despite its southern origin, *Didelphis* is widespread in the north-central region and is common throughout the southern half.

Two species are herein assigned to a Southwestern faunal element. They are:

> Big free-tailed bat, *Tadarida macrotis*
> Western harvest mouse, *Reithrodontomys megalotis*

Jones et al. (1983) included *Reithrodontomys megalotis* in a Chihuahuan faunal unit, characterized by a center of distribution in northern Mexico. The alternative would be to include it as a Plains/Grassland species, as it does occupy primarily grassland habitats, but the total distribution differentiates this arid desert or desert grassland species from our other grassland taxa. Like its neotropical congener, *Tadarida macrotis* is known from our area only as a wanderer or accidental. It conceivably could have been included with our Neotropical group.

The subject of zoogeography is both fascinating and frustrating. Although we have relied primarily on present distributions to assign the 99 north-central species to their respective faunal elements, a knowledge of fossils and of geologic and vegetative history is also helpful in attempting to reconstruct past distributions and dispersal routes of species. Though imperfect, we hope that our attempts to subdivide and categorize the mammals of the large and environmentally diverse north-central region into units of common distribution and perhaps common zoogeographic history will stimulate interest and appreciation for the role of the past in creating the present. Similarly, the world and its environments and organisms of the future will reflect the events, both climatic and human induced, of today.

MAMMALS OF THE
NORTH-CENTRAL STATES

Mammals of the North-Central States

Checklist of Mammals

The following checklist of wild mammals occurring in the north-central states serves as a ready reference to the 99 native (exclusive of man) and five introduced species (marked with an asterisk here and in the keys that follow) treated in this handbook. Page references to species accounts are given. Orders, families, and genera are listed in currently accepted phylogenetic sequence, but species within each genus are listed alphabetically, as they are in the text.

Key to Orders of Mammals

1. First toe on hind foot thumblike, opposable; marsupium present
   in females; incisors 5/4 ....Marsupialia
1'. First toe on hind foot not thumblike or opposable; marsupium
   absent; incisors never more than 3/3 2
2. Forelimbs modified for flight ....Chiroptera
2'. Forelimbs not modified for flight 3
3. Upper incisors absent; feet with hooves.................Artiodactyla
3'. Upper incisors present; feet with claws 4
4. Toothrows continuous (no conspicuous diastema); canines present 5
4'. Toothrows having conspicuous diastema between incisors
   and cheekteeth; canines absent..................................6
5. Canines approximately equal in size to adjacent teeth;
   size small ....Insectivora
5'. Canines conspicuously larger than adjacent teeth;
   size medium to large ....Carnivora
6. Ears of approximately same length as (or longer than) tail;
   incisors 2/1 ....Lagomorpha
6'. Ears much shorter than tail; incisors 1/1 ....Rodentia

Order Marsupialia

Marsupials

Aside from the egg-laying monotremes, marsupials constitute the most primitive grouping of living mammals. They have the longest recorded fossil history of any extant order, being first known from the middle Cretaceous of North America (about 110 million years ago). Living representatives of the order occur naturally in two disjunct geographic regions—Australia and adjacent areas and the temperate and tropical parts of the Americas.

There currently is controversy as to the higher classification of marsupials. Most recent authors claim at least supraordinal status for Marsupialia, which is reasonable in that it reflects the evolutionary diversity within this group. However, there is little agreement to date on a biologically meaningful system of classifying marsupials above the family level. The schemes most often used would place the Virginia opossum in one or another of the orders Didelphiformes, Marsupicarnivora, or Polyprotodonta. All families assigned to these names may or may not represent descendants of a single common ancestor. This fact, together with our opinion that a handbook is not an appropriate forum for taxonomic controversy, leads us to retain Marsupialia following Marshall (1984), who summarized the history and problems of ordinal classification of marsupials.

Recent marsupials are represented by 16 families, 75 genera, and 260 species. They primitively have three premolars and four molars both above and below (the reverse of the primitive condition in placental mammals), and the number of upper and lower incisors is never equal. Offspring are poorly developed at birth and females of most species have a pouch (marsupium) in which the young develop. The reproductive tract of females is bifid and males have a bifurcate penis, to which the scrotum is anterior.

Didelphis virginiana

Virginia Opossum

Distribution. This opossum occurs naturally from southeastern Canada and the eastern and central United States southward to Nicaragua. It has been introduced at several places in western North America. *D. virginiana* is found throughout the north-central states save for northern Michigan and Minnesota, and it has expanded its range northward in the past century.

Description. Snout pointed, legs short, ears naked, tail long, scaly, sparsely haired, and prehensile. Dorsum usually dark grayish overall, venter somewhat paler and lacking guard hairs. Total length, 640–830; tail, 250–370; hind foot, 60–80; ear, 45–55; weight, 1.5–6 kg, usually 2–3.5.

Natural History. This hardy animal is principally a denizen of wooded areas, especially near water, but may be found anywhere in our region. It is omnivorous, the diet consisting of a wide variety of organic materials including carrion, feed grains, invertebrates, fruits and berries, small vertebrates, and eggs. Opossums are primarily nocturnal, denning by day in such places as abandoned burrows, brush piles, hollow logs or trees, and haystacks, and beneath farm buildings. They are occasionally nuisance predators in henhouses.

One litter, usually born in March, is the rule to the north in this region, whereas two litters, one in midwinter and another in late spring, is usual in the south. Four to 20 or more poorly developed young are produced after only 12 or 13 days of gestation. These climb without direct maternal assistance to the mother's pouch, where each attaches firmly to a teat. Females normally have 13 mammae, and any neonate that fails to attach to one perishes. One to 13 pouch young have been reported, but the average is about eight. Young remain in the marsupium for about two months and with the female for another month or more. Longevity in the wild rarely exceeds two years.

Home ranges have been variously estimated as about 10 to more than 100 acres, depending on habitat, season, and other factors. Opossums are eaten by humans in some places and taken also for the pelt, which is not especially valuable. Carnivores and large raptors prey on *D. virginiana*, and it hosts a variety of ectoparasites and endoparasites.

Selected References. Gardner (1973, 1982); McManus (1974).

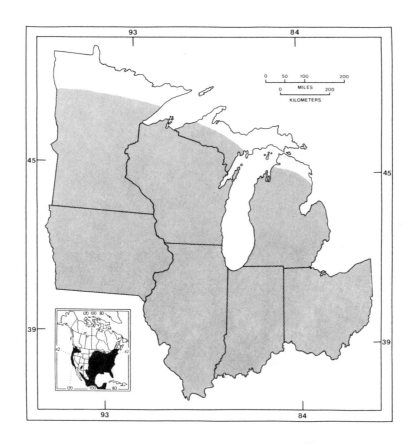

Order Insectivora

Insectivores

This order includes the most primitive of living placental mammals, although some are highly specialized, and represents the general stock from which more advanced placentals are thought to have evolved. Insectivores occur on all continents except Antarctica, Australia, and Greenland; in South America, however, they are distributed only in the northwestern part.

Modern members of Insectivora (in the now restricted sense) are representative of six families, 61 genera, and about 375 species. Of these, two families—Soricidae (shrews) with three genera and 10 species and Talpidae (moles) with three monotypic genera—are found in the north-central states. The fossil record of the order extends back to late Cretaceous times in North America, some 75 million years ago.

All insectivores have the primitively five-toed feet, and most retain a well-developed W-shaped cusp pattern on the molar teeth. Many are insectivorous, as implied by the ordinal name, but other invertebrates, such as earthworms, centipedes, slugs, and snails, are eaten, and some species take small vertebrates and other animals as well as plant material.

Key to Insectivores

1. Front feet developed for burrowing, more than twice as broad as hind feet; zygomatic arches and auditory bullae present (Talpidae) . .2
1'. Front feet not developed for burrowing, much less than twice as broad as hind feet; zygomatic arches absent; tympana ringlike, lacking auditory bullae (Soricidae) 4

2.   Tail more than 50 in length; fleshy tentacles on snout; first upper
     incisor projecting noticeably anteriorly...........*Condylura cristata*

2'. Tail less than 50 in length; no fleshy tentacles on snout; first
     upper incisor not projecting anteriorly...........................3

3.   Tail essentially naked; auditory bullae complete; total of 36
     teeth...*Scalopus aquaticus*

3'. Tail densely haired; auditory bullae incomplete; total of
     44 teeth.....................................*Parascalops breweri*

4.   Tail short, less than 30 percent of length of head and body; four
     or five unicuspids in each upper jaw; if five upper unicuspids
     present (only four visible in lateral view), then first two much
     larger in bulk than third, second the largest, fifth minute and
     internal to other teeth..5

4'. Tail relatively long, 30 percent or more of length of head and body;
     five unicuspids in each upper jaw (three or five visible in lateral
     view); first two unicuspids not much larger than third and fourth, or
     if so second not larger than first; fifth small but visible in lateral
     view except in *Sorex hoyi* 8

5.   Dorsal pelage brownish to reddish brown, venter noticeably paler;
     weight less than 8 g (usually 6 or less); four unicuspids in each
     upper jaw, three visible in lateral view ....*Cryptotis parva*

5'. Dorsal pelage grayish to grayish black, venter about same color
     as dorsum; weight more than 8 g (usually more than 10); five
     unicuspids in each upper jaw, four visible in lateral view...........6

6.   Total length rarely less than 120; condylobasal length rarely less
     than 21.5; occurring in all north-central states ....*Blarina brevicauda*

6'. Total length rarely more than 120; condylobasal length 21.5 or less
     (usually less than 21.0); occurring only in southern parts of
     Iowa and Illinois...7

7.   Total length more than 100; weight about 15 g; condylobasal length
     usually 20.0 or more; occurring in southern Iowa ..*Blarina hylophaga*

7'. Total length usually less than 100; weight about 9 g; condylobasal
     length usually less than 20.0; occurring in southern
     Illinois ....*Blarina carolinensis*

8.   Pelage dark grayish to blackish dorsally; length of hind foot
     more than 18, foot fringed with stiff, whitish hairs; condylobasal
     length usually more than 19.5 ....*Sorex palustris*

8'. Pelage brownish to grayish dorsally; length of hind foot less
     than 18, foot not fringed with stiff hairs; condylobasal length
     usually less than 19.5..9

9.   Total length more than 102; condylobasal length more than 17.5... 10
9'.   Total length less than 102; condylobasal length less than 17.5......11
10.   Pelage often with tricolored pattern; first two upper unicuspids essentially equal in size and larger than third and fourth; cranial breadth usually more than 9.1 .... *Sorex arcticus*
10'. Pelage almost the same color throughout, only slightly paler ventrally than above; first four upper unicuspids decreasing progressively in size from front to rear; cranial breadth usually less than 9.1 .... *Sorex fumeus*
11.   Length of hind foot usually 10 or less; third upper unicuspid much compressed, disklike; only three upper unicuspids visible in lateral view .... *Sorex hoyi*
11'. Length of hind foot usually 10 or more; third upper unicuspid not compressed and disklike; five upper unicuspids normally visible in lateral view 12
12.   Third upper unicuspid smaller than fourth; length of tail usually less than 32; longest hairs at tip of tail (unworn) 2–3 in length..................................... *Sorex longirostris*
12'. Third upper unicuspid larger than fourth; length of tail usually more than 32; longest hairs at tip of tail (unworn) 4–6 in length .... *Sorex cinereus*

Sorex arcticus
Arctic Shrew

Distribution. This species ranges from the north-central United States northward into much of Canada; it or a closely related species also is found in Alaska and over much of Siberia. In the seven-state region, the arctic shrew is known from northern and central Minnesota and the Upper Peninsula of Michigan southward to southeastern Wisconsin.

Description. A relatively large shrew, exceeded in size among *Sorex* in this region only by *S. palustris*. Pelage distinctly tricolored in adults, especially in winter; rich, dark brown to blackish brown dorsally, paler brownish on sides, grayish brown ventrally. Total length, 105–125; tail, 36–46; hind foot, 12–15; weight 7–12 g.

Natural History. Although *S. arcticus* occurs over a large geographic area and is not uncommon at many places within its range, relatively little of a definitive nature has been published on the ecology of this species. Preferred habitats seem to be swamps, bogs, marshes, and the margins of lakes and streams, but some drier areas also are occupied. In Wisconsin, this insectivore has been reported to occur mostly in wet spruce and tamarack swamps and in alder or willow marshes. Most specimens in a study in northeastern Minnesota, however, were taken in nonforested sites or clearings in forested areas.

Densities of arctic shrews have been reported as high as five per acre, but about three per acre probably is the average in good habitat. Home ranges have a radius of approximately 150 feet. These animals are principally nocturnal, but may be active by day as well. Foods include larval, pupal, and adult insects, including aquatic species, and other invertebrates. Fleas, mites, and ticks have been reported as ectoparasites. Adults molt in May or June to summer pelage and in late summer or early autumn to winter pelage. The life span probably rarely exceeds 15 months.

The breeding season extends from late winter through much of the summer. Some females bear two or more litters annually. Litter size ranges from four to 10, averaging about six. Early young of the year sometimes breed in late summer, but most reproduce first in the following year.

Selected References. Baird et al. (1983); Wrigley et al. (1979); van Zyll de Jong (1983).

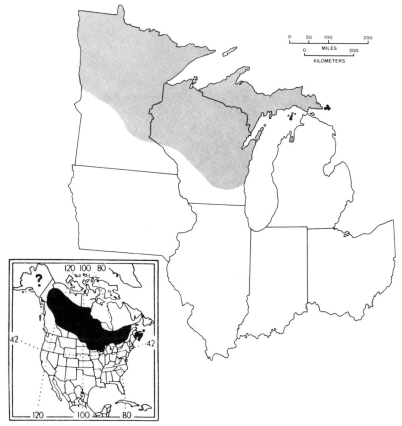

Photo by Elmer C. Birney

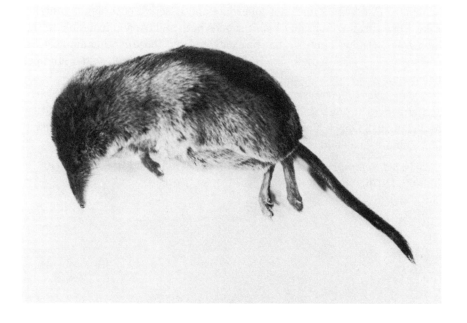

Sorex cinereus
Masked Shrew

Distribution. The masked shrew, sometimes referred to as the cinereous shrew, is distributed over much of northern North America, south in mountainous regions to Georgia and New Mexico, and in eastern Siberia. In the north-central states, it evidently occurs in all but parts of southern Indiana, Illinois, and Ohio. The systematics of the *S. cinereus* complex are not well understood, and two distinct species rather than one may occur in this region.

Description. A small-sized *Sorex*. Pelage dark brownish in summer, paler on sides, and grayish white ventrally; longer, slightly paler, and more tricolored in winter. Total length, 80–98; tail, 30–44; hind foot, 10–13; weight usually 3–5 g.

Natural History. This shrew is found in a wide variety of habitats, but most often in locally mesic areas, both grassy and forested. It feeds on a broad array of invertebrates, including beetles, moths, ants, flies, grasshoppers, earthworms, centipedes, spiders, mollusks, and sowbugs, and occasionally on small vertebrates. Vegetable matter also may be consumed, and fungi are a common component of the diet in winter. Owls and certain carnivores prey on this and other soricids, although the foul-tasting scent glands may discourage larger mammals from eating them. Other reported predators include large frogs, fish, snakes, short-tailed shrews, and weasels.

Because the masked shrew is widely distributed and occupies many habitats, it frequently associates with other shrews and many other small mammals. *S. cinereus* does not hibernate and is active both day and night. Like other shrews, individuals emit sounds both audible and inaudible to the human ear. Shallow burrows may be excavated, but those of other animals are used as well. Nests, four to five inches in diameter, are built under stumps, fallen logs, rocks, debris, and in similar situations.

This species breeds throughout the warm months, from late winter or early spring to midautumn. A litter of four to 10 young is born after a gestation period of 19–22 days. Young, quite altricial at birth, weight about a quarter of a gram. Females may bear two or more litters a year.

Selected References. Buckner (1964, 1966); Diersing and Hoffmeister (1981); Forsyth (1976); van Zyll de Jong (1976, 1980, 1983).

Sorex fumeus
Smoky Shrew

Distribution. The smoky shrew is known from southeastern Canada and the northeastern United States, south to northern Georgia and west to the north-central states. In our region, it occurs principally in eastern and central Ohio westward to southern Indiana. *S. fumeus* has been reported also from Racine, Wisconsin, on the basis of a single specimen taken in 1853, and from northeasternmost Michigan (Sugar Island). Western limits of the range of this species are poorly known.

Description. Size medium among species of *Sorex* in region, approximating that of *S. arcticus.* Color of dorsum slaty gray to near blackish in winter, dull brownish in summer; venter somewhat paler, sometimes slightly silvery; tail bicolored. Total length, 110–126; tail, 40–52; hind foot, 12–15; weight 6–10 g.

Natural History. This is primarily an animal of the forest floor, both deciduous and coniferous, but is known also from such habitats as swamps and bogs, grassy swales, and rocky slopes. Favored microhabitats include leaf mold and humus, mossy rocks, old logs and stumps, and brush piles. Although it prefers moist situations, *S. fumeus* occasionally is taken in relatively xeric areas such as dry deciduous woodlands; shrews from Indiana were taken primarily on steep slopes and in ravines of deep woods along with *S. hoyi.* Little is known about the population biology of this shrew. Estimated densities range from a few to more than 50 per acre. *Blarina* and other species of *Sorex* are common associates.

Smoky shrews may not construct tunnels and runways, but individuals readily use those made by other small mammals. Spherical nests, three to four inches in diameter, are constructed from mammal hair and soft vegetable matter in hollow logs, under stumps, within tunnels, or beneath debris. A wide variety of invertebrates makes up most of the diet. Adults molt twice annually, in spring and autumn. Maximum life span is about a year and a half.

The breeding season extends through the warm months, from late March to early October, and females are thought to produce two or three litters a year. Litter size ranges from two to eight, averaging about five. These shrews evidently do not breed in their first year.

Selected References. Owen (1984).

Sorex hoyi
Pygmy Shrew

Distribution. This species ranges across much of boreal North America, from Labrador and northern Quebec to Alaska. In the United States, it occurs in the Northeast, south in the Appalachians to northern Georgia, in all north-central states and the adjacent Dakotas, and in parts of the northern and central Rockies.

Description. Smallest of North American *Sorex*; tail relatively short. Dorsum reddish brown to grayish brown, grayer in winter; sides paler than back; venter whitish to grayish. Total length, 78–91; tail, 27–34; hind foot, 8–11; weight, 2–4 g. Because of the unique, tiny, third upper unicuspid tooth, this species was classified for years in a separate genus, *Microsorex*.

Natural History. This soricid seemingly tolerates a fairly wide variation in moisture, temperature, vegetative type, and ground cover. Thus it has been taken in a variety of ecological situations, but it probably prefers mesic surroundings, as do most of its relatives. Like many other shrews, *S. hoyi* is difficult to trap by conventional means and can be taken most easily in pitfalls (a frequent technique is number 10 cans buried flush with the ground). Food consists mostly of invertebrates.

Pygmy shrews are active year round. They are adept climbers and can run rapidly when disturbed. They burrow in soft substrate, especially under fallen logs, stumps, and the like, but also readily use burrows of other animals. Adults usually molt in April or May to summer pelage and in October to winter pelage, but molting animals have been taken at other times of year. Females may bear only one litter (of three to eight young) annually.

The distribution of *S. hoyi* in the north-central states is not well documented, particularly in the south. Probably it ranges throughout most of Minnesota, Wisconsin, and Michigan, but records are spotty. From Iowa it is known only from one station in the north, and from Illinois only from the extreme northeast. The recent capture of specimens in southern Indiana, however, suggests that this species may be found over much of the seven-state region. It probably inhabits most of Ohio, for example, although it is recorded only from the eastern part of that state.

Selected References. Diersing (1980); Long (1974).

Photo by John O. Whitaker, Jr.

Sorex longirostris
Southeastern Shrew

Distribution. This species, as its vernacular name suggests, inhabits the southeastern United States from Florida north to Maryland and westward to Arkansas, Louisiana, and Missouri. In the seven-state region, it is known only from Illinois and Indiana, but it probably occurs also in at least southern Ohio.

Description. A small shrew resembling *S. cinereus* in size. Dorsum brownish to reddish brown, venter paler brown (sometimes tending toward ochraceous); tail indistinctly bicolored. Total length, 77–92; tail, 26–33; hind foot, 9–11; weight, 3–6 g. Principal differences from *S. cinereus*: skull smaller but rostrum broader; teeth more lightly pigmented; third unicuspid usually smaller than fourth.

Natural History. The southeastern shrew is known from a variety of habitats ranging from swamps and bogs to upland forested and grassy areas. Generally, however, it seems to prefer moist to wet areas bordering swamps, marshes, rivers, and streams. In any event, *S. longirostris* usually is associated with a heavy ground cover of grasses, sedges, rushes, low-growing brushy vegetation, or thick leaf litter. Like many other shrews, it is readily taken in pitfalls (which, incidentally, should be filled in at the conclusion of any study). In a study in Alabama, populations were estimated at 12–18 shrews per acre.

Pregnant females have been taken from late March to early October, strongly suggesting that they bear two or more litters annually. It is not known whether young of the year breed later in the season of their birth. Reported litter size ranges from one to 10, but the average seems to be about four. Young have been found in leaf-lined nests under or within rotting logs.

Important foods are spiders, insects (especially Lepidoptera larvae), slugs, snails, centipedes, earthworms, and vegetable matter. Owls are the most active of predators on this and other shrews. *S. longirostris* is known to be parasitized externally by a variety of mites and at least one species of tick and internally by nematodes, cestodes, and protozoans.

An individual kept in captivity burrowed in moist soil and was active both day and night. Occasionally the animal emitted a series of soft, birdlike chirps. It defecated in only one corner of the enclosure.

Selected References. French (1980*a*, 1980*b*, 1982).

Photo by T.W. French

Sorex palustris
Water Shrew

Distribution. This interesting species has a broad North American distribution, occurring from Labrador to southern Alaska, southward in the Appalachians to eastern Tennessee, and in the montane West to California, Arizona, and New Mexico. In our states, it is known from the northern halves of Minnesota, Wisconsin, and Michigan.

Description. Largest *Sorex* in north-central region. Hind feet relatively broad; feet fringed with stiff whitish hairs (for swimming). Pelage dense and soft, blackish to grayish brown dorsally, sometimes iridescent; venter paler, grayish to silvery white; tail distinctly bicolored. Total length, 136–164; tail, 63–76; hind foot, 18–21; weight, 11–19 g.

Natural History. The water shrew, as its name implies, usually is closely associated with permanent water such as swamps, bogs, potholes, lakes, and streams. Cold, fast-running creeks bordered by rocks, logs, roots, and overhanging banks may be the preferred habitat throughout much of the range. These shrews are excellent swimmers and divers; they can move easily along the bottom of streams and pools and are said to be able to run on the surface for short distances. The pelage is resistant to soaking. Nearly half the diet consists of aquatic insects and their larvae, but planaria, small fish, spiders, worms, small terrestrial vertebrates, and some vegetable matter also are eaten.

These shrews are primarily nocturnal, but individuals may be active at any time. They are secretive, however, and rarely seen. As in most other shrews, sight is poorly developed but this is compensated for by well-developed senses of touch and smell. As in other *Sorex*, there is but one maturational molt from the thin juvenile pelage to the appropriate adult seasonal coat; thereafter there are two molts annually, one in late spring and the other in middle to late summer.

This species probably breeds from late winter through early autumn. Females may bear two or three litters a year, and some born early in the year breed later in the same season. Males, however, do not breed until their second year. Litter size ranges from five to eight, six being most common. The normal life span evidently is about 18 months.

Selected References. Conaway (1952); Jackson (1928); Sorenson (1962).

Blarina brevicauda
Northern Short-tailed Shrew

Distribution. This short-tailed shrew ranges throughout the northeastern United States and adjacent Canada, west to Saskatchewan and Nebraska and south to Georgia. It occurs over the entire seven-state region except possibly in southwestern Illinois.

Description. A relatively heavy-bodied shrew with a short tail; largest species of the genus. Dorsum grayish to grayish black, venter slightly paler; color variants, including albinos, are known. Total length, 118–140; tail, 21–30; hind foot, 14–18; weight, 15–30 g.

Natural History. This insectivore occupies a variety of habitats, including woodlands, grasslands, brush fencerows, marshy areas and bogs, and even relatively dry uplands, and is one of the common small mammals in many places. Populations, which may vary locally and annually, usually range from three to 20 or so shrews per acre, but much higher densities have been reported.

B. brevicauda is active both day and night, but subdued light is sought in daytime. Home ranges of males may be as large as four and a half acres. Foods include earthworms, slugs, snails, larval and adult insects, centipedes, other invertebrates, the fungus *Endogone*, vegetable matter, and small vertebrates. Seeds spilled from bird feeders attract *Blarina*.

These animals move about with apparent rapidity but little actual speed, with the tail elevated as in other shrews. Burrows and tunnels are at two levels, a few inches below the surface or under logs or litter, and deeper – to about 20 inches below ground; the two levels in the same system are joined at irregular intervals. Burrows of other small mammals also are used. Both breeding and resting nests, the former the larger, are constructed from available plant material. Nests are hollow balls four to eight inches in diameter.

Reproduction usually commences in late winter or early spring and litters of four to 10 young (average six to seven) are born after 21–22 days of gestation. There is little breeding in early summer and midsummer, but another peak occurs later in the warm season. Young of early litters may breed in the year they are born. Longevity rarely exceeds two years. Adults molt twice annually.

Selected References. Dapson (1968); George et al. (1986); Pearson (1944, 1945); Platt (1976).

Blarina carolinensis
Southern Short-tailed Shrew

Distribution. This species is found in the southeastern United States, ranging northward to Virginia and southern Illinois (see area labeled 1 on map). It may occur also in the north-central region in southwestern Indiana. The inset map on the facing page depicts the distribution of this species.

Description. Smallest species of *Blarina*; measurements not overlapping, or only barely so, those of *B. hylophaga* (see below). Total length, 72–95; tail, 13–22; hind foot, 10–14; weight about 9 g. Color as described for *B. brevicauda*. The shrew illustrated to the right represents *B. carolinensis*.

Notes. Shrews of the genus *Blarina* treated in this handbook were thought for many years to represent a single, morphologically variable species. Recent studies have revealed, however, morphological and especially chromosomal differences among populations that strongly argue for recognition of at least two and probably three species in this region. The distribution of the southern short-tailed shrew is known to overlap that of *B. brevicauda* only in southern Illinois. Differences in natural history among the species, if any, are unknown.

Selected References. Ellis et al. (1978); George et al. (1982); Lowery (1974); Schmidly (1983).

Blarina hylophaga
Elliot's Short-tailed Shrew

Distribution. This shrew is recorded as occurring from northeastern Colorado and the southern parts of Nebraska and Iowa southward to the Gulf Coast in Texas (see area labeled 2 on map).

Description. Medium-sized among the three species of the genus; smaller than *B. brevicauda* but larger than *B. carolinensis*; color as described for *B. brevicauda*. Total length, 103–120; tail, 19–25; hind foot 12–16; weight, 13–17 g.

Notes. See discussion under *B. carolinensis*. In a recent publication, it was noted that considerable mensural overlap is found in geographic areas of sympatry between *B. hylophaga* and *B. brevicauda*, evincing the need for additional karyotypic and morphometric studies of these two shrews.

Selected References. George et al. (1981, 1982); Moncrief et al. (1982).

Photo by R. Altig

Cryptotis parva
Least Shrew

Distribution. This diminutive shrew ranges from southernmost Ontario and the northeastern United States, westward to Colorado and South Dakota, and southward through much of Texas, eastern and central Mexico, to western Panama. In the north-central states, it has been taken as far north as extreme southeastern Minnesota and the southern parts of Wisconsin and Michigan. [After this account was prepared, a shrew of this species was taken in Pipestone County, Minnesota, indicating that it may be found elsewhere in southern Minnesota and adjacent Iowa and South Dakota in areas not shaded on our maps.]

Description. A small shrew, solidly built, with a short tail. Winter pelage dark brown (sometimes reddish brown) dorsally, dark grayish ventrally; summer pelage somewhat shorter and paler. Total length, 68–86; tail, 13–18; hind foot, 9–12; weight, 4–6.5 g.

Natural History. The least shrew evidently is not so much dependent on mesic habitats as are many other insectivores, being more an animal of upland prairies, weedy fencerows and fields, meadows, grassy roadsides, and the like. Although its range overlaps those of several species of *Sorex*, it is rarely captured with them. This animal is gregarious, perhaps even colonial, because several adults often occupy a single nest (31 were found nesting together under a log in Texas). Individuals utter clicks and high-pitched chirps, as well as other sounds beyond the range of human hearing.

C. parva feeds on a variety of animal and vegetable material; important items seem to be insects, earthworms, spiders, centipedes, snails, and slugs. Individuals have been reported to consume as much as 60 to 100 percent of their own body weight each day. Owls probably are the most important natural enemy. Hawks and snakes also prey on these shrews, and carnivores sometimes kill them. Chiggers, mites, and fleas are known ectoparasites; cestodes, nematodes, and trematodes are recorded endoparasites.

The breeding season extends from early spring to midautumn. Females bear several litters a year, and early young may breed later in the season. Litter size ranges from two to seven but normally is four to six. The gestation period lasts 21–23 days. Young weigh about a third of a gram at birth and are naked and blind. They mature rapidly and reach essentially adult size in only about two weeks. As in other shrews, the juvenile pelage is thin and "fuzzy" in contrast to that of adults.

Selected References. Whitaker (1974).

Parascalops breweri

Hairy-tailed Mole

Distribution. This species is known only from the northeastern United States and adjacent southeastern Canada, west to south-central Ontario, central Ohio, and eastern Kentucky, and south to southwestern North Carolina.

Description. Color blackish dorsally, slightly paler ventrally; tail thick, fleshy, constricted at base, and covered with long, coarse hairs. Snout relatively short, nostrils laterally directed. Dental formula 3/3, 1/1, 4/4, 3/3, total 44. Total length, 145–175; tail, 25–38; hind foot, 17–21; weight, 40–65 g. Males average slightly larger than females.

Natural History. This mole, like others, is primarily fossorial, although individuals occasionally forage above ground, particularly at night. It is not restricted to any particular habitat, being found in both coniferous and deciduous woodlands, pasturelands, cultivated fields, and grassy roadsides. It favors sandy loam soils with good surface cover and at least modest moisture content. Dry soils or those high in clay content are avoided.

P. breweri is mostly solitary except during the breeding season and when young are with females, but several moles may utilize the same system of tunnels. Individuals are active the year around, but they remain below ground when the surface is frozen. Main tunnels are smooth and well packed, usually dug from four to eight inches underground. Some deeper tunnels, up to a foot and a half below ground, also are constructed, and smaller, ill-defined tunnels are formed while foraging. The latter sometimes result in surface ridges, but not as conspicuous as those formed by *Scalopus*. A spherical nest, located in a deep tunnel, is built of grass and shredded leaves. Deep tunnel systems are marked by mounds at the surface, as are those of other moles, especially in autumn.

Earthworms evidently are the principal food of this mole; insects, other invertebrates, and rootlets also are eaten. Fleas, mites, and lice parasitize this species, as do spiny-headed worms and nematodes internally.

Mating takes place in early spring. Females bear a single litter of four or five young annually. The gestation period has been estimated as four to six weeks. Young remain in the natal nest for about a month. Juvenile pelage is grayer and much shorter than the summer pelage of adults.

Selected References. Hallett (1978).

Scalopus aquaticus
Eastern Mole

Distribution. The eastern mole has the broadest distribution of any New World talpid, ranging throughout most of the eastern and central United States, northward to Massachusetts, Michigan, and Minnesota, and westward to Colorado, Texas, and northernmost Mexico. It occurs in much of the southern part of our region, north to central Minnesota and Wisconsin and the Lower Peninsula of Michigan (and adjacent southernmost Ontario).

Description. A robust mole with a short, essentially hairless tail. Pelage dark brownish through silvery gray to blackish above, slightly paler ventrally; whitish to yellowish ventral blotching not uncommon. Dental formula 3/2, 1/0, 3/3, 3/3, total 36. Total length, 165–205; tail, 25–38; hind foot, 22–27; weight, 70–120 g. Males average significantly larger than females.

Natural History. This mole spends most of its life underground. Tunnels are of two types, those used for foraging near the surface, which result in the characteristic ridges so familiar to gardeners and grounds keepers, and those constructed more permanently six to 10 inches below ground. A nest four to six inches in diameter is built of grass, leaves, and fine rootlets in the permanent burrow system, typically in a well-drained site. Moist loose soils are preferred by this species, but all but the driest and hardest substrates are occupied, in both forested and nonforested habitats. Individuals may be active at any time of day or night. In a recent study in Kentucky, home ranges of adult males averaged about 2.7 acres, whereas those of females averaged less than an acre in extent.

The diet of the eastern mole consists mostly of earthworms and adult and larval insects, but some vegetable matter also is taken. Even though adults swim well, flooding may be an important cause of mortality in some places, particularly among young. Predation on *S. aquaticus* is minimal because it spends so little time above ground. Large birds of prey take some and carnivores probably kill a few. Like other moles, adults molt twice a year.

Females give birth to a single litter per year, in spring, after a gestation period estimated to be about five weeks. Litters consist of two to five young, usually four.

Selected References. Yates and Schmidly (1978).

Condylura cristata
Star-nosed Mole

Distribution. This unique mole is found in the eastern parts of Canada and the United States, from Labrador south to Georgia and west to Manitoba and Minnesota. It occurs in the eastern and northern parts of the seven-state region, but the southern limits of its range there are imperfectly documented.

Description. Nose ringed by 22 fleshy appendages. Pelage blackish throughout, dense and shiny. Tail long, constricted at base, covered with coarse black hairs. Dental formula same as *Parascalops*; cranial bones exceptionally thin. Total length, 160–205; tail, 58–82; hind foot, 23–30; weight, 35–70 g. Males do not average larger than females, but individuals in northern populations are larger than those from farther south.

Natural History. The star-nosed mole is both diurnal and nocturnal but is most active at night and in early morning hours. It is a gregarious, perhaps even colonial, animal, and there are numerous records of multiple captures in a single burrow system. This species is much less fossorial than other moles and is an excellent swimmer, spending much time in the water. It is active under snow in winter and even has been observed swimming under ice; there is some evidence that more time is spent in water in winter than in summer.

Burrows, from just under the surface to two feet or so in depth, typically are constructed near water, in or near marshy areas and along streams, and sometimes have underwater openings. They most commonly are located around fallen logs, stumps, roots, and rocks. Nests usually are built in some naturally elevated spot so as to avoid flooding during periods of high water. These are composed of unshredded leaves and grasses.

Aquatic annelids and insects make up the bulk of the diet when available, but grubs, earthworms, and other invertebrates also are eaten. A variety of raptors prey on *Condylura*; carnivores and perhaps large fish probably take a few. Mites and fleas are known ectoparasites, and cestodes and nematodes, including ascarid worms, have been reported as endoparasites.

Females are thought to produce only one litter annually, consisting of two to seven young (average about five), in spring or early summer.

Selected References. Petersen and Yates (1980).

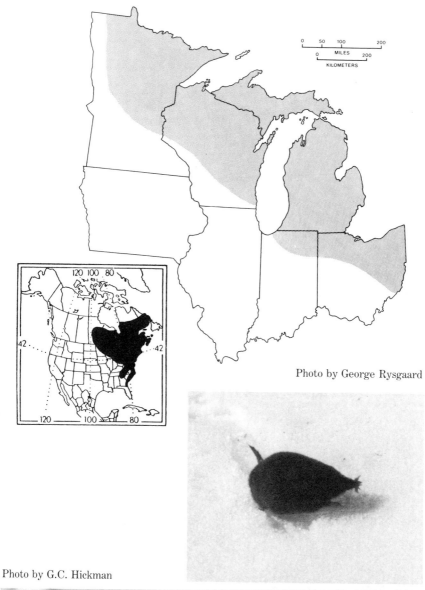

Photo by George Rysgaard

Photo by G.C. Hickman

Order Chiroptera

Bats

Bats are volant and thus unique among mammals. The flying surface consists of the wings and the interfemoral membrane (uropatagium), double-layered extensions of skin that encompass the forelimbs, hind limbs except the feet, and, in all species in the north-central states, most or all of the tail. Elongate bones of the fingers and hand support the wing, with the exception of the thumb, which is small, clawed, and not included in the wing membrane. All bats of this region feed on insects; the W-shaped cusps of the molars are not much modified from the condition found in most Insectivora.

The fossil record of the Chiroptera is sketchy, but, oddly enough, one of the earliest known bats is a completely preserved skeleton from early Eocene deposits in Wyoming. Modern chiropterans are divided into two suborders (only one, Microchiroptera, occurs in the New World) and are representative of 17 families and about 170 genera and 900 species. Only two families, Vespertilionidae and Molossidae, and 15 species occur in the seven states covered by this handbook.

Because insects, the source of food for all bats of north-temperate and boreal environments, are scarce or unavailable in the colder months of the year, bats of this region have developed strategies to cope with this situation. Some migrate many miles in autumn to warmer habitats to the south, returning again in spring; others hibernate over winter; and some species apparently exhibit both types of behavior.

Rabies has been detected in all species of bats in this region. The incidence of infection is low in natural populations, however, and few human cases of rabies have been attributed to bats. As a precaution, bats found on the ground or in other unusual places, especially in daylight when they normally would be roosting, should be avoided or handled with extreme care.

Key to Bats

1. Tail extending conspicuously beyond posterior border of uropatagium; anterior border of ear with horny bumps; lower incisors bifid (Molossidae) 2

1'. Tail not extending conspicuously (5 at most) beyond posterior border of uropatagium; anterior border of ear relatively smooth; lower incisors trifid (Vespertilionidae) 3

2. Size large, forearm 55 or more; ears joined at base, extending well beyond nose when laid forward; incisors 1/2 . . . . . . *Tadarida macrotis*

2'. Size medium, forearm less than 50; ears not joined at base, extending little if at all beyond nose when laid forward; incisors 1/3 . . . . *Tadarida brasiliensis*

3. Single pair of upper incisors (incisors 1/3); total number of teeth 30 or 32, if 32 uropatagium thickly furred 4

3'. Two pairs of upper incisors (incisors 2/3); total number of teeth 32–38, if 32 uropatagium essentially naked 6

4. Premolars 1/2, total of 30 teeth; overall color dark brown; uropatagium essentially naked . . . . *Nycticeius humeralis*

4'. Premolars 2/2, total of 32 teeth; overall color not dark brown; uropatagium thickly furred 5

5. Dorsal pelage dark brownish tipped with grayish white; forearm more than 45; greatest length of skull more than 17 . . . . . *Lasiurus cinereus*

5'. Dorsal pelage reddish orange to chestnut; forearm less than 45; greatest length of skull less than 15 . . . . *Lasiurus borealis*

6. Dorsal pelage blackish frosted with white or, if not, ear tremendously enlarged (27 or more in length from notch); premolars 2/3, total of 36 teeth 7

6'. Dorsal pelage dark brown through reddish brown to yellowish; ear not noticeably enlarged (21 or less in length from notch); premolars 1/2, 2/2, or 3/3, total of 32, 34, or 38 teeth 8

7. Upper surface of uropatagium furred proximally from a third to half its length; dorsal pelage blackish frosted with white; ear from notch less than 15 . . . . *Lasionycteris noctivagans*

7'. Upper surface of uropatagium only thinly furred at base; dorsal pelage brownish; ear from notch 27 or more . . . . . *Plecotus rafinesquii*

8. Upper surface of uropatagium furred proximally, sometimes thinly,

for a third to half its length; premolars 2/2, total of 34
teeth ....*Pipistrellus subflavus*

8'. Upper surface of uropatagium only thinly furred at base; premolars
1/2 or 3/3, total of 32 or 38 teeth.................................9

9. Total length usually more than 110 (average about 120); greatest
length of skull more than 18; premolars 1/2, total of 32
teeth ....*Eptesicus fuscus*

9'. Total length less than 110 (usually less than 100); greatest length
of skull less than 18; premolars 3/3, total of 38 teeth 10

10. Wing attached at ankle; forearm usually more than 40; greatest
length of skull usually more than 15.5 ....*Myotis grisescens*

10'. Wing attached at base of toe; forearm usually less than 40;
greatest length of skull usually less than 15.5 11

11. Ears and membranes dark brownish to blackish, contrasting
noticeably with color of dorsum, distinct dark facial mask; forearm
less than 34; hind foot small, usually 8 or less ....*Myotis leibii*

11'. Ears and membranes brownish, not contrasting noticeably with
color of dorsum, no distinct facial mask; forearm more than
34; hind foot usually 9 or more 12

12. Ear relatively long, usually 16–17 from notch; tragus long (about 9)
tapering to a pointed tip; greatest length of skull averaging more
than 15.0 ....*Myotis septentrionalis*

12'. Ear of moderate length from notch, usually 13–15; tragus moderate
in length (6–7), less tapered at tip; greatest length of skull
rarely exceeding 15.0...13

13. Braincase low, rising only gradually from rostrum; hairs on hind foot
not extending beyond toes; calcar strongly keeled .....*Myotis sodalis*

13'. Braincase higher, rising moderately to abruptly from rostrum;
hairs on hind foot extending beyond toes; calcar not keeled
or indistinctly so...14

14. Braincase rising moderately abruptly from rostrum; dorsal pelage
glossy in appearance, ventral pelage not tipped with white
or tan ....*Myotis lucifugus*

14'. Braincase rising abruptly from rostrum; dorsal pelage "woolly"
in appearance, ventral pelage tipped with white
or tan ....*Myotis austroriparius*

Myotis austroriparius

Southeastern Myotis

Distribution. This bat, as the vernacular name suggests, inhabits the southeastern United States. It is found from Florida westward to southeastern Oklahoma and eastern Texas, and it reaches the northern limit of its range in the southern parts of Illinois and Indiana.

Description. Medium-sized member of genus with an abruptly rising and globose braincase. Dorsum grayish to russet, even orangish before annual molt, pelage somewhat "woolly" in appearance; venter tan to whitish. Total length, 80–95; tail, 35–45; hind foot, 8–11; ear, 14–15; forearm, 36–41; weight, 4–9 g.

Natural History. This species hibernates over winter in the northern part of its range, principally in caves and mines. Clusters of 50–100 have been reported but populations of the southeastern myotis have declined noticeably in some places in recent years, and single individuals or small groups now are the rule in Indiana, for example. Hibernating bats can be found in the open, hanging on ceilings or walls of caves, but many times they are wedged into a hole, crack, or crevice, sometimes in association with *M. lucifugus*. This bat may be active all year in the South, where groups have been reported congregating by day in such sites as buildings, culverts, storm sewers, hollow trees, and under bridges.

Wintering habitats, including hibernacula, are evidently in the same general vicinity as summer haunts. Thus, this species probably does not exhibit the local to regional seasonal movements seen in many other species of *Myotis*. Homing ability does not seem to be as well developed as in most other species of the genus.

In active periods during the warm months, *M. austroriparius* is said to be closely associated with water. Individuals emerge at dusk, usually foraging only a few feet above streams or ponds. The flight pattern has been described as "low, rapid, and stable." Mites, chiggers, and batflies have been reported as ectoparasites. Predators include carnivores, owls, and snakes, the latter preying on roosting bats.

Uniquely among American *Myotis*, females usually produce twins, which are born in maternity colonies in late April or May. Bats of this species have been observed copulating in both autumn and spring.

Selected References. Barbour and Davis (1969); LaVal (1970); Lowery (1974).

Myotis grisescens
Gray Myotis

Distribution. This species is found only in the south-central part of the eastern United States, from northwestern Florida northward to the southern part of the region covered by this handbook, eastward to the Appalachians, and westward to eastern Oklahoma and southeastern Kansas. In the north-central states, it is known from the southern parts of Illinois and Indiana and from one locality along the southern boundary of Ohio.

Description. Largest species of myotis in north-central states. Grayish brown dorsally, pelage relatively sparse and "woolly" in appearance; grayish white ventrally. Wing membrane attached at ankle rather than at base of toe as in other *Myotis*. Total length, 90–107; tail, 32–47; hind foot, 9–13; ear, 12–16; forearm, 40–45; weight usually 8–12 g.

Natural History. The gray myotis has been described as a "true" cave bat. This is a reasonable statement because this species finds retreats principally in caves both in summer and winter. A few man-made cavelike structures, such as storm sewers, occasionally are inhabited, but, surprisingly, no reports are on record of *M. grisescens* occupying abandoned mines. In summer, females form maternity colonies usually in large, deep, well-watered caves and frequently including many thousands of individuals, whereas males and barren females congregate in other reaches of the same structure or in different caves.

This is a migratory species in that individuals rarely remain over winter in the same cave occupied in summer; rather they usually move a hundred miles or more to relatively inaccessible, deep caves in which they hibernate, clustering in the thousands on ceiling and walls. Flocking is thought to characterize seasonal movements. Populations of the gray myotis have declined in recent years owing primarily to disturbance by humans. Caves in which they hibernate or spend the summer have been vandalized or converted to commercial exploitation, and these and other insectivorous bats are susceptible to poisoning indirectly through human use of various insecticides.

As in other hibernating species, copulation takes place in autumn prior to hibernation and probably occasionally over winter. Females bear a single young in June.

Selected References. Barbour and Davis (1969); Tuttle (1975, 1976a, 1976b, 1979); Tuttle and Stevenson (1977).

Myotis leibii
Eastern Small-footed Myotis

Distribution. The eastern small-footed myotis, which occurs from the Ozarks northeastward to New England and southeastern Canada, is known from but one locality in the north-central states. A large, disjunct western population (found from southwestern Canada to central Mexico and east to the western Great Plains) currently is recognized as a separate species, *M. ciliolabrum*, but until recently was considered to be conspecific with *M. leibii*. The inset map on the facing page shows the combined distributions of the two species.

The one known specimen from our region was taken more than a century ago in Erie County, Ohio, but this species is to be looked for in the southern tier of states and in the eastern part of Michigan's Upper Peninsula.

Description. Smallest species of *Myotis* in the seven states. Yellowish brown dorsally, hairs with shiny tips giving a burnished appearance; paler, more buffy ventrally. Ears and membranes dark blackish brown; distinct blackish facial mask. Calcar keeled. Total length, 75–85; tail, 32–40; hind foot, 7–9; ear, 13–15; forearm, 30–34; weight, 3.5–6 g.

Natural History. This bat is known as a saxicolous species, and thus is restricted primarily to rocky areas with fissures, caves, and abandoned mines. In hibernation, individual *M. leibii* tend to roost singly or in small groups, wedged into cracks or crevices in a cool, dry cave or mine. In the warm months, daytime retreats may be in such sites as man-made structures, under rocks, in abandoned swallow nests, and even in holes in banks and hillsides, in addition to the usual haunts. Females with their young normally roost alone, but small maternity colonies of up to a dozen or so females have been reported.

This myotis emerges early in the evening from its diurnal roost, coursing over streams and ponds and along cliffs, ledges, and riparian woodland in search of insects. Nocturnal activity may be interrupted one or more times by periods of rest.

As in other hibernating bats, most mating takes place in autumn prior to hibernation, sperm being held in the female until time for fertilization in spring. Occasional overwinter and spring breeding probably also occurs. Females bear a single young from late May to early July.

Selected References. Barbour and Davis (1969, 1974); Mohr (1933, 1936); van Zyll de Jong (1985).

Myotis lucifugus
Little Brown Myotis

Distribution. This widespread North American species is found from Alaska and Labrador southward to northern and perhaps central Mexico. It occurs throughout the north-central states.

Description. Medium-sized member of genus *Myotis*. Dorsum dark brown, pelage sleek and glossy (often with a metallic coppery sheen); venter paler, sometimes slightly grayish. Ears and membranes brownish. Total length, 83–100; tail, 33–42; hind foot, 9–12; ear, 13–16; forearm, 34–40; weight usually 5.5–9.5 g.

Natural History. Because it is widely distributed and is common in many areas, and because it frequently inhabits man-made structures, this is one of the best known of American bats. These myotis begin foraging for their insect prey at late dusk, frequenting the same areas night after night. The usual flight pattern is over water, such as streams and rivers, ponds, and lakes; along the borders of copses and riparian growth; and in nearby open areas. A variety of insects, such as flies, moths, and small beetles, is eaten. Summer retreats are in such places as hollows in trees, caves, crevices, and a variety of human structures.

Maternity colonies of up to several thousand females form in late spring and early summer, frequently in warm buildings; the same sites may be used year after year. Males and barren females usually roost singly or in small groups in warm weather. All roosts are near available water. Dispersal in summer from hibernation sites ranges from a short distance to 300 miles or more.

Hibernation takes place from September or early October to April or May, depending on latitude. Typical hibernacula are in caves or mines that have a relatively high humidity and temperatures varying from 40° to 60°F. The bats hang singly or in small clusters or wedge themselves into cracks or crevices.

Most mating may take place prior to entry into hibernation; in large hibernacula, however, copulating pairs may be found throughout the colder months. Parturition dates vary with latitude, but the single young (rarely twins) usually is born from late May to early July. Known longevity in this species is slightly more than 30 years, the longest recorded for any bat.

Selected References. Fenton and Barclay (1980).

Myotis septentrionalis
Northern Myotis

Distribution. The northern myotis occurs in southern Canada (from Labrador to western Saskatchewan) and the eastern United States (west to the Great Plains and south to the Florida Peninsula) and is found throughout the north-central states. A disjunct population in western British Columbia and adjacent Washington, now recognized as a separate species, *M. keenii*, until recently was considered to be conspecific with *M. septentrionalis.* The inset map on the facing page shows the combined distributions of both species.

Description. A medium-sized myotis with relatively long ears and a long, pointed tragus. Dorsum dull brownish, venter pale grayish brown; membranes slightly darker than dorsal pelage; calcar slightly keeled. Total length, 78–95; tail, 32–34; hind foot, 8–10; ear, 16–18; forearm, 32–37; weight, 5–9.5 g.

Natural History. This bat, although widely distributed, usually is not especially common locally. Thus its biology is not so well known as that of some other species of *Myotis.* It hibernates in caves and mines where individuals may hang in the open, sometimes with other species, but also wedge themselves into cracks, crevices, or holes in the ceiling or walls. Precise information as to the duration of hibernation is unavailable, but probably it lasts from early October to late March or April in the southern part of the region, longer in the north.

In the warm months, a few males may remain in and around the winter hibernaculum, but females and other males disperse to summer haunts up to 100 miles or more away. Maternity colonies usually contain fewer than a dozen females but may range upward to 30 or more. Daytime retreats in summer are in abandoned or little-used man-made structures, behind loose bark of trees or shutters of buildings, beneath shingles, in tree hollows, and even in such places as birdhouses.

A single offspring is born in late spring or early summer. Lactation has been recorded well into August in the northern parts of the range, suggesting that young bats there may have minimal time to accumulate adequate fat reserves for hibernation. Adults molt once a year in midsummer. Known longevity from banding studies is 18.5 years.

Selected References. Fitch and Shump (1979); Jones et al. (1983); van Zyll de Jong (1979, 1985).

Myotis sodalis
Social Myotis

Distribution. The social myotis is distributed throughout much of the eastern United States, from New Hampshire and Vermont south to northern Florida, and westward to eastern Oklahoma. It occurs in the southern part of the seven-state region, northward to central Iowa and southern Michigan.

Description. Medium-sized myotis, relatively dark in color. Pelage fine and fluffy, dull in appearance. Dorsum dark pinkish gray (usually) to blackish brown, the individual hairs tricolored; venter somewhat paler. Calcar slightly keeled; hairs on hind foot short and inconspicuous. Total length, 77–95; tail, 35–43; hind foot, 7–10; ear, 13–15; forearm, 34–41; weight usually 5–8 g.

Natural History. This species appears to be most common, at least in hibernacula in the colder months, in southern Indiana, Kentucky, and the Ozarks of Missouri. It hibernates in caves, usually in tight clusters, sometimes in association with *M. lucifugus*. Swarming occurs around hibernating sites prior to dispersal in spring and prior to entry into torpor in autumn. Males occupy hibernacula later than females, ordinarily in early or mid-November, and usually remain there later in the spring, until mid-April or so. Like other hibernating bats, individuals may be active within a cave from time to time during winter.

Upon quitting hibernacula in spring, females form maternity colonies, evidently mostly in tree hollows and behind loose slabs of bark. Males probably disperse in small groups in the warm months, finding daytime retreats in caves, mines, and similar sites. Nighttime foraging patterns frequently are over or near water. In one study in Indiana, individuals were observed feeding near the foliage of riparian and floodplain trees from about six feet above the ground to as high as 100 feet.

As with many other bats that hibernate, most mating takes place in autumn, prior to hibernation, but it has been observed also in hibernacula in both winter and spring months. Females evidently give birth to a single offspring in June or early July. Known longevity in this species, based on records of banded bats, is about 14 years. Like all other bats in this region, *M. sodalis* molts once a year, in summer.

Selected References. Humphrey et al. (1977); Thomson (1982).

Lasionycteris noctivagans
Silver-haired Bat

Distribution. This species occurs in temperate North America, from southern Alaska and Canada southward to northeastern Mexico. It may be found as a migrant anywhere in the north-central states; as a summer resident it is known from all but the southern part of the region, and torpid individuals have been taken in Illinois, Indiana, Michigan, and Minnesota in winter.

Description. A handsome, distinctively colored bat. Upper parts blackish brown overall, the long, silky pelage frosted with silvery white; venter somewhat paler and less frosted; membranes blackish brown. Ears short, rounded, and naked; uropatagium furred dorsally on basal half. Total length, 90–108; tail, 38–45; hind foot, 7–10; ear, 12–17; forearm, 38–43; weight, 8.5–12.5 g.

Natural History. This is a migratory species, and for many years it was thought to vacate most of the northern parts of its range in the colder months. Although a wintering specimen has been taken as far south as the San Carlos Mountains in northeastern Mexico, and there are abundant records of spring and autumn migrants at localities where this bat does not otherwise occur, little is known of its whereabouts in winter. Evidence is accumulating that at least some individuals hibernate at middle latitudes in such places as caves, mines, buildings, and hollow trees, and it may be that both migration and hibernation are strategies available to *L. noctivagans.*

During the warm months, silver-haired bats roost singly, principally under loose bark and in tree hollows, but also in such places as buildings, bird nests, and dense canopy. Migrants have been found in various shelters, including piles of boards and bricks. In many places, this species begins foraging in early evening, but it has been characterized as a late flier in other areas; also, a marked bimodality of nocturnal activity may be present. Activity patterns may depend on the presence or absence of other species of bats. *L. noctivagans* is apparently an opportunistic feeder, judging from the variety of insects thus far identified as food items.

Mating takes place in autumn, and the young, usually twins, are born in June or early July. Following delayed fertilization, gestation lasts 50–60 days.

Selected References. Kunz (1982).

Pipistrellus subflavus
Eastern Pipistrelle

Distribution. The eastern pipistrelle ranges over much of eastern North America, from southeastern Canada south to Honduras and westward to the plains states. In our region, it occurs as far north as central Minnesota and the Upper Peninsula of Michigan, but apparently is absent from eastern Wisconsin and most of Lower Michigan. [While this account was in press, a bat of this species was captured in northeastern Minnesota, north of the shaded area on the distribution maps.]

Description. One of the smallest bats in north-central states (about same size as *Myotis leibii*). Dorsal color varies from yellowish brown or reddish brown to grayish brown; underparts paler; ears and membranes generally darker than dorsum. Uropatagium furred dorsally, sometimes thinly, on basal third. Total length, 75–90; tail, 33–41; hind foot, 8–10; ear, 12–14; forearm, 31–35; weight, 4–8 g.

Natural History. A hibernating species, *P. subflavus* usually seeks winter quarters in caves, mines, and rock crevices. These same structures may be used as both day and night roosts in summer, but daytime retreats in the warm months probably are primarily in the foliage of trees or in tree hollows; small maternity colonies have been found in buildings. These bats are thought to forage beginning at early dusk, mostly in open wooded areas and along woodland borders, frequently in the vicinity of water, but surprisingly little is known of the warm-weather biology of the eastern pipistrelle. In Indiana, 16 general groups of insects have been identified as food items, with leafhoppers, beetles, and dipteran flies amounting to almost 50 percent by volume.

Seasonal movements of this bat are not well known, but it evidently does not stray far in summer from hibernation sites. During torpor, individual bats usually roost singly (although small hibernating groups have been reported). They seek relatively warm, humid parts of the hibernaculum, and beads of water frequently are found on them. In Indiana, hibernation lasts from late September or early October to early May.

Females give birth to one to three young (usually twins) in June or early July. Mating takes place in autumn and occasionally in winter. As with most other bats, offspring can fly within three to four weeks. Known longevity, based on a male banded in Illinois in 1957 and recovered in 1971, is 14.8 years.

Selected References. Barbour and Davis (1969); Fujita and Kunz (1984); Jones and Pagels (1968).

Eptesicus fuscus
Big Brown Bat

Distribution. This widespread species is found in southern Canada and across the United States, southward to northern South America and on many Caribbean islands. It is distributed throughout the north-central states.

Description. A large bat, medium brownish to dark brownish above, venter somewhat paler; ears and membranes dark brown. Total length, 112–130; tail, 39–50; hind foot, 9–13; ear, 16–20; forearm, 42–50; weight, 13–25 g or more. The average male is about five percent smaller than females.

Natural History. One of the most common North American bats, *E. fuscus* is to be looked for anywhere in our region. Favorite warm-weather roosts are in buildings, but a variety of sites such as in caves, mines, rock crevices, and hollow trees and behind loose bark and other objects may be used. Hibernacula usually are in man-made structures or caves, frequently where temperatures are just above freezing. This hardy bat is active later in autumn and earlier in spring than most other species and may be active on warm winter days; there may be movement within and even between hibernacula in winter.

Torpid individuals may hang singly or in small groups, but also are found in clusters of 100 bats or more; or they may wedge themselves into holes or crevices, normally in relatively cold places in the hibernaculum. Movements from winter to summer quarters are frequently less than 50 miles. Males and nonpregnant females are mostly solitary in summer, but gravid females form maternity colonies.

Big brown bats are ordinarily early flyers that are recognized by their strong, relatively slow and steady flight; activity may continue intermittently throughout the night. There is some audible chattering while in flight. As with other bats, water is sought after leaving the daytime roost; foraging then takes place over water or clearings in woods, along riparian vegetation, and in similar situations. A variety of insects is consumed, but several kinds of beetles and true bugs seem to be preferred.

Two is the usual number of young in this region. These, weighing 3-4 g, are born in June or early July and become volant in four weeks. Known longevity is 19 years.

Selected References. Barbour and Davis (1969); Burnett (1983); Goehring (1972).

Lasiurus borealis

Red Bat

Distribution. This species ranges from southern Canada southward throughout much of South America, having the broadest distribution of any American bat. It occurs throughout the north-central region.

Description. Medium-sized bat with long, pointed wings. Dorsum bright reddish orange to chestnut (females usually duller in color than males); venter paler than dorsum; uropatagium completely and heavily furred dorsally. Ears short, rounded, and furred outwardly; shoulder patch of yellowish white. Total length, 105–125; tail, 45–60; hind foot, 8–10; ear, 10–14; forearm, 37–42; weight, 6–14 g (pregnant females to 20 or more).

Natural History. This bat is migratory in the northern part of its range. In southern Michigan, for example, the earliest record of occurrence is 30 April and the latest is early November. Thus, this species vacates the northern part of the region in the colder months, but some individuals evidently hibernate in the southern part. Those that overwinter may be active on warm winter days. Presumed hibernating sites are in hollow trees or under loose bark, but there are a few records from mines and caves. Individuals may become lost in the later retreats, however, and perish if they stray too far from the entrance.

In warm months, red bats roost by day in trees, singly or a female with young. Maples and elms are preferred but a variety of trees and tall shrubs is used, typically located in "edge" situations. While roosting, bats cling by one foot to a leaf petiole, twig, or branch and thus resemble a dead leaf. Roost sites are from a few feet to more than 40 feet high. *L. borealis* begins flight early in the evening, foraging near woodlots, along riparian growth, in trees bordering city streets and golf courses, and the like. Most activity takes place within a few hours of sunset. Females leave nonvolant young at the roost while foraging. Little is known of the distribution and habits of males in summer.

Mating takes place in autumn or on wintering grounds and has been observed between bats in flight. One to five (usually three or four) young, more than in any other bat, are born in June or early July.

Selected References. Shump and Shump (1982a).

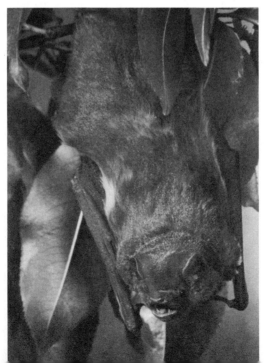

Lasiurus cinereus
Hoary Bat

Distribution. In North America, the hoary bat is found from central Canada southward at least to Guatemala. It occurs throughout the north-central states in the warm months. Disjunct populations of this species occur in South America and on the Hawaiian Islands.

Description. A large bat with long, narrow wings; ears short, rounded, furred outwardly, and edged with black; uropatagium heavily furred dorsally; membranes dark brown. Upper parts yellowish brown to mahogany but washed with silver (thus hoary in overall color); venter whitish to yellowish; yellowish white shoulder patch. Total length, 133–150; tail, 46–65; hind foot, 10–14; ear, 17–20; forearm, 52–57; weight, 15–35 g.

Natural History. This species is strongly migratory, vacating most of the seven states in the colder months. Wintering grounds are thought to be mostly in Mexico, but little precise information is available on migration. A few winter records exist for the southern part of the north-central region and, like the red bat and silver-haired bat, some individuals may remain there through the cold months.

Like other members of the genus, this bat seeks daytime retreats in tall, woody vegetation, roosting in sites that are covered from above but open below. It emerges to drink and forage later than most other species and rarely is seen before nightfall. The flight pattern is swift, and individuals may chatter audibly in flight. In a study in Iowa, greatest activity of hoary bats was from three to seven hours after sunset, with a second period of foraging before daylight. Except in migration and females with young, this bat is solitary. Males and females tend to be segregated in summer, the former apparently more common at higher altitudes. As for many migratory species, there are a number of records from well outside the normal range.

Moths evidently are the principal food, but beetles, bugs, flies, and other insects also are taken. Like most other noncolonial bats, *L. cinereus* has few ectoparasites. Internally, cestodes, nematodes, and trematodes have been reported.

Females bear offspring (usually twins) from late May to early July, depending somewhat on latitude. As with other *Lasiurus*, there are four mammae.

Selected References. Shump and Shump (1982*b*).

Nycticeius humeralis
Evening Bat

Distribution. The evening bat occurs in much of the eastern United States, from Pennsylvania southward to Florida and westward to the Great Plains. It is distributed also in northeastern Mexico, and a related species is found on Cuba. In the north-central states, *N. humeralis* ranges northward as far as southern Michigan and Wisconsin.

Description. Medium-sized bat with dark brown dorsum and slightly paler venter; ears and membranes blackish. Resembles big brown bat but smaller and incisors 1/3 instead of 2/3. Also resembles some species of *Myotis* but only 30 instead of 38 teeth. Total length, 80–96; tail, 30–40; hind foot, 7–9; ear, 12–14; forearm, 30–37; weight, 7–14 g.

Natural History. This is a bat of the eastern deciduous forest. It roosts by day in hollow trees, behind loose bark, and also in a variety of human structures. Maternity colonies of females and young, sometimes containing hundreds of individuals, have been found in old buildings and in hollow trees. In one case in Indiana, a nursery colony was shared with big brown bats. *N. humeralis* usually begins to forage in twilight, coursing over clearings, farm ponds, and along the borders of woodlands and watercourses. It is rather slow and deliberate in flight, rarely venturing above treetop level.

This is a migratory bat, quitting the northern part of its range in late summer or autumn and returning again in spring. Records from Indiana are from early April to mid-November. Males normally do not accompany females northward in spring, apparently remaining instead on the wintering grounds, but few precise data are available. Torpid individuals have been taken in winter in southern Arkansas, but *N. humeralis* is known to be active in all months in the Southeast; much remains to be learned about winter habits.

As with many other bats, a sense of homing is well developed. Evening bats removed as much as 100 miles from their home roosts have returned to them within a few days. Ectoparasites include mites and batbugs, whereas flatworms, roundworms, and tapeworms have been found internally. Females bear one to three young, usually twins, in June or early July.

Selected References. Watkins (1972); Watkins and Shump (1981).

Plecotus rafinesquii

Rafinesque's Big-eared Bat

Distribution. This species occurs only in the southeastern United States, westward to Oklahoma and Texas. It reaches the northern known extent of its distribution in central Indiana.

Description. A relatively pale-colored, medium-sized bat with tremendously enlarged ears and two large lumps on nose. Upper parts brownish gray overall, underparts whitish, individual dorsal hairs dark brown or blackish basally, pale reddish or brownish distally. Long hairs on feet project beyond toes. Total length, 85–105; tail, 43–50; hind foot, 9–12; ear, 27–37; forearm, 38–45; weight, 8–13 g.

A related species, *Plecotus townsendii*, ranges northward nearly to the north-central states (northern Kentucky and West Virginia) and may one day be found there. From it, *P. rafinesquii* differs in that the first upper incisors are bicuspid (rather than unicuspid), the hairs on the hind feet project beyond the toes, the underparts are whitish (rather than brownish), and the dorsum is more grayish and the hairs distinctly bicolored.

Natural History. This species is relatively rare in the northern part of its range. It remains there in winter, choosing caves or mines as hibernacula. In the South, however, at least some individuals are active in every month of the year. Summer roosts include unoccupied buildings, crevices, hollows in trees, behind loose bark, and similar situations in addition to caves and mines. Females form maternity colonies ranging in size from a few bats up to 100 or more; these are frequently in dilapidated buildings. Males are usually solitary in summer.

P. rafinesquii prefers to roost in dimly lighted places. In winter, torpid individuals may be found near the entrance to the hibernaculum; in summer, day roosts tend to be more open and lighted than those of most other bats. Foraging takes place after dark and individuals return to daytime quarters before dawn. Little is known of the insect food of this species. Adults molt once a year, from July to September, males and barren females earlier than females that rear young.

Mating takes place in autumn and winter. A single offspring, weighing about 2.5 g, is born in late May or June. The young are volant in three to four weeks.

Selected References. Barbour and Davis (1969); Jones (1977).

Tadarida brasiliensis
Brazilian Free-tailed Bat

Distribution. This free-tailed bat occurs from the western and southeastern United States southward into South America and on Caribbean islands (see inset map). It is known by accidental records in the north-central states only from one locality in Illinois and two in Ohio, well to the north of the normal range of the species (see half symbols on map).

Description. Small among members of genus. Color usually dark grayish brown above, slightly paler below; membranes dark brown. Ears not joined at base. Total length, 90–100; tail, 30–40; hind foot, 8–11; ear, 13–18; forearm, 40–45; weight, 8–14 g.

Notes. This is a migratory colonial species. Adults migrating northward in spring occasionally overshoot the intended destination within the usual range, accounting for some records far to the north of known colonies. Dispersing young also may wander in unusual directions in late summer and early autumn.

Selected References. Barbour and Davis (1969); Jones et al. (1983).

Tadarida macrotis
Big Free-tailed Bat

Distribution. This species is distributed from the western United States (north to Colorado and Utah and east to Kansas, Oklahoma, and Texas) southward to southeastern Mexico (no inset map). It is known in the north-central states only from Iowa, where autumn stragglers were taken at Cedar Rapids in 1910 and at Marshalltown in 1914 (see solid symbols on map).

Description. Largest of American *Tadarida*. Upper parts usually dark brown, ranging from reddish brown to almost black; venter slightly paler than dorsum. Ears joined basally at midline. Total length, 125–138; tail, 46–54; hind foot, 12–16; ear, 28–30; forearm, 58–64; weight to 20 g or more.

Notes. The two Iowa specimens are from far northeast of the normal distribution of this migratory species and probably represent young of the year that wandered northward during autumn migration.

Selected References. Barbour and Davis (1969); Easterla (1973).

Tadarida brasiliensis.

Tadarida
macrotis.

Order Lagomorpha
Hares and Rabbits

Lagomorphs and rodents once were thought to be closely related and to belong to the same order. Basically this resulted from certain shared characteristics, including such things as a large pair of incisors both above and below and a long diastema between incisors and cheekteeth. More recent studies have shown, however, superficial resemblance aside, that the two groups have had a long, independent history in the fossil record and that the ancestors of modern hares and rabbits probably diverged from early rodentlike stock as far back as the Paleocene. There are two familes of Recent Lagomorpha – the Ochotonidae (pikas) and the Leporidae. Only leporids occur in the north-central states, represented by three species of hares (*Lepus*), one introduced, and two of rabbits (*Sylvilagus*).

In addition to the large pair of upper incisors, there is a second, smaller pair directly behind the first. The skull is fenestrate, lightening it somewhat, which aids in balance and locomotion. As mentioned, there is a diastema between the incisors and the high-crowned cheekteeth; the dental formula of all leporids in this region is 2/1, 0/0, 3/2, 3/3, total 28. There are 12 modern genera of lagomorphs and 65 recognized species. The order is nearly worldwide in distribution but has been introduced in a number of places where it did not occur natively, such as on Australia and New Zealand. The classical distinction between hares and rabbits is that the young of the former are precocial, whereas those of the latter are altricial.

Key to Hares and Rabbits

1. Interparietal bone distinct, not fused to parietals;
   hind foot less than 115 2
1'. Interparietal bone indistinct, fused to parietals; hind foot usually
   more than 120 (slightly less in smallest *Lepus americanus*)..........3
2. Anterior projection of supraorbital process minute or lacking,
   posterior projection completely fused to braincase; size large, hind
   foot usually more than 100 ....*Sylvilagus aquaticus*
2'. Anterior projection of supraorbital process distinct, posterior
   projection reaching (but not fused or incompletely fused with)
   braincase; size medium, hind foot usually less than
   100 ....*Sylvilagus floridanus*
3. Ear less than 90; no (or small and indistinct) anterior projection on
   supraorbital process ....*Lepus americanus*
3'. Ear more than 90; large, distinct anterior projection
   on supraorbital process..4
4. Tail mostly white (at most a middorsal line of grayish black); pelage
   white in winter; rostrum relatively narrow and shallow; length
   of nasal bones usually less than 42 ....*Lepus townsendii*
4'. Tail blackish above; pelage brown in winter; rostrum broad and
   deep; length of nasal bones usually more than 42 .....*Lepus capensis*

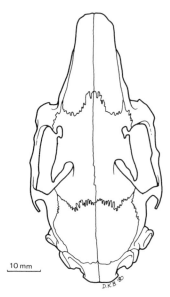

10 mm

D.K.B. '80

Figure 1. Dorsal view of the skull of a snowshoe hare, *Lepus americanus*. Note lack of an interparietal bone, typical of the genus *Lepus*, and the small anterior projections of the supraorbital processes, typical of this species.

Sylvilagus aquaticus
Swamp Rabbit

Distribution. The swamp rabbit occurs only in the southern United States, from Georgia and western South Carolina westward to central Texas. To the north, the range barely reaches southeastern Kansas, southern Missouri, and the southern parts of Illinois and Indiana.

Description. A large rabbit, largest member of genus *Sylvilagus*. Upper parts brownish, blackish brown middorsally, dull rusty patch on nape; venter whitish; upper surface of hind feet tan. Total length, 450–540; tail, 60–75; hind foot, 95–115; ear, 60–80; weight, 1.65–2.65 kg.

Natural History. This species occurs mostly in floodplain forests, bottomlands, and canebrakes. It favors areas with a damp to wet substrate. Swamp rabbits are excellent swimmers and readily enter water when pursued or to move from one area to another in search of food or homesites. Because of their size and delicious meat, they are regularly sought by hunters.

In captivity, swamp rabbits are territorial and males form a linear social hierarchy so that the dominate male does most of the breeding; there is more tolerance among females. In Indiana, the reproductive season has been estimated to last from February to September, with peaks in April and July. In the South, these rabbits breed in all months. Females bring forth several litters annually; litter size ranges from one to five, averaging two to three. Gestation lasts 35–40 days. The young, blind but furred at birth, are reared in a nest usually built under a log or roots of a tree. There are distinct nestling, juvenile, and subadult pelages prior to acquiring the adult coat, which thereafter is shed twice a year.

The diet includes a variety of grasses, sedges, leaves of vines and other woody plants, twigs and stems, and occasionally bark. These rabbits have a habit of defecating on logs and stumps, thus revealing their presence to the keen observer. They rest by day in "forms" under bushes and logs, in hollows, and the like. Activity is mostly in subdued light or at night. Home ranges average 10 acres or less. Hunting, severe winter weather, and a variety of predators take a toll of swamp rabbits, and flooding probably kills nestlings.

Selected References. Chapman and Feldhamer (1981).

Sylvilagus floridanus
Eastern Cottontail

Distribution. This cottontail has the broadest distribution of any lago-morph in this region, occurring in southern Canada and the eastern and cen-tral United States, in the Southwest, and southward through much of Middle America to Costa Rica. It is found throughout the north-central states except in extreme northern Minnesota and the eastern part of Michigan's Upper Peninsula.

Description. A medium-sized cottontail with dark, buffy brown to grayish brown upper parts, sprinkled with black; reddish patch on nape; rump grayer than in swamp rabbit; underparts and underside of tail white; throat and legs dark reddish brown. Total length, 360–450; tail, 35–60; hind foot, 85–102; ear, 50–62; weight, 0.9–1.5 kg.

Natural History. This rabbit is common over much of its range and is a popular game mammal. About two million are harvested annually in Indiana, for example. *S. floridanus* is primarily crepuscular in activity, but may be ac-tive at night and occasionally by day. Most of the day is spent in a "form," a shallow depression on the ground, usually in good cover; abandoned burrows of other mammals sometimes are used as retreats. Eastern cottontails are heavily parasitized externally by fleas, ticks, mites, and larval botflies. A vari-ety of endoparasites also has been reported. Carnivores and large raptors are, aside from humans, the principal predators; snakes take young cottontails.

Eastern cottontails are mostly solitary, although populations are occasion-ally high enough locally that the rabbits appear to be almost colonial. Forbs and grasses make up most of the diet in the warm months, but a good deal of browsing on twigs, buds, and bark of trees takes place in winter. Occasionally, serious girdling of trees occurs, especially in orchards. As in other lago-morphs, reingestion of the soft, green fecal pellets is commonplace, a phenomenon known as coprophagy. Water is obtained mostly from ingested foods.

The breeding season extends through all but the coldest months. Mating takes place after a vigorous courtship. Females bear several litters a year, each containing one to eight (usually four or five) young, after a gestation period of about 30 days.

Selected References. Chapman et al. (1980, 1982).

Lepus americanus
Snowshoe Hare

Distribution. This hare ranges across boreal America, from Newfoundland and Labrador to Alaska. It occurs southward in the Appalachians to Tennessee and in the montane West to New Mexico and central California. In the north-central states, it is distributed from northern and eastern Minnesota southward to south-central Michigan and Wisconsin. Within historical times, *L. americanus* was found even farther south, to approximately the southern boundaries of the latter two states and in northeastern Ohio.

Description. Smallest of New World hares. Dorsum generally rusty brown in summer with blackish brown wash, especially middorsally; venter grayish white; tail blackish above, white below. Pelage white in winter save for black-tipped ears. Total length, 370–460; tail, 25–45; hind foot, 110–140; ear, 65–90; weight, 0.7–2.1 kg.

Natural History. Snowshoe hares are generally solitary, although they may be seen in groups when populations are high. They are mostly crepuscular and nocturnal, resting during the day in a secluded spot. Foods consist of grasses, forbs, and shrubs in the warm months, bark, buds, twigs, and conifer needles in winter. Molt from the white winter coat to brown summer pelage begins in March or April, triggered by increasing amount of daylight; autumn molt begins in September or October.

These hares are of economic importance, being hunted for sport and for their meat and fur. As many as three-quarters of a million are taken in good years in Michigan, for example. Populations vary greatly, reaching a peak every nine to 10 years or so, followed by a drastic "crash." The causes of this phenomenon are not well understood, but it has a trailing effect on populations of carnivores, especially lynx, for which *L. americanus* serves as an important food source. Large raptors also take this hare.

Females bear one to seven (usually two to four) young after a gestation of about 35 days. The breeding season lasts from early spring to late summer, and females may produce three or four litters annually. The young are furred at birth and their eyes are open; they are fully active within about a week and are weaned at the age of about three weeks.

Selected References. Bittner and Rongstad (1982); Keith and Windberg (1978).

Lepus townsendii
White-tailed Jackrabbit

Distribution. The white-tailed jackrabbit is typically an inhabitant of the northern and central Great Plains and the intermontane West, occurring from the Prairie Provinces of Canada southward to northern New Mexico and central California. In our region, it is found throughout Iowa, in western and southern Minnesota, and in extreme northwestern Illinois (introductions not shown on map). There is some evidence that this hare has shifted its range northeastward within historical times. It has been widely introduced in Wisconsin, but it is not known whether native populations ever reached the western part of that state.

Description. A large hare with pale grayish brown dorsum; under parts white; tail white or at most with thin brownish to grayish black middorsal stripe. Coat white in winter except for blackish ears. Total length, 560–650; tail, 70–100; hind foot, 135–160; ear, 95–110; weight to 4.5 kg, usually 3–3.5.

Natural History. This denizen of open grasslands is a characteristic mammal of the northern plains. It is primarily crepuscular, feeding in the early morning and evening hours, but may be active at night as well. The day is spent under a bush or shrub or simply hidden in tall grass. Speed, up to 40 miles per hour in bursts, rather than concealment is principally relied upon to escape predators. Nonetheless, coyotes and other large carnivores take a toll of this hare, as do large birds of prey. Young animals are especially prone to capture. Diseases and parasites are important controls on populations. *L. townsendii* also is hunted by humans for sport and meat.

The diet consists of a variety of green vegetation in summer, including clover, alfalfa, and other crops. Twigs, buds, and dried plant material are eaten in winter. Reingestion of soft fecal pellets (coprophagy) occurs in hares, as it does in rabbits.

The breeding season begins in late February, and females bear up to four litters of one to nine (usually two to four) young each year. The latter are precocial at birth, weighing about 100 g, and are concealed in an abandoned burrow, cavity, or shallow "form." They reach adult weight in three to four months.

Selected References. Bear and Hansen (1966); James and Seabloom (1969a, 1969b); Jones et al. (1983).

Photo courtesy of U.S. Fish and Wildlife Service

Order Rodentia

Rodents

This order represents the most diverse grouping of living mammals, being represented by more than 30 families and approximately 490 genera and 1,620 species. Seven families are native to the north-central states, encompassing 37 species, and representatives of two other families have been introduced there. Because of this large number, a key first is given to families, followed by keys to species in the four native families (Sciuridae, Geomyidae, Cricetidae, Zapodidae) that contain more than one taxon. While we retain Cricetidae as distinct from Muridae as a matter of convenience, there is controversy as to whether this recognition is justified on biological grounds.

Rodents are first known in the fossil record from the late Paleocene. Modern members of the order are indigenous to all major land areas in the world except Antarctica and New Zealand, and they also have been widely introduced by humans. Rodents are characterized by having a single pair of ever-growing incisors, both above and below; a distinct diastema between the incisors and the cheekteeth; and a dental formula that never exceeds 1/1, 0/0, 2/1, 3/3, total 22. Most are primarily herbivorous, but many also eat insects and other small animals. Most are strictly terrestrial, but the range in habits stretches from species that are fossorial and semiaquatic to those that are scansorial and even some that glide.

Key to Families of Rodents

1. Modified for semiaquatic life, hind feet webbed; lower incisor more than 6.0 in width at alveolus 2

1'. Not especially modified for semiaquatic life (except *Ondatra*), hind feet not webbed; lower incisor less than 5.5 (less than 4.0 in all except Erethizontidae) in width at alveolus 3

2. Tail flattened dorsoventrally, its breadth approximately 25 percent of its length; infraorbital canal smaller than foramen magnum . . . . .Castoridae

2'. Tail not flattened dorsoventrally, its breadth less than 10 percent of its length; infraorbital canal larger than foramen magnum . . . .*Myocastoridae

3. Sharp quills on dorsum and tail; infraorbital canal larger than foramen magnum . . . . .Erethizontidae

3'. No quills on any part of body; infraorbital canal never larger than foramen magnum 4

4. Hairs on tail usually distichous; skull with distinct postorbital processes . . . . .Sciuridae

4'. Hairs on tail not distichous; skull lacking distinct postorbital processes 5

5. External fur-lined cheek pouches present; cheekteeth 4/4 6

5'. No external fur-lined cheek pouches; cheekteeth 4/3 or 3/3 7

6. Tail more than three-fourths length of head and body; hind feet larger than forefeet; tympanic bullae exposed on posterodorsal part of skull . . . . .Heteromyidae

6'. Tail much less than three-fourths length of head and body; hind feet smaller than forefeet; tympanic bullae not exposed on posterodorsal part of skull . . . . .Geomyidae

7. Tail much longer than head and body; hind feet noticeably elongate; cheekteeth 4/3 (*Zapus*) or 3/3 (*Napaeozapus*) . . . . .Zapodidae

7'. Tail about equal to, or shorter than, head and body; hind feet not noticeably elongate; cheekteeth 3/3 8

8. Annulations of scales on tail nearly or completely concealed by pelage (except in *Ondatra*, in which the tail is laterally flattened); cheekteeth with two longitudinal rows of cusps or prismatic . . . . .Cricetidae

8'. Annulations of scales easily visible on sparsely haired tail; cheekteeth with three longitudinal rows of cusps . . . .*Muridae

Key to Sciurids

1.   Skin between forelimbs and hind limbs noticeably loose, forming gliding membrane; narrow interorbital region V-shaped 2

1'.   Skin between forelimbs and hind limbs not noticeably loose; interorbital region not V-shaped 3

2.   Hair of venter white to base; total length less than 260; greatest length of skull less than 36 .... *Glaucomys volans*

2'.   Hair of venter gray, white only at tips; total length more than 260; greatest length of skull more than 36 ...... *Glaucomys sabrinus*

3.   Size large, length of hind foot more than 70; skull relatively massive, greatest length more than 70 .... *Marmota monax*

3'.   Size smaller, length of hind foot less than 65; skull smaller and relatively delicate, greatest length less than 70 4

4.   Dorsal pelage always striped, but without spotting; stripe(s) continuing onto face; infraorbital foramen (no extensive canal) piercing zygomatic plate 5

4'.   Dorsal pelage striped (some stripes containing spots), dappled, grizzled, or plain; if striped, the stripes not continuing onto face; distinct infraorbital canal passing between zygomatic plate and rostrum 6

5.   Dorsal stripes not continuing to base of tail; total length more than 225; cheekteeth 3/3 .... *Tamias striatus*

5'.   Dorsal stripes continuing to base of tail; total length less than 225; cheekteeth 4/3 .... *Tamias minimus*

6.   Total length less than 340; greatest length of skull less than 50 7

6'.   Total length more than 340; greatest length of skull more than 50 (except in some *Tamiasciurus*) 8

7.   Dorsum marked with series of alternating dark and pale brown stripes, the dark stripes broken with pale spots; maxillary toothrow less than 8.5 .... *Spermophilus tridecemlineatus*

7'.   Dorsum buffy yellowish, more or less uniform; maxillary toothrow more than 8.5 .... *Spermophilus richardsonii*

8.   Dorsum somewhat dappled or speckled, overall olivaceous to tawny buff; tail less than 40 percent of total length; crown of second upper molar noticeably wider than long ..... *Spermophilus franklinii*

8'.   Dorsum reddish, reddish brown, or grayish, sometimes grizzled; tail more than 40 percent of total length; crown of second upper molar as long as wide 9

9.   Total length less than 400; greatest length of skull less than 55; anterior border of orbit opposite P4 . . . . *Tamiasciurus hudsonicus*

9'. Total length more than 400; greatest length of skull more than 55; anterior border of orbit opposite M1 10

10. Pelage grayish overall dorsally, white ventrally; tips of hairs on tail white; premolars usually 2/1 (P3 much reduced and sometimes absent) . . . . *Sciurus carolinensis*

10'. Pelage orangish brown overall dorsally, yellowish or buff ventrally; tips of hairs on tail orangish; premolars 1/1 . . . . *Sciurus niger*

Key to Geomyids

1.   Face of upper incisor smooth (or occasionally with faint groove along median margin); dorsal pelage dull brownish to brownish gray . . . . *Thomomys talpoides*

1'. Face of upper incisor with two distinct longitudinal grooves; dorsal pelage rich reddish brown to blackish . . . . *Geomys bursarius*

Key to Cricetids

1.   Total length more than 300; greatest length of skull more than 42 . . 2

1'. Total length less than 300; greatest length of skull less than 42 3

2.   Tail laterally flattened, scaly; greatest length of skull more than 55 . . . . *Ondatra zibethicus*

2'. Tail rounded, furred; greatest length of skull less than 55 . . . . *Neotoma floridana*

3.   Cheekteeth cuspidate; tail more than 40 percent of total length (except *Onychomys*) 4

3'. Cheekteeth prismatic; tail less than 35 percent of total length 13

4.   Pelage somewhat harsh to touch; claws brown; molars nearly equal in size, squared . . . . *Sigmodon hispidus*

4'. Pelage soft to touch; claws pale, translucent; first molar nearly twice as long as third, molars not squared 5

5.   Tail less than half length of body; coronoid process of mandible prominent . . . . *Onychomys leucogaster*

5'. Tail more than half length of body; coronoid process of mandible not especially well developed 6

6.   Face of upper incisor conspicuously grooved; greatest length of skull less than 22.5 7

6'. Face of upper incisor smooth; greatest length of skull more than 22.5 8

7. Total length usually less than 125; tail relatively short, usually less than half total length; distinct labial ridge, often with cusplets on first two lower molars ....*Reithrodontomys humulis*

7'. Total length usually more than 125; tail relatively long, half total length or more; no labial ridge on lower molars ....*Reithrodontomys megalotis*

8. Total length 225 or more; cusps on upper molars opposite ....*Oryzomys palustris*

8'. Total length less than 225; cusps on upper molars alternate 9

9. Ears same color as head, reddish to golden buff; posterior palatine foramina nearer posterior edge of palate than anterior palatine foramina....................................*Ochrotomys nuttalli*

9'. Ears different in color from head, somewhat more grayish and usually rimmed with white; posterior palatine foramina about equidistant between anterior palatine foramina and posterior edge of palate 10

10. Size relatively large; hind foot 22 or more; greatest length of skull averaging more than 28 ....*Peromyscus gossypinus*

10'. Size smaller; hind foot 22 or (usually) less; greatest length of skull averaging less than 28....................................11

11. Hind foot usually 19 or less; greatest length of skull less than 25; tail averaging about 40 percent of total length ....*Peromyscus maniculatus bairdii*

11'. Hind foot usually more than 19; greatest length of skull more than 25; tail averaging more than 40 percent of total length............12

12. Tail long, averaging about 90, sharply bicolored; rostrum not much expanded laterally at base ...*Peromyscus maniculatus gracilis*

12'. Tail averaging less than 80, darker above than below but not sharply bicolored; more or less pronounced lateral bulbous expansion at base of rostrum ....*Peromyscus leucopus*

13. Tail short, approximately same length as hind foot; distinct groove on face of upper incisor 14

13'. Tail relatively long, longer than hind foot (only barely so in some *Microtus pinetorum*); face of upper incisor smooth (or at most with a shallow, faint groove) 15

14. Females with four pair of mammae; hairs at base of ear brighter than surrounding pelage; outer (labial) edges of lower molars lacking distinct angles ....*Synaptomys borealis*

14'. Females with three pair of mammae; hairs at base of ear same color as surrounding pelage; outer (labial) edges of lower molars having distinct angles . . . . *Synaptomys cooperi*

15. Dorsum with broad reddish to reddish brown stripe, contrasting with grayish flanks; posterior border of palate shelflike . . . . *Clethrionomys gapperi*

15′. Dorsum lacking reddish to reddish brown stripe, more or less same color as flanks; posterior border of palate rounded or with median spine 16

16. Lingual reentrant angles of lower molars deep, extending more than halfway across tooth; cheekteeth rooted in adults; dorsum generally grayish brown . . . . *Phenacomys intermedius*

16′. Lingual reentrant angles of lower molars not extending more than halfway across tooth; cheekteeth ever-growing; dorsum lacking grayish shading 17

17. Nose yellowish to orangish; third upper molar with four reentrant angles on each side . . . . *Microtus chrotorrhinus*

17′. Nose essentially same color as dorsum, not yellowish or orangish; third upper molar with three or fewer reentrant angles on each side 18

18. Dorsal pelage molelike (soft and smooth), reddish to reddish brown; tail less than 29; skull wide and flat; last upper molar with two reentrant angles on each side . . . . *Microtus pinetorum*

18′. Dorsal pelage relatively coarse, grizzled brownish to blackish; tail more than 26 (usually more than 29); last upper molar with two or three reentrant angles on each side, if two then skull high and narrow 19

19. Venter buff to ochraceous; third upper molar with two reentrant angles on each side . . . . *Microtus ochrogaster*

19′. Venter silvery to grayish; third upper molar with three reentrant angles on each side . . . . *Microtus pennsylvanicus*

Key to Zapodids

1. Tip of tail usually white; flanks with distinct orangish tinge; cheekteeth 3/3 . . . . *Napaeozapus insignis*

1′. Tip of tail not white; flanks olivaceous; cheekteeth 4/3 . . . . *Zapus hudsonius*

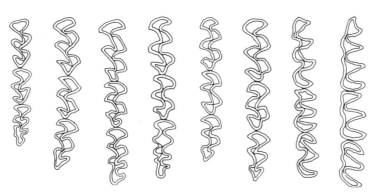

Figure 2. Diagramatic views of cheekteeth of selected microtines from the north-central states (after Hazard, 1982). From left to right: upper molars of *Clethrionomys gapperi, Phenacomys intermedius, Microtus pennsylvanicus, M. chrotorrhinus,* and *M. pinetorum;* lower molars of *Synaptomys cooperi* and *S. borealis.*

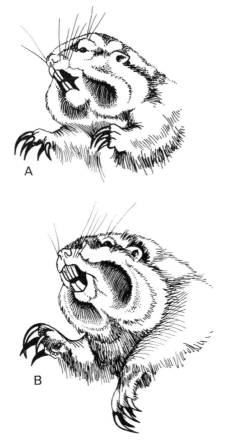

Figure 3. Head and forefeet of pocket gophers of the north-central states (after Wrigley, 1971). A, *Thomomys talpoides;* B, *Geomys bursarius.*

Tamias minimus
Least Chipmunk

Distribution. This chipmunk occurs from western Quebec to the Yukon in Canada, south to the northern Lake States and west to Arizona and New Mexico. In the north-central region, it is found southward to central Minnesota and Wisconsin and on Michigan's Upper Peninsula.

Description. Smallest member of genus *Tamias*. Dark middorsal stripe extending from base of head to base of tail; lateral dorsal stripes alternating pale and dark, the outermost whitish; flanks buffy; venter grayish white to pale buffy gray; tail grizzled brownish above, dark tipped, orangish below. Tail held vertical when running. Total length, 195–220; tail, 90–105; hind foot, 29–33; ear, 14–18; weight, 35–50 g. Member of subgenus *Eutamias*, which includes all American chipmunks except *Tamias striatus* and is recognized at the generic level by some mammalogists.

Natural History. This sciurid is common in the boreal forest of the northern part of our region, where its range overlaps that of the eastern chipmunk and the two species occur together locally. The least chipmunk, however, favors more open areas, especially in coniferous forest, than does *T. striatus*, but it occupies varied habitats. The diet of this chipmunk is made up of a variety of vegetable matter, including nuts, fruits, berries, and seeds, as well as insects, especially beetles, grasshoppers, and caterpillars. Nuts and seeds are cached for winter.

Tamias minimus hibernates from October until March or April in the north-central states. When active, it is diurnal and primarily terrestrial, although individuals climb shrubs and trees in search of food and occasionally nest in stumps and tree holes. These chipmunks are preyed upon by hawks, snakes, and a number of carnivores. Parasites include nematodes and spiny-headed worms internally and fleas, ticks, mites, and lice externally.

Mating takes place soon after emergence from hibernation. There is one litter each year of two to seven (usually five or six) young, born after a gestation of about 30 days. The offspring are weaned in less than two months, and populations are highest at this time (up to 30 per acre reported from Wisconsin, but usually five to 15 per acre). Adults molt twice annually.

Selected References. Forbes (1966); Manville (1949); Sheppard (1968, 1972).

Tamias striatus

Eastern Chipmunk

Distribution. As the name implies, this is a mammal of eastern North America. It occurs westward to the edge of the plains and from southeastern Canada southward to Louisiana and northern Florida. The species is found throughout the seven north-central states except in northwestern Iowa and adjacent Minnesota.

Description. A large chipmunk with a rufous rump. Dorsal stripes less extensive than in *T. minimus*, not reaching base of tail; venter whitish; tail grizzled brownish gray above, dark tipped, buffy orange below. Tail directed backward when running. Total length, 230–275; tail, 85–105; hind foot, 32–40; ear, 15–20; weight, 90–130 g.

Natural History. This chipmunk prefers forested areas with a dense canopy and sparsely covered forest floor, but it also occurs in riparian forest and brushy areas. Burrow systems, up to 30 feet long and three feet deep, frequently are complex, containing several storage chambers and a nest of chewed or crushed leaves. Like other chipmunks, these are diurnal animals, most active at midday or earlier, depending on temperature. They readily climb trees but evidently rarely nest in them. *T. striatus* eats principally nuts, flowers, berries, seeds, fruits, a variety of invertebrates (mostly insects), some small vertebrates, and bird eggs. Individuals cache nuts and seeds for winter; like other northern *Tamias*, they hibernate but may awaken during warm periods to eat stored food and even appear above ground.

Eastern chipmunks defend the territory around the home burrow. Home ranges, however, may overlap broadly, those of males the larger (up to about two acres). Population highs of 20 or so per acre have been reported, but the usual density in good habitat is 10 or fewer per acre. Like other members of the genus, these are vocal animals, and their characteristic calls can be heard during periods of activity. Record longevity in captivity is about 12 years, eight in the wild, but the average lifespan of an animal that reaches maturity probably is less than two years.

Females bear one or two litters annually, one in April and a second (if produced) in midsummer. Gestation lasts 31 or 32 days. Two to eight (usually four or five) young comprise a litter.

Selected References. Snyder (1982).

Marmota monax
Woodchuck

Distribution. The woodchuck is distributed in the eastern United States (south to Arkansas and central Alabama), westward to the edge of the plains. To the north, it occurs over much of Canada to east-central Alaska. *M. monax* is found throughout the north-central states.

Description. Largest sciurid of region, heavy bodied, with relatively short legs and tail. Dorsum grizzled brownish, venter paler; feet dark brown to blackish. Head broad and short, ears small, rounded. Total length, 500–650; tail, 120–175; hind foot, 75–100; ear, 22–34; weight, which varies seasonally as in all hibernating squirrels, 2.5–5.5 kg.

Natural History. Woodchucks are typically inhabitants of forest edges and openings, the bases of rocky bluffs, stone walls, and the like, never far from cover. Their burrows are marked by a mound of earth at the main entrance (there may be one or more secondary entrances, hidden in vegetation) and may be 20–30 feet long. The nest chamber is about 10 by 18 inches; the hibernating chamber is similar but is plugged to isolate the occupant. Length of hibernation varies from four to six months, depending on latitude, but usually lasts from October to March.

The diet includes native grasses and forbs, clover, and alfalfa. Although mostly ground dwelling, woodchucks climb trees in search of food or to sun themselves. They are solitary except for females with young, although home ranges, which generally are restricted to several hundred feet around the burrow, may overlap broadly in good habitat. Territoriality is well developed among neighboring animals.

Natural enemies include large carnivores such as foxes, coyotes, and badgers as well as large raptors, and mustelids prey on young. Humans hunt woodchucks for sport and because they sometimes are pests in gardens and other plantings. They are eaten in some areas. A variety of ectoparasites and endoparasites has been reported.

Breeding takes place in early spring. Females bear a single litter of two to nine (usually four or five) young after 30–32 days of gestation. Offspring are weaned at about a month and a half of age. Longevity rarely exceeds six years.

Selected References. de Vos and Gillespie (1960); Grizzell (1955); Hamilton (1934).

Spermophilus franklinii
Franklin's Ground Squirrel

Distribution. This squirrel is typical of the tallgrass prairie. It occurs from Alberta and Saskatchewan southeastward to Kansas, Missouri, and the western north-central states. It is known from most of Minnesota, throughout Iowa, southern Wisconsin, northern and central Illinois, and northwestern Indiana, and it possibly occurs in southwesternmost Michigan.

Description. Largest member of genus in our region. Dorsum olive buff to tawny buff overall, actually grayish with both pale and dark speckles; underparts yellowish white to olivaceous; tail relatively long and bushy. Total length, 360–410; tail, 120–145; hind foot, 45–58; ear, 13–18; weight, 320–500 g.

Natural History. Although diurnal like its relatives, this highly secretive squirrel is not as readily observed. This results from concealment in its favored tallgrass habitat, particularly "edge" situations between grassy and wooded areas, and because it is uncommon in many places. It is not considered a colonial species but is often found in loose aggregations. In good habitat and good years, concentrations of four to eight animals per acre may be attained, but higher numbers have been reported. Populations fluctuate, apparently peaking every four to six years.

The home range is usually an area no more than 300 feet in diameter. Burrows are excavated to a depth of eight feet; there may be several entrances, the main one marked by a mound of soil, with secondary openings usually plugged. Excavations are always in well-drained sites. A nest made of vegetative material is constructed in a side branch of the burrow system.

Like other ground squirrels, individuals develop a heavy layer of fat in preparation for hibernation, which lasts from late summer or early autumn until late March or April. Young animals enter torpor later than adults; males emerge before females in spring. *S. franklinii* is omnivorous, eating a wide variety of both plant and animal materials. It is, for example, an important predator on ducklings and duck eggs on northern prairie wetlands.

Mating takes place in spring. Females bear a single litter, ranging from two to 13 young, usually six to nine, after about 28 days of gestation.

Selected References. Iverson and Turner (1972); Murie (1973); Sowls (1948); Turner et al. (1976).

Spermophilus richardsonii
Richardson's Ground Squirrel

Distribution. This species ranges from the southern parts of the Canadian Prairie Provinces southward through Montana to the Dakotas, western Minnesota, and northwesternmost Iowa.

Description. Medium-sized ground squirrel, somewhat resembling *S. franklinii* but with shorter tail and buffy yellowish dorsum. Underparts pale pinkish to yellowish; tail brownish above, buff to yellowish below, fringed with black-tipped hairs. Total length, 290–330; tail, 70–82; hind foot, 41–48; ear, 10–15; weight usually 250–500 g, but some more than 600.

Natural History. This is the famous "picket pin" of the northern prairies, so named because of its habit of standing erect to survey the surroundings. Like other ground squirrels, these animals are diurnal. They are active in spring during the warmer middle of the day, but in summer are about mostly in the morning and late afternoon. The species is colonial, and large colonies may cover many acres. Adult males are highly territorial, vigorously defending their harem of females during the breeding season. The largest, oldest males occupy territories in the center of the colony, less dominant males those toward the periphery.

Adult males enter torpor first, in early summer, followed in turn by non-reproductive adult females, reproductive females, juvenile females, and finally, by early October, juvenile males. Hibernation lasts until March; males emerge about a week before females. Breeding takes place shortly after emergence, and the single litter of from three to 11 (usually six to eight) young is born after a gestation period of some 23 days.

These squirrels seemingly prefer to construct burrows in sandy loam or gravelly soils. Burrow systems may be up to 50 feet long and five feet deep. These contain a nest chamber, about nine inches in diameter and lined with dry vegetation, and similar chambers for food storage, although little is known of caching food in this species. The diet of both vegetable and animal material, including carrion, varies seasonally.

Badgers and a number of other carnivores regularly prey on *S. richardsonii*, as do hawks, falcons, and eagles. Snakes and weasels enter burrows to take young animals. Adults molt but once annually. Longevity rarely exceeds four years.

Selected References. Lampe et al. (1982); Michener and Koeppel (1985); Murie and Michener (1984).

Spermophilus tridecemlineatus
Thirteen-lined Ground Squirrel

Distribution. This widely distributed sciurid is found from Michigan and Ohio westward to Arizona, Montana, and Utah, and from central Alberta, Manitoba, and Saskatchewan on the north to the Texas Gulf Coast. It inhabits all but the eastern, northern, and southern edges of the north-central region.

Description. Smallest ground squirrel in region. Dorsum with 13 stripes from nape to base of tail (seven narrow, yellowish stripes alternating with six broader, dark brown stripes, the latter with pale yellow spots in the middle); venter yellowish to yellowish orange. Total length, 245–290; tail, 75–100; hind foot, 34–38; ear, 8–11; weight, 100–220 g.

Natural History. This animal occurs in open areas with relatively short grass – well-grazed pastures and regularly mowed golf courses, cemeteries, parks, fencerows, and roadsides, for example. There is ample evidence that *S. tridecemlineatus* has moved eastward in the north-central states within historical times, following clearing of forested areas for agricultural and other human purposes. Its movement into northern Wisconsin, Michigan, and south-eastward across Indiana has been documented; the first recorded occurrence in Ohio was published in 1930.

This rodent prefers well–drained sites for location of burrows, often in sandy or loose loamy soils. These animals are not colonial, but may concentrate in certain favored habitats. Populations range from one to about 20 individuals per acre, depending on place and season, being highest when young first leave the maternal burrow. Home ranges of less than two acres to more than 11 have been reported; these may overlap, but home burrows are defended.

S. tridecemlineatus is preyed upon by carnivores, raptors, and snakes. Its diet consists of a variety of plant foods and invertebrates, as well as occasional small vertebrates and carrion. Ectoparasites include fleas, lice, mites, and ticks, and several kinds of endoparasites are known. Hibernation lasts from August or September (later in juveniles) to March. Adults molt twice annually.

Females bear only one litter a year, of up to 13 offspring (usually eight or nine). Mating takes place shortly after emergence from hibernation and gestation lasts 27 or 28 days. The neonates are pink, naked, and helpless, weighing about 4 g.

Selected References. Murie and Michener (1984); Streubel and Fitzgerald (1978).

Sciurus carolinensis
Gray Squirrel

Distribution. This squirrel inhabits forested areas in southernmost Canada and the eastern United States, west to Saskatchewan and the Dakotas in the north and Texas in the south. It occurs throughout the north-central states, except in northwestern Iowa and adjacent Minnesota, and possibly parts of northern Minnesota.

Description. Dorsum grayish, usually with a tawny to brownish wash; venter whitish, often with a suffusion of fulvous or reddish orange, or even slightly grayish; hairs of tail buff basally, black medially, tipped with white. Total length, 440–500; tail, 190–230; hind foot, 62–70; ear, 29–35; weight, 380–700 g.

Natural History. This shy, diurnal squirrel is typical of the hardwood forests of eastern North America, but it also inhabits mixed deciduous-coniferous forests. The species tends to be more an animal of subdued light than the fox squirrel, foraging mostly in the early morning and evening, on overcast days, and in heavily shaded forest. Holes in trees are preferred as den sites, but when hollows are unavailable a spherical, waterproof nest of interwoven leaves and twigs is constructed in the fork of a tree or entwined high in the branches. Nest boxes also are occupied.

Food is sought both in trees and on the ground. Nuts, such as acorns and beechnuts, are harvested in summer and autumn and buried singly or in small lots, a practice known as "scatter hoarding". In winter, the nuts are relocated by a keen sense of smell. In season, the diet also consists of seeds, flowers, buds, fruits, inner bark, leaves, and even some insects, young birds, and eggs.

Gray squirrels are parasitized externally by fleas, lice, mites, ticks, and botfly larvae and internally by a variety of cestodes, nematodes, protozoans, and acanthochephalans. Large raptors and a number of carnivores prey on *S. carolinensis*, and it is also a popular game animal over much of its range. Despite all this, longevity may be up to 12 years in the wild, even longer in captivity.

Mature females often produce two litters each year – one in late winter or early spring and another in midsummer – containing one to eight (usually two to four) young.

Selected References. Allen (1952); Longley (1963); Packard (1956); Uhlig (1955).

Photo by George Rysgaard

Sciurus niger

Fox Squirrel

Distribution. This species occurs over most of the eastern United States (from New York and Pennsylvania south to Florida) westward to the Great Plains and northeasternmost Mexico. It inhabits much of the seven-state region, being absent only in the extreme northern areas of Minnesota and Wisconsin and from part of Michigan's Upper Peninsula.

Description. Larger and more brownish or orangish overall than gray squirrel, tail fringed with buffy orange. Dorsum grizzled tawny brown; underparts rufous to yellowish, occasionally whitish. Total length, 480–590; tail, 220–270; hind foot, 62–76; ear, 22–32; weight, 0.5–1.1 kg.

Natural History. The fox squirrel, although an inhabitant like the gray squirrel of broad-leafed deciduous forest, is more characteristic of open stands of trees such as woodlots, riparian communities, forest edge situations, and the like. Both species, however, adapt well to urban environments. *S. niger* evidently has occupied the northern part of its range in the north-central states within historical time in response to clearing of forests and at least partly as a result of introductions by humans.

Fox squirrels feed on walnuts, acorns, and other nuts when available and scatter hoard them for winter as do gray squirrels. They are not so dependent as the latter on such foods, however, and eat a wider variety of items in both summer and winter, including corn and other grains.

This squirrel forages on the ground more than does *S. carolinensis* and thus is more susceptible to predation by terrestrial carnivores. Home ranges tend to be elliptical and, of course, are three dimensional, averaging (depending on age, sex, and habitat) about 12 acres. Both species "bark" and issue other sounds when disturbed or frightened. Parasites are similar to those of *S. carolinensis*. Adults of both species molt but once a year, in the warm months. Maximum longevity in the wild probably is less than 10 years for this popular game species.

There are two breeding peaks, one in winter and the second in spring. After a gestation period of about 45 days, a litter of one to six (average about three) young is produced. Neonates weigh an average of 15 g.

Selected References. Allen (1943); Longley (1963); Moore (1957); Packard (1956).

Tamiasciurus hudsonicus
Red Squirrel

Distribution. This squirrel is found across northern North America, from Labrador to Alaska; it occurs southward in the Rockies to Arizona and New Mexico and in the Appalachians to the western Carolinas. In our region, *T. hudsonicus* ranges south to northern Illinois and Iowa and over most of Indiana and Ohio.

Description. Smallest tree squirrel in north-central states. Dorsum reddish gray (brighter in winter), somewhat darker on head, eye-ring white; venter whitish, separated from flanks by blackish line; ears prominent, tufted (especially in winter). Tail rufous medially, hairs with black subterminal bands and tawny tips; underside grayish buff. Total length, 280–350; tail, 105–145; hind foot, 42–54; ear, 18–26; weight, 150–250 g.

Natural History. This animal is typical of the North American boreal coniferous forest. In the southern part of its range in our region, however, it occurs in deciduous woodlands, and evidence suggests that at least part of that area has been occupied within historical times. The distributional status of the species there is somewhat uncertain; it no longer may inhabit Illinois, for example, but evidently is widespread in Indiana.

This is a conspicuous mammal in places where it occurs, not only because it is diurnal, highly active, curious, and vocal, but also because it caches food in one place, frequently resulting in large middens. Conifer seeds are preferred, but a variety of nuts and other seeds is eaten as well as (in season) buds, flowers, fruits, insects, and the like. Home ranges may be large in deciduous forest, up to 10 acres or more, but are much smaller in preferred habitat. These animals are highly territorial and vigorously defend their home area. Both holes and tree nests are used.

Unlike their larger cousins, adults molt twice annually. Fleas, lice, mites, and ticks are known ectoparasites and various worms are endoparasites. Within its range, the marten is an important predator, but many other carnivores as well as raptors take *S. hudsonicus*. Females produce one or two litters a year, depending on environmental conditions. One to 10, usually three to five, young are born after 35–38 days of gestation.

Selected References. Layne (1954); Reichard (1976); Smith (1968, 1970, 1978).

Photo by George Rysgaard

Glaucomys sabrinus
Northern Flying Squirrel

Distribution. This flying squirrel occurs in northern North America from Alaska to Labrador. It ranges southward in the Appalachians, in the western mountains to California, Utah, and the Black Hills, and to the Lake States. In our region, *G. sabrinus* is found only in Michigan, Minnesota, and Wisconsin.

Description. Larger than *G. volans*; pelage thicker and more richly colored. Upper parts cinnamon brown, sometimes slightly smoky, sides of head smoky gray; underparts grayish white, sometimes washed with buff, the individual hairs gray basally; tail grayish buff, darker toward the tip. Total length, 250–310; tail, 110–150; hind foot, 35–40; ear, 18–27; weight, 70–125 g.

Natural History. Like its southern counterpart, this flying squirrel is nocturnal and has large, rounded eyes. *G. sabrinus* thrives in heavy forest of mixed conifers and northern hardwoods. In Quebec, for example, optimal habitat has been reported to be mature mixed forest of yellow birch, sugar maple, hemlock, balsam fir, and white spruce. Home ranges vary from less than 10 to more than 30 acres, depending on habitat. One author estimated densities of three to four individuals per acre in favored sites in Wisconsin, but other studies have revealed lower numbers. The animals are active year-round.

Because of their nighttime habits, flying squirrels rarely are seen by humans. Sometimes, however, they take up residence in the attic of a cabin or summer home, their nocturnal activities frequently disturbing the occupants. Otherwise, they do little harm. The diet consists of a variety of nuts and seeds, fruits and berries, buds, mushrooms, fungi, insects and other invertebrates, and even young birds. Tree hollows and abandoned woodpecker holes are preferred nesting sites, but outside nests also are built.

Both species of flying squirrels molt but once a year, in early autumn. *G. sabrinus* is parasitized externally by lice, mites, and fleas and internally by nematodes, cestodes, and protozoans. Carnivores, such as foxes, martens, and weasels, and owls are known predators. Females usually bear only one litter a year – in spring – but some may reproduce again in late summer. The one to six young (average three) are born after a gestation period of about 37 days.

Selected References. Wells-Gosling and Heaney (1984).

Photo by R. Altig

Glaucomys volans
Southern Flying Squirrel

Distribution. This species occurs in eastern North America, from southernmost Canada to Florida and west to Nebraska and Texas; it also is found in the mountains of Mexico southeastward to Honduras. In the north-central states, the southern flying squirrel is absent only from the western part and some northern areas, where the distribution is spotty.

Description. Smaller of the two flying squirrels. Pelage silky; dorsum drab brownish or brownish gray; venter creamy to white, with individual hairs white basally; tail pale brownish above, not dark tipped, somewhat paler below. Total length, 215–250; tail, 80–110; hind foot, 28–33; ear, 15–20; weight, 45–80 g.

Natural History. This species prefers mature broad-leaved forests, but also occurs in mixed coniferous-deciduous forests. Flying squirrels do not fly, of course, but glide, using the outstretched fold of skin (patagium) between the front and hind feet as the gliding surface, along with the flattened tail. In this manner, they travel from the top of one tree to the base of another, sometimes covering distances of 100 feet or more. Gliding allows for rapid long-distance movement and a means of escaping predators. Foraging takes place both in trees and on the ground.

Southern flying squirrels are more dependent on tree holes (or nest boxes) for denning than are their northern counterparts and also are more dependent on nuts, such as those of oak and hickory, as a staple food source. Reported population densities range from less than one per acre up to about five in good habitat. These docile animals make good pets. In winter, many may den together in the same tree cavity to conserve energy, but breeding females are territorial.

G. volans usually breeds twice a year, once in late winter and again in midsummer. Litters, which number two to seven young but most often three or four, are born in April or May and in August or September after about 40 days of gestation. The neonates, pink and hairless at birth, weigh 3–5 g; they mature slowly, becoming completely independent of the female at four months of age. Captive animals have lived 13 years.

Selected References. Dolan and Carter (1977); Weigl (1978).

Thomomys talpoides
Northern Pocket Gopher

Distribution. This is the most widely distributed pocket gopher, occurring from Alberta and Saskatchewan to Arizona and New Mexico and from northwestern Minnesota to Washington.

Description. Smaller than plains pocket gopher, front feet somewhat smaller and with shorter claws. Upper parts brownish to grayish brown, lacking the distinct sheen of *G. bursarius*; venter paler. Total length, 220–250; tail, 58–75; hind foot, 27–33; ear small and inconspicuous, 7–10; weight, 115–195 g. Males are larger than females.

Natural History. Pocket gophers are well adapted for fossorial life. The body is fusiform, lacking a distinct neck region, and the eyes and ears are small. The tail is relatively short, thinly haired, and has a sensitive tip. The large incisors, which pierce the lips so that the mouth can be closed behind them, and the powerful front feet are used in burrowing. These animals travel both forward and backward in burrows with ease. The fur-lined cheek pouches, which open on either side of the mouth, are used for transporting food, which consists entirely of vegetation.

T. talpoides is a somewhat less efficient burrower than the larger plains pocket gopher. The burrow system, which may reach lengths of 400–500 feet, is constructed on two levels. The upper level is composed of foraging tunnels, usually six to eight inches below the surface. The deep level may descend to six feet or more and contains the nest and storage areas. Side branches of shallow tunnels are used for deposit of dirt and feces. Excess dirt is thrown out of the system, forming the characteristic earthen mounds, which tends to be fan-shaped because the passageway leading to them from a main tunnel is oblique. Burrow systems are kept plugged except when opened for airing or on the few occasions the occupant forages above ground.

Badgers and large owls are the most important predators, but other carnivores and snakes also take a toll. Except for a female with young, these rodents are solitary. They may be active under snow in winter. Females give birth to one litter of four to seven young annually. The maximum life span may be about five years.

Selected References. Andersen (1978); Reid (1973); Tryon (1947).

Photo courtesy of U.S. Fish and Wildlife Service

Geomys bursarius
Plains Pocket Gopher

Distribution. This pocket gopher is found in prairie and plains habitats from Indiana and Illinois to the foothills of the Rockies and from Manitoba to south-central Texas. In the seven-state region it occurs in all of Iowa, much of Minnesota, in western Wisconsin, and in central Illinois and adjacent northwestern Indiana.

Description. Larger than *T. talpoides*, front feet larger and with longer claws. Dorsum usually dark brown, black in some populations; underparts slightly paler; tail sparsely haired. Face of each upper incisor with two deep longitudinal grooves. Total length, 235–315; tail, 65–90; hind foot, 31–37; ear, 6–9; weight, 190–420 g. Adult males are significantly larger than females.

Natural History. This large gopher is a common inhabitant of roadsides, pasturelands, and alfalfa fields within its range in this region. Locally, the distribution is determined primarily by soil type in that this species prefers moist, deep sandy loam; it is generally absent from areas of hard, dry soils. The burrow system may cover as much as 5,000 square feet but in good habitat may be only half that size. Males tend to range more widely than females. Population densities of up to 15 or so individuals per acre in preferred areas have been reported. These animals are beneficial because of the soil they turn over; it has been estimated that a single individual may move as much as 52 cubic feet of earth a year (about two and a half tons). They can be pests, however, in agricultural plantings, especially alfalfa and sweet clover, where they not only eat the crops but may cause damage to farm machinery with their mounds.

Various carnivores, owls, and snakes prey on pocket gophers. They are known to be parasitized externally by fleas, lice, and mites and internally by cestodes, nematodes, trematodes, and protozoans.

The gestation period of *G. bursarius* is thought to be about a month and a half. The single annual litter of one to six (average two to three) young is born in late winter or early spring. Pocket gophers live in solitude (except for a female with young); maximum longevity may be five or six years.

Selected References. Burns et al. (1985); Downhower and Hall (1966); Heaney and Timm (1983); Vaughan (1962).

Perognathus flavescens
Plains Pocket Mouse

Distribution. The plains pocket mouse, as the name implies, inhabits the grasslands of central North America, from Minnesota and the Dakotas southward to northernmost Mexico. In the north-central region, it is known only from western and northern Iowa and western and southern Minnesota.

Description. Only mouse in region with external fur-lined cheek pouches and four cheekteeth both above and below. Upper parts usually cinnamon buff with strong admixture of blackish hairs; buffy patch behind ears and around eyes; lower flanks and venter yellowish orange to cinnamon buff, belly frequently with creamy white blotches, rarely all white. Total length, 115–130; tail, 50–62; hind foot, 16–18; ear, 5–7; weight, 7–12 g.

Natural History. Relatively little is known of the biology of this beautiful little mouse. Like other pocket mice, it is a nocturnal granivore; seeds found in caches in Minnesota included those of sedges, spiderwort, wild buckwheat, puccoon, yellow foxtail, and green foxtail, along with trace quantities of sweet clover, switchgrass, ragweed, and knotweed. Small grains such as wheat and oats also are eaten, as probably are insects on occasion. Plains pocket mice hibernate in winter, but individuals evidently awaken from time to time to feed on their cached stores. Water is metabolized from the food.

This mouse prefers well-drained, sandy soil in grassland habitats with some bare, open areas. It often is found along roadsides and the margins of grain fields. The tiny burrows have several entrances (which are plugged when the occupant is within) and contain a nest and chambers for food storage. Of 100 feet or so of burrows excavated in Minnesota, all were parallel to the surface at a depth of six to eight inches. Deeper burrows obviously would be needed for hibernation. Home ranges evidently are small, about a tenth of an acre. Owls, small carnivores, and snakes are the principal predators.

The breeding season extends from spring to late summer and females probably bear two or three litters of two to five young each year. Known longevity (in captivity) is a year and a half, but adults may live twice that long.

Selected References. Beer (1961); Hibbard and Beer (1960); Jones et al. (1983); Williams (1978).

Photo by Barbara Clauson

Castor canadensis
Beaver

Distribution. The beaver ranges over much of North America, from central Alaska and northern Canada to northern Mexico. It occurs in suitable aquatic habitats throughout the north-central states, but is not now so commonly distributed as in early historical times.

Description. Largest rodent in temperate North America; highly modified externally for semiaquatic habits. Color dark brown, sometimes reddish brown, throughout; tail scaly, flattened, and nearly naked; feet webbed. Total length, 940–1,200; tail, 290–370; hind foot, 170–190; ear, 30–35; weight usually 15–30 kg, but large individuals to 45.

Natural History. The beaver is one of the most familiar of rodents. Although principally crepuscular and nocturnal, it is sometimes active by day and, in any event, its presence in an area is generally evident because of its tree-cutting behavior and construction of its characteristic dwellings and dams. Long sought for its valuable fur, the beaver was driven nearly to extinction in much of the southern part of the seven-state region by the turn of the last century. Protective legislation, restocking, and natural emigration have resulted in reoccupancy of most of its former range. Now there is a controlled trapping season in some areas; the price of a pelt in recent years has averaged about 35 dollars.

This animal is a strict vegetarian. Grasses and other greens are eaten in the warm months along with bark from materials used in dam- and lodge-building. Branches and saplings, especially those of willow, cottonwood, and alder, are stored for winter food. Typically, lodges are constructed in quiet ponds, frequently formed behind dams. A colony consists of one or more pairs of adults with yearlings and young. On water courses that cannot be dammed, a lodge may be built against the bank or bank dens with underwater openings may be used.

Beavers have few natural enemies. Mink take young, and large carnivores, especially wolves, prey on adults; but humans, through destruction or modification of habitat, are probably of greatest importance. These rodents are susceptible to rabies and tularemaia and host a variety of parasites. Females bear one litter annually of one to six (usually three or four) young in spring.

Selected References. Jenkins and Busher (1979).

Oryzomys palustris
Marsh Rice Rat

Distribution. The marsh rice rat inhabits the southeastern United States, northward to New Jersey, Pennsylvania, Illinois, and Missouri, and westward to Oklahoma and the Texas Gulf Coast. A related species occurs throughout the tropical and subtropical parts of Mexico southeastward to Panama. In the north-central states, *O. palustris* is found only in southern Illinois.

Description. Medium-sized rat with dense, soft, water-repellent underfur. Dorsum dark brownish to brownish gray, slightly paler on flanks; underparts grayish white, sometimes washed with pale buff; tail darker above than below, scales visible under hairs. Total length, 225–260; tail, 110–145; hind foot, 25–37; ear, 12–16; weight, 45–80 g.

Natural History. Rice rats are semiaquatic and typically are inhabitants of wetlands such as marshes, swamps, wet meadows, grassy borders of lakes, and the like. Common rodent associates are the hispid cotton rat and meadow vole. This rat is an excellent swimmer (both on the surface and under water) and diver. It is an omnivorous rodent, eating seeds, green vegetation, fungi, insects and other invertebrates, small fish, nestling birds and eggs, young turtles, and carrion. Owls, especially the barn owl, may be the chief predators of *O. palustris*, but marsh and other hawks, mink, weasels, raccoons, skunks, red foxes, and water moccasins and other snakes all take a toll.

These rats are primarily nocturnal. Their grapefruit-sized nests of woven grasses and sedges usually are on high ground under debris or some other protective cover, or at the base of a bush, or in a shallow burrow. Home ranges average between half an acre and an acre in size. Population densities ranged from less than one to more than seven rats per acre in a study in Louisiana, but far higher figures have been reported. Mites, ticks, lice, and fleas are known ectoparasites. A variety of endoparasites also has been reported, some of which are the result of eating fish and crustaceans.

Breeding may occur throughout the year. Gestation lasts 21–28 days depending on whether the female is also lactating. Litters average four or five young, each weighing about 3.5 g at birth. Sexual maturity is reached at 50–60 days of age. Longevity is not certainly known.

Selected References. Wolfe (1982).

Reithrodontomys humulis
Eastern Harvest Mouse

Distribution. This mouse is distributed in the southeastern United States, except southern Florida, west to Oklahoma and Texas. It reaches the northernmost point of its range in central Ohio, the only state in the north-central region from which it is known.

Description. Smallest mouse in seven-state region. Upper parts brownish, washed with blackish hairs; whitish to grayish white ventrally; tail darker above than below but not strikingly bicolored, less than half total length. Total length, 110–130; tail, 45–60; hind foot, 15–17; ear, 8–9; weight, 6–10 g.

Natural History. This is a mouse, like its relatives, of overgrown pastures, abandoned fields, weedy fencerows, and brushy clearings. It is not strongly territorial, and individuals are highly tolerant of each other. In cold weather, groups of up to six or more may huddle together in the same nest, thereby conserving energy. Globular nests are constructed of woven grasses and are suspended from plants or built on the ground in tall grass. In one study, it was found that each individual had two to four nests and that these tended to be located at or near the periphery of the home range. This small mouse does not burrow and evidently rarely uses abandoned burrows of other rodents except in winter. *R. humulis* is nocturnal except in cold weather, when foraging may take place during the warmer daylight hours. The diet is composed mostly of seeds, but some green vegetation and insects also are eaten.

Owls, snakes, and a variety of small carnivores prey on eastern harvest mice, and they are parasitized by small arthropods and internally by helminths. Mortality is greatest among nestlings; known longevity is slightly more than 15 months. This species seems to be nowhere especially abundant, population densities averaging two to three per acre.

Reproduction is concentrated in spring and early summer but may take place at any time of year. Litters average about three young (range one to eight) and are born after a gestation period of about three weeks. Neonates weigh little more than a gram, but they mature rapidly and are weaned before they are a month old.

Selected References. Dunaway (1968); Kaye (1961*a*, 1961*b*); Layne (1959).

Reithrodontomys megalotis
Western Harvest Mouse

Distribution. This harvest mouse occurs over much of western North America, from southern Canada to southern Mexico. In the north-central states, it is found in Iowa, southern Minnesota, southwestern Wisconsin, northern and central Illinois, and northwestern Indiana. It has extended its range eastward within this century, probably as a result of clearing of woodlands; the species first was taken in Indiana in 1969, for example.

Description. Larger of two harvest mice in the region. Dorsum dark brownish overall, somewhat grizzled; flanks and side of head with slightly fulvous wash; venter whitish with buffy pectoral spot in some populations; tail bicolored, brownish above, white below. Total length, 120–150; tail, 55–70; hind foot, 15–17; ear, 10–12; weight averaging about 10 g.

Natural History. This species is an inhabitant of grassy and weedy habitats where it is frequently one of the most common small mammals. It is mainly granivorous, but green vegetation and insects are eaten. The spherical nest, about five inches in diameter, woven of grasses and other fibers and lined with finer "down," usually is located on the ground under heavy grass, bushes, weeds, or similar cover; occasionally nests are built in small shrubs (up to about three feet above the ground) or in a burrow. Density estimates vary considerably, depending on habitat and season, but four or five individuals per acre seems to be about average.

Reithrodontomys megalotis, like most other mice, has three distinctive maturational pelages—juvenile, subadult, and adult. The latter is shed twice a year, in spring and autumn; winter adult pelage is much longer and somewhat paler than the summer coat. Owls, hawks, snakes, and small carnivores prey on harvest mice. Fleas and mites are known as ectoparasites and cestodes, nematodes, spiny-headed worms, and protozoans as endoparasites.

Most reproduction occurs from early spring to midautumn, with reduced activity in midsummer, but it takes place year-round in some areas. Females are polyestrous (two in captivity each gave birth to 14 litters in one year); litter size ranges from one to nine, averaging about four. In a study in California, only a few individuals lived as long as 12 months.

Selected References. Webster and Jones (1982).

Photo by Thomas H. Kunz

Peromyscus gossypinus
Cotton Mouse

Distribution. This is a species of the southeastern United States, ranging from Virginia to Florida and westward to the eastern parts of Oklahoma and Texas. In the north-central states, it is known only from southern Illinois.

Description. A relatively large *Peromyscus*. Upper parts dark brown, venter white; tail bicolored, brown above and whitish below. Total length, 160–205; tail, 70–95; hind foot, 22–26; ear, 16–18; weight, 20–40 g. Most closely resembles *P. leucopus*, which has a shorter hind foot (usually less than 22).

Natural History. The cotton mouse is a rodent of wooded stream banks and bottomlands, swamps, brushy thickets, and similar situations. Rocky ledges, caves, and abandoned or little-used buildings also are occupied. Much of the preferred habitat is subject to annual flooding; thus, nest sites tend to be hidden under debris and the like on locally high ground or placed in stumps or hollow trees. These mice are agile climbers and adept swimmers. They sometimes occur together with the white-footed mouse, but the latter tends to inhabit somewhat higher, better-drained woods and brushlands.

These are more carnivorous mice than their near relatives, animal matter such as adult and larval insects, spiders, and slugs making up more than half the diet. A variety of plant material, including the fungus *Endogone*, also is taken. Home range size varies but seems to average about an acre or a little less; ranges of males are larger than those of females and may broadly overlap, whereas ranges of females tend to be more or less exclusive. Reported population estimates range from less than one mouse per acre up to about 20 depending on habitat and season.

Like other mice, *P. gossypinus* is eaten by a variety of avian and mammalian predators and by snakes. This species breeds throughout the year in Florida but may not do so in our region. Litter size ranges from one to seven, averaging about four. Neonates are essentially hairless and have eyes and ears closed. Weaning takes place in the third or fourth week. These mice probably have two maturational molts–from juvenile to subadult to adult pelage. Known longevity is two years.

Selected References. Wolfe and Linzey (1977).

Peromyscus leucopus
White-footed Mouse

Distribution. The white-footed mouse ranges from southeasternmost Canada and over much of the eastern United States, westward to Arizona and the southern Canadian Prairie Provinces and southward into Mexico as far as the Yucatan Peninsula. In the seven-state region, it occurs in all but northern Minnesota and parts of northern Wisconsin and Michigan's Upper Peninsula.

Description. Medium-sized among *Peromyscus* in north-central states. Upper parts dark brown to rich reddish brown; underparts white; tail less distinctly bicolored than that of *P. maniculatus* except in winter. Total length, 160–200; tail, 65–95; hind foot, 19–22; ear, 15–18; weight, 17–30 g.

Natural History. Like its relatives, this species is nocturnal and does not hibernate. Typically, this is a mouse of woodland habitats where it frequently is one of the most common small mammals. The diet consists of acorns and other nuts and seeds, berries and fruits, and insects and other small invertebrates. Water is obtained mostly from green vegetation and dew. *P. leucopus* climbs well, foraging in brushy vegetation and trees as well as on the ground. The home range, which actually is three-dimensional, varies from less than half an acre up to two acres; territoriality is but weakly developed.

Nests are built of almost any soft material under logs, roots, and rocks, in hollows and crevices, and occasionally in burrows abandoned by other small mammals. This mouse is taken by virtually all woodland predators. Fleas, lice, mites, ticks, and botfly larvae parasitize it externally, whereas flatworms, roundworms, and tapeworms infest it internally.

The white-footed mouse breeds throughout the warmer months. Females bear several litters annually; young may become pregnant while still in juvenile pelage. Gestation lasts 22 or 23 days in nonlactating females (about 30 days in those that are nursing one litter while pregnant with the next). Litter size ranges from one to seven, averaging about four. Juvenile mice have the gray dorsal pelage typical of all young *Peromyscus*, which is replaced by a subadult coat between 40 and 50 days of age. Adult *P. leucopus* are reported to molt but once a year, in spring or early summer.

Selected References. Lackey et al. (1985); Metzgar (1973).

Peromyscus maniculatus bairdii
Deer Mouse

Distribution. As a species, *Peromyscus maniculatus* has one of the broadest distributions of any small, terrestrial mammal in the New World. It occurs over much of central and southern Canada, throughout the United States (except in the Southeast), and southward in Mexico to Oaxaca. The species ranges all across the north-central states, where it is represented by distinctive, noninterbreeding woodland and grassland populations. These are treated separately in this handbook.

Description. Smallest *Peromyscus* in north-central region. Dorsum dark grayish brown, darkest middorsally; venter white; tail distinctly bicolored, dark above and white below. Total length, 125–160; tail, 42–65; hind foot, 15–19; ear, 13–15; weight, 12–25 g.

Natural History. This creature is common to abundant in open habitats over much of the north-central region. In fact, this subspecies of deer mouse is to be looked for almost anywhere except in woodlands and wet, swampy lowlands. It thrives in grassy areas and weedy fields, along overgrown fencerows and roadsides, and in similar situations. It has expanded its range in our region as a result of clearing of forests.

A wide variety of both animals and plants makes up the diet. Insects, especially moth larvae, and other invertebrates are eaten as are seeds of wild plants and those of small grains such as wheat, soybean, sorghum, and corn. More than 50 different food items have been identified in studies in Indiana. These mice rarely drink free water in the wild, meeting their needs from dew and the water in their food. Because it is both widely distributed and common, *P. maniculatus* is one of the most studied of American small mammals. For the same reasons, it is a staple food for many raptors, small carnivores, and snakes.

Nests are constructed just below ground level in a burrow dug by the occupant or abandoned by another small mammal, or under rocks, debris, or similar cover on the ground. As with most mice, males are promiscuous and opportunistic breeders. Females bear several litters annually, usually in the warmer months, but pregnant animals have been taken in every month in Indiana. Litters number one to 11 offspring, usually four to six.

Selected References. Blair (1940); King (1958, 1968).

Peromyscus maniculatus gracilis
Deer Mouse

Distribution. This long-tailed race of *Peromyscus maniculatus* is found from the northern Lake States and adjacent southern Canada northeastward to south-central Quebec and hence southward to Pennsylvania. It interbreeds with other long-tailed subspecies to the north and east of its range and in the northern Appalachians. In our region, it occurs over much of the northern parts of Michigan, Minnesota, and Wisconsin. A related race, *Peromyscus maniculatus maniculatus*, is known from Isle Royale in Lake Superior.

Description. About the size of *P. leucopus*; tail long, sharply bicolored. Color much as in *P. maniculatus bairdii*. Total length, 165–200; tail, 80–105; hind foot, 19–22; ear, 18–21; weight, 18–30 g. Much larger than the subspecies *bairdii*. Most closely resembles *P. leucopus*, from which it differs principally in having a sharply bicolored tail (darker top blends into paler underside in *leucopus*), braincase flattened and parallel sided instead of rounded, and third upper molar narrower than first two instead of nearly as wide.

Natural History. This is a mouse of woodlands, both coniferous and mixed, but it also occurs in nearby brushy to grassy habitats and often invades newly burned or clear-cut areas in large numbers. It is partly arboreal, in contrast to its grassland-inhabiting relative; the long tail is an adaptation for climbing. Nests may be located on the ground, under logs or roots, or in stumps or hollows. Where competition with *P. leucopus* is keen, the latter tends to nest on the ground, whereas *P. m. gracilis* tends to nest in trees. This may be the most common small mammal in some woodlands, but populations seem to decrease noticeably every four years or so and then build back up to peak numbers.

Like other *Peromyscus*, this mouse is nocturnal. Owls and forest-dwelling carnivores are its principal enemies. Fruits, nuts, pine seeds, and insects make up much of the diet. Deer mice are parasitized by fleas, lice, mites, ticks, botfly larvae, protozoans, flatworms, roundworms, tapeworms, and spiny-headed worms. They have lived more than eight years in captivity but rarely live more than one year in the wild. The reproductive season of *P. m. gracilis* probably extends from March to November.

Selected References. Hooper (1942); King (1968); Klein (1960).

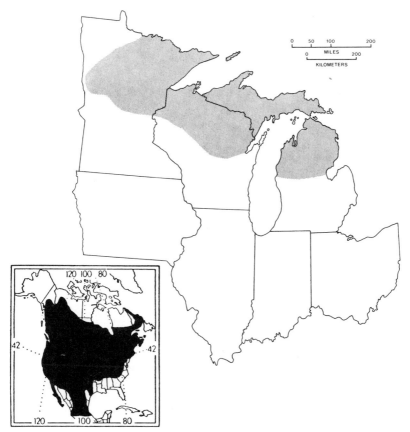

Photo by Elmer C. Birney

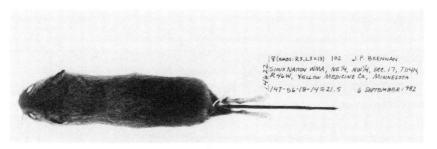

Peromyscus maniculatus bairdii

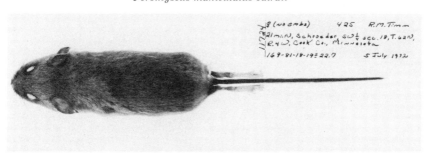

Peromyscus maniculatus gracilis

Ochrotomys nuttalli
Golden Mouse

Distribution. The golden mouse ranges in the southeastern United States from central Florida northward to Virginia and westward to Oklahoma and Texas. In the seven-state region, it is known only from southern Illinois but also should be looked for in the southern parts of Indiana and Ohio.

Description. Unique among rodents in this region in golden to tawny upper parts and ears; venter creamy white, usually with ochraceous wash; pelage dense and soft. Total length, 140–170; tail, 62–80; hind foot, 17–20; ear, 14–17; weight, 15–25 g. For many years, *Ochrotomys* was regarded as a subgenus of *Peromyscus*.

Natural History. Golden mice occur from densely forested lowlands and floodplain communities to thickets and pine uplands on sandy soils with heavy undergrowth, and in a variety of local woody or brushy habitats. The greatest populations evidently are in deciduous lowland forests. Reported densities range from about one to more than 15 mice per acre, arranged in loose communities; local distribution may be spotty, however, with no mice sometimes found in what appears to be suitable habitat. Home range size seems to average about an acre to an acre and a half. This mouse is among the longest lived of small rodents; five individuals kept in captivity survived six years or longer, and one, a female, lived almost 8.5 years.

Nests, globular structures of leaves, shredded bark, and grass, usually are built four to 15 or so feet above the ground in trees or vines, as are feeding platforms. Occasionally nests are located at ground level in stumps or under logs or rocks. The food consists mostly of seeds and invertebrates. Mites, fleas, ticks, lice, and botfly larvae are known ectoparasites, whereas single-cell organisms, cestodes, nematodes, and trematodes are known internally.

Golden mice breed throughout the year in captivity, but in the northern part of the range they do so in the wild from late winter to early autumn. Females produce several litters a year of one to four young, averaging between two and three. Gestation lasts from 25 to 30 days.

Selected References. Linzey and Packard (1977); Packard (1969).

Onychomys leucogaster
Northern Grasshopper Mouse

Distribution. This species occurs from the Prairie Provinces of Canada to northern Mexico and from the grasslands of the central United States westward to Washington and California. In this region, it is found only in western Minnesota and adjacent northwestern Iowa.

Description. A stocky mouse with a short, thick tail. Pelage distinctly bicolored; upper parts usually brownish to brownish gray; underparts white; tail white distally and ventrally, brownish above near base, tapering to relatively blunt tip. Total length, 140–165; tail, 35–45; hind foot, 19–23; ear, 14–17; weight, 30–50 g.

Natural History. This mouse inhabits grassy or weedy areas, usually those with sandy, sandy loam, or silty soils. Pastures, abandoned fields, weedy roadsides and fencerows, and the like are preferred in this region. *O. leucogaster* is an obligate dustbather, and some bare areas thus are necessary within the home range; dustbathing helps maintain the pelage in a clean, nonoily condition.

Grasshopper mice have adapted as active predators. In the warm months, fully 80 percent of the diet may consist of animal matter – mostly larval and adult insects but also other invertebrates, carrion, and even vertebrates up to three times their size. Forbs, grasses, sedges, and seeds, including small grains, also are consumed. As a predator, the home range is large for a rodent of this size, averaging between five and six acres in extent. These mice are highly territorial and rarely are they locally common.

A male and female form a pair bond, somewhat unusual among rodents, and nest burrows are jointly excavated. Other burrows are used to cache food and as temporary retreats. The typical nest burrow is U-shaped, about 18 inches long and some six inches deep. Many predators take these nocturnal mice, but never in great numbers. A variety of external and internal parasites has been reported.

Gestation lasts about 27 days, up to 32 in lactating animals. Females are polyestrous and have a postpartum estrus. Most litters are born in spring and summer; number of young ranges from one to six, averaging between three and four. The male provisions the nursing female. These mice may live two years or more.

Selected References. Engstrom and Choate (1979); McCarty (1978).

Sigmodon hispidus
Hispid Cotton Rat

Distribution. This cotton rat occurs in the southeastern United States and from Nebraska south to Panama. Westwardly it extends to New Mexico and Arizona, and there is an isolated population just north of the Gulf of California. In the north-central region, this species is recorded only from owl pellets from extreme southwestern Iowa; it has been expanding its range northward in this century, however, and is to be looked for elsewhere in southern Iowa and in southern Illinois.

Description. A medium-sized rat with long, coarse pelage. Upper parts grizzled yellowish brown, frequently with a salt-and-pepper appearance; venter grayish, sometimes with buffy wash; tail sparsely haired. Total length, 225–265; tail, 95–110; hind foot, 29–32; ear, 16–18; weight, 50–100 g or more.

Natural History. This rat is one of the few mammals of neotropical affinity that occurs in the seven-state region. To the west, its northward movement has been calculated at seven miles per year in Kansas in this century; it was first recorded from Nebraska in 1958 and had reached the Platte River by the mid-1960s. *S. hispidus* occupies a variety of relatively mesic habitats— woodland borders, brushy areas, riparian communities, weedy margins of fields and pasturelands, stands of tall grass in roadside ditches, and the like. These are primarily herbivores, and they clip quantities of vegetation, especially in autumn and winter, which they pile at intervals along their well-marked runways. Seeds, including small grains, are eaten in quantity along with small amounts of vertebrate flesh, invertebrates, and eggs of ground-nesting birds.

Cotton rats are primarily crepuscular and nocturnal. The home range averages about an acre for males, half that for females. A globular nest of shredded plant material is built beneath logs, rocks, debris, or matted vegetation or may be located in a burrow dug by the rat or abandoned by some other small mammal.

In this region, breeding occurs only from April to October. Litter size is larger northwardly, averaging eight to 10. Gestation lasts about 27 days and postpartum estrus occurs. Neonates are precocial for a rodent, well haired and weighing 6–8 g, and they mature rapidly.

Selected References. Cameron and Spencer (1981).

Neotoma floridana
Eastern Woodrat

Distribution. The eastern woodrat is found throughout much of the eastern United States, westward to Colorado and Texas; there is also an isolated subspecies in north-central Nebraska. The known distribution in our region is curious in that this species has been recorded only from extreme southwestern Illinois and the south-central parts of Indiana and Ohio. Perhaps additional study will reveal a somewhat broader, more contiguous range.

Description. Largest of native rats and mice. Upper parts brownish to brownish gray; underparts grayish white; tail bicolored, but usually not sharply so, brownish above and pale below. Total length, 350–420; tail, 140–185; hind foot, 38–44; ear, 24–27; weight, 250–360 g.

Natural History. In this region, the woodrat is principally an inhabitant of wooded areas with rocky ledges, cliffs, bluffs, outcroppings, and rough ravines. It frequently lives in crevices, fissures, and caves in such habitats or among rocks at the base of ledges and cliffs. The characteristic dwelling, however, may be built at the base of a tree, under fallen timber, or in some other convenient location, even in unused shelters and buildings.

Woodrats are unique rodents in that they build conspicuous "houses" from items found within their home range or pack the items into their home in a crevice or fissure. Sticks and small rocks usually form the matrix for the house, but anything the rat can carry may be incorporated into the waterproof structure – spent shotgun shells, corncobs, leaves, cow dung, husks of nuts, bones, trash, and the like. One or more spherical nests, about nine inches in diameter and composed of soft materials, and storage areas are located deep within. A variety of invertebrates and small vertebrates also may reside in parts of the house without disturbing the resident rat.

Woodrats are vegetarians, eating a variety of plant material. They are nocturnal and forage both on the ground and by climbing into bushes and trees. Food is stored for winter, but *N. floridana* does not hibernate. Predators include owls, carnivores, and snakes. Females are polyestrous and breed throughout the warm months. Gestation lasts about 35 days; litter size varies from one to five, averaging between two and three.

Selected References. Wiley (1980).

Clethrionomys gapperi
Southern Red-backed Vole

Distribution. This vole occurs across Canada in boreal forest and south-ward in the Appalachians to northern Georgia, to the Lake States and adjacent Dakotas, the Black Hills, and in the western mountains to Arizona and New Mexico. In the seven-state region, the range extends southward to north-central Iowa, southern Wisconsin, and central Michigan, and also extreme eastern Ohio.

Description. Small vole with relatively long tail and conspicuous ears. Dorsum with broad band of reddish brown pelage; flanks grayer; venter grayish to grayish white. Total length, 120–150; tail, 32–42; hind foot, 17–19; ear, 12–16; weight, 15–35 g.

Natural History. This species is typically an inhabitant of cold, moist forests, but it may be found in nearby, more open mesic environments as well. Water requirements (about half a gram of water per gram of body weight daily) generally restrict local distribution to areas where free water is available. Staple foods include nuts, seeds, fruits and berries, fungi, green foliage, and some invertebrates. Bark of small trees and shrubs and roots also are eaten in winter. This species does not hibernate but caches seeds for winter use; it also raids caches of other small mammals, such as those of red squirrels.

Like other voles, these animals may be active at any time, although they are usually crepuscular and nocturnal, at least in the warm months. Population densities probably average four or five voles per acre in good habitat, but numbers three times that high have been reported. Home ranges vary from one-quarter to three-quarters of an acre. In moist surroundings, *C. gapperi* tunnels under rotting logs and stumps, in moss, and in the humus of the forest floor; in drier situations, runways of other small mammals may be used.

Breeding extends from late winter into autumn. After 17–19 days of gestation, a litter of two to 10 young (usually four to six), each weighing about 2 g, is born. Postpartum mating, frequently within 12 hours, follows. Juvenile pelage is replaced by subadult pelage beginning at about 33 days of age, and adult pelage is acquired by 120 days. Thereafter, there are two molts annually as in other voles. Maximum longevity probably is less than three years.

Selected References. Merritt (1981).

Phenacomys intermedius
Heather Vole

Distribution. The heather vole is found all across Canada, from Labrador to the Yukon, and in the mountains of the western United States south to California and New Mexico. In our region, the species is known only from one specimen taken in 1940 in northeastern Minnesota.

Description. Small to medium-sized vole; cheekteeth usually black. Dorsum grizzled ochraceous brown, distinct tawny to yellowish patch on both nose and rump; tips of ears also tawny; venter and feet silvery gray; tail bicolored, brownish gray above and whitish below, sparsely haired. Total length, 135–155; tail, 25–35; hind foot, 17–19; ear, 12–16; weight, 30–45 g.

Natural History. The heather vole is a solitary animal in the warm months, but in winter groups share a nest that is about six inches in diameter and built on the ground at the base of a shrub or stump, or wedged between rocks; tunnels under the snow radiate from the nest site. Summer nests are constructed a few inches below ground beneath a log or stump, under roots, or at the base of a bush; short burrows lead to the surface in several directions. This rodent is primarily crepuscular and nocturnal. Food is cached for winter use, but these voles do not hibernate.

P. intermedius is found in a fairly wide array of habitats—coniferous forest, willow thickets, rocky hillsides, meadows, brushy forest edge, and the like—usually in fairly dry areas. Little is known of population densities, except that they seem to fluctuate at irregular intervals; the vole may be common at a locality in one year and rare a year or two later. The diet in summer consists of greens of forbs and shrubs along with berries and seeds. In winter, cached food and bark and buds are eaten. Raptorial birds and small carnivores are potential predators.

Females are seasonally polyestrous. Litters ranging from two to eight (average about five) young are born from June through early September. Neonates weigh about 2.5 g. Young females become sexually active in four to six weeks after birth, but males do not do so until the following spring. There are three maturational pelages—juvenile, subadult, and adult.

Selected References. Banfield (1974); Foster (1961); Foster and Peterson (1961); Peterson (1966).

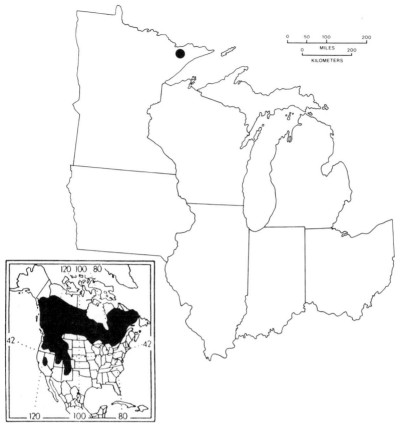

Photo by J.B. Foster

Microtus chrotorrhinus
Rock Vole

Distribution. This species ranges from Labrador westward to central Ontario and southward in the Appalachians to eastern Tennessee. In the north-central region, it is known only from extreme northeastern Minnesota.

Description. Medium-sized vole with distinctive yellowish orange patch on nose. Upper parts yellowish brown, face yellowish; venter grayish to grayish white. Total length, 140–180; tail, 42–60; hind foot, 18–22; ear, 13–17; weight, 30–45 g.

Natural History. As its name implies, this vole is closely associated with rocky habitats, including talus, throughout its range, in or near forested areas and frequently characterized by an abundance of mosses and forbs. In Cook County, Minnesota, a colony inhabiting a boulder field appeared to be limited to a narrow zone of ecological transition between the open rocks and mature forest. There, a system of interconnecting runways was found beneath and between boulders. Occasionally, this vole becomes abundant and may be found in a variety of habitats, especially newly clear-cut areas. Permanent populations appear to be isolated. Much of the activity of this microtine apparently is subterranean. The red-backed vole, *Clethrionomys gapperi*, is a frequent associate.

Rock voles feed primarily on plant material, but insects also are taken on occasion. Stems and leaves of shrubs and forbs, berries, grasses, mushrooms, roots, fungi, and the like make up most of the diet. Individuals may be active at any time of day or night but evidently prefer crepuscular and nocturnal periods. Predators thus far reported are bobcats, rattlesnakes, and copperheads, although other small carnivores and snakes, as well as raptorial birds, probably take a toll. Ectoparasites include fleas, mites, ticks, and botfly larvae, whereas cestodes and nematodes are known internally.

The breeding season extends from March to October in the southern part of the range, but for a shorter period in Minnesota. Females have a postpartum estrus, common among members of the genus, and bear several litters each year; those born in spring themselves produce young later in the year. One to eight fetuses per pregnancy have been reported, averaging about four in all studies. The gestation period is 19–21 days.

Selected References. Kirkland (1977); Kirkland and Jannett (1982); Timm et al. (1977).

Microtus ochrogaster
Prairie Vole

Distribution. Prairie voles inhabit grasslands from the southern Prairie Provinces of Canada south to Oklahoma and northern New Mexico, and eastward to West Virginia and northern Alabama. They occur throughout the southern states of our region, north to southwestern Michigan, central Wisconsin, and western Minnesota.

Description. Medium-sized vole; stocky and with compact body. Upper parts grizzled brownish to grayish brown, having a somewhat salt-and-pepper appearance; venter usually buff to ochraceous, sometimes silvery; tail dark above, pale below. Total length, 120–165; tail, 25–45; hind foot, 17–22; ear, 11–14; weight, 20–70 g. Northern populations average noticeably smaller than those to the south.

Natural History. As suggested by its name, this is an animal of grassy to weedy areas, railroad grades, and overgrown fencerows—usually well-drained sites. Where prairie voles and meadow voles occur together, the latter occupy more mesic habitats, with the former in the drier uplands with a greater mixture of plant species. Populations of both voles fluctuate greatly, often reaching peaks every three to four years. Densities in peak years can be as high as 30–50 animals per acre.

A common small mammal in grassland habitats, *M. ochrogaster* is taken by many predators—hawks and owls, various snakes, coyotes, foxes, weasels, skunks, badgers, bobcats, raccoons, and even occasionally by opossums, short-tailed shrews, and grasshopper mice. These voles form pair bonds, and both males and females care for the young. Nests are constructed by the male and lined by the female, usually in a relatively shallow underground burrow. A system of well-marked runways is used within the home range. Food consists of green vegetation in the warmer months, roots, seeds, tubers, bark, and cached items in winter. These animals sometimes seriously damage orchards by girdling trees.

Breeding extends from late winter into autumn and may be year-round in the southern part of the range. Litter size varies for several reasons, ranging from one to seven (average three to four). The reproductive rate is high in this and many other voles, but so is the mortality rate.

Selected References. Choate and Williams (1978); Gaines and Rose (1976); Jameson (1947); Thomas and Birney (1979).

Microtus pennsylvanicus
Meadow Vole

Distribution. This species has the broadest distribution of any New World vole, occurring from Alaska across most of Canada and southward to Utah and New Mexico, the central Great Plains, and Georgia. It is found throughout the north-central states except in southwestern Illinois.

Description. Largest vole of region on the average. Dorsum rich dark brown to blackish brown, pelage soft and dense, not so coarse as in *M. ochrogaster*; venter usually silvery gray; tail relatively long and not sharply bicolored. Total length, 150–185; tail, 35–55; hind foot, 18–24; ear, 12–16; weight, 35–60 g, averaging about 45.

Natural History. Meadow voles typically inhabit moist to wet meadows, marshes, stream banks, and lakeshores, living in dense stands of vegetation. Occasionally they are found in drier situations if vegetative cover is sufficient. Like many other voles, *M. pennsylvanicus* may be active at any time but is primarily crepuscular and nocturnal. Greens and seeds of grasses, sedges, and herbaceous plants make up most of the diet; in a study in Newfoundland, more than 70 different plant species were eaten. Bluegrass is a staple in some areas. Runways permeate the habitat, with piles of characteristic *Microtus* plant clippings scattered along them. The nest, five to six inches in diameter, which is constructed of dry leaves and stems and lined with dry, shredded plant material, usually is located on the ground because of the mesic habitats occupied. Unlike prairie voles, in which a pair bond may be formed, males are promiscuous breeders and compete for females in estrus.

Densities fluctuate over periods of two to five years; in peak periods they may reach 100 or more voles per acre. Home ranges vary in size with season (larger in summer), habitat, and population size, but generally vary from a tenth of an acre up to about an acre.

Breeding takes place through the warm months. Pregnancy lasts 21 days. Litters range from one to 11 young, averaging between four and six. Females have eight mammae and tend to have larger litters than prairie voles, which have only six mammae. Average longevity is only a month or two, but individuals have lived for almost three years in captivity.

Selected References. Reich (1981).

Microtus pinetorum
Woodland Vole

Distribution. The woodland vole is distributed in eastern North America, from southernmost Canada to northern Florida and from the East Coast to the Plains States. In this region, it is absent only from northwestern Iowa, most of Minnesota, northern Wisconsin, and the Upper Peninsula of Michigan.

Description. Small vole with short tail. Dorsum reddish to brownish chestnut, pelage soft, dense, and velvety; venter grayish buff; tail only faintly bicolored. Total length, 120–140; tail, 18–25; hind foot, 16–20; ear, 10–13; weight, 20–45 g. *M. pinetorum* has been placed in the genus *Pitymys*, which also has Old World representatives, by some investigators, or in the genus *Pedomys* (with *M. ochrogaster*) by others. In a recent study, it was suggested that two closely related species occur in the north-central states.

Natural History. Unlike other voles of this region, *M. pinetorum* is primarily an inhabitant of woodlands – coniferous, deciduous, and mixed. The vernacular name *pine vole* sometimes is used. Well-drained wooded slopes are favored where the animals burrow under leaf litter, roots, and logs. The wavy pelage enables them to move both backward and forward in a burrow with ease, and they are in many ways semifossorial. Brushy habitats near forested areas sometimes are occupied.

Woodland voles are highly tolerant of each other, and it is thought that males and females form monogamous pairs, sharing their burrow system with offspring. Nests are located in subterranean tunnels or beneath logs or other ground cover. Home ranges overlap broadly, averaging about half an acre. Populations usually are 10 or fewer per acre, but can be much higher. These voles are active both day and night, feeding on a variety of nuts, seeds, roots, tubers, grasses, bark, and other vegetation. Food is cached for winter. Orchards sometimes are damaged when trees are girdled just beneath ground level.

Like other voles, adults molt twice a year – in spring and early autumn. Their semifossorial habits give them some protection from predation, but only about half the animals in a population survive from one year to the next. Breeding extends from late winter to midautumn. Litters are small, averaging less than three offspring (females have only four mammae).

Selected References. Smolen (1981).

Ondatra zibethicus
Muskrat

Distribution. The muskrat occurs over much of boreal and temperate North America, from Alaska and Labrador south through most of the United States to northernmost Mexico. It is found throughout the north-central region.

Description. Largest of microtine rodents; body heavyset, tail laterally compressed, hind feet partly webbed. Pelage of upper parts dense and glossy, especially in winter, dark brown; flanks paler and more yellowish; underparts generally silvery gray; tail scaly, nearly hairless. Total length, 470–630; tail, 200–260; hind foot, 70–90; ear, 20–25; weight, 0.7–1.5 kg.

Natural History. The muskrat is semiaquatic, inhabiting streams, rivers, marshes, sloughs, ponds, lakes–almost any place where sufficient food and permanent water are present. This is a valuable furbearer, and a million or more are taken for their pelts each winter in the north-central states. The price per pelt, somewhat dependent on the overseas market, has averaged about five dollars over the past decade.

In relatively quiet water, muskrats build conspicuous, conical lodges of aquatic plant material and mud, sometimes as much as five feet high, each of which houses a family group. These are constructed in shallow water, on islands, and sometimes against the bank. In other places, muskrats dig bank burrows with an entrance usually beneath water level. In winter, they swim and forage under ice, their home range marked by a plug of vegetation pushed up through the ice every 100 feet or so. Densities range from one animal per acre up to about 25, but may average 15 an acre in optimum habitat. Foods include stems, leaves, bulbs, and roots of aquatic plants; animals such as fish, frogs, crayfish, and snails also are eaten, especially in winter.

A temporary mating bond is formed in the breeding season. Females bear two (northwardly) to three litters per year of two to nine young, beginning in early spring. Gestation lasts 29–31 days. Young females may breed later in the year of birth. Mink are probably the most important predator, but raptors and many other carnivores take *O. zibethicus*, and snapping turtles and large predatory fish capture young. Muskrats have a heavy parasite load and may suffer from tularemia and a hemorrhagic disease, which can decimate populations.

Selected References. Willner et al. (1980).

Photo by R. Altig

Synaptomys borealis
Northern Bog Lemming

Distribution. This bog lemming is found from Alaska across much of Canada to Labrador. Its distribution barely reaches the United States in the extreme Northwest, northern Minnesota (known only from a few localities), and northern New England.

Description. Solidly built, with short tail, closely resembling *S. cooperi* externally (see key). Dorsum dark brownish to chestnut brown, slightly grizzled in appearance, pelage long and lax; venter overall pale grayish brown; buffy orange patch at base of ear; flank glands of males whitish; tail brownish. Total length, 110–140; tail, 18–25; hind foot, 17–22; ear about 13; weight, 20–40 g. In one recent study, it was recommended that *S. borealis* be included in a distinct genus, *Mictomys*.

Natural History. Little is known of the biology of this microtine. It apparently occurs principally in bogs and marshy areas, but it also has been taken in more xeric habitats including dry woods and sagebrush hillsides. *S. borealis* digs short burrows and also uses conspicuous runways through vegetation. Globular nests are constructed of dry vegetation; these are underground in summer but under snow on the surface in winter. Like other microtines, bog lemmings do not hibernate and may be active at any time.

Food of bog lemmings consists of grasses and sedges, which are cut and piled along runways. The fecal pellets of *Synaptomys* are bright green in color, distinguishing them from those of voles, which are dark olivaceous to blackish. The middle two claws on the feet of *S. borealis* enlarge noticeably in winter, a phenomenon not seen in *S. cooperi*; presumably this is an adaptation to burrowing in snow.

The breeding season is said to extend from May to August. Females produce several litters a year. The recorded number of young per litter varies from two to eight, averaging about four. In a study in the Yukon, for example, 10 pregnant females carried three to six fetuses (average 4.4). Females have four pair of mammae (two pectoral and two inguinal) as opposed to three pair in *S. cooperi*. There are presumably three maturational pelages and two seasonal molts in adults, as in other microtines.

Selected References. Banfield (1974); Peterson (1966); Youngman (1975).

Photo by R.E. Wrigley

Clethrionomys gapperi   *Phenacomys intermedius*   *Synaptomys borealis*   *Microtus pennsylvanicus*

Synaptomys cooperi

Southern Bog Lemming

Distribution. This is a species of the eastern United States and adjacent southeastern Canada. It occurs southward to North Carolina and northeastern Arkansas and westward to Manitoba, Nebraska, and Kansas. In the north-central states, it is absent only from western Minnesota and possibly extreme northwestern Iowa.

Description. A chunky, volelike rodent resembling *S. borealis* except averaging slightly larger. Color essentially as in *borealis*, except possibly somewhat more yellowish overall dorsally and with a pale buffy wash ventrally in some specimens; no orangish patch at base of ear. Median front claws do not enlarge in cold months. Total length, 115–140; tail, 18–25; hind foot, 18–24; ear, 10–13; weight 20–45 g.

Natural History. This bog lemming occurs in a variety of habitats but seems partial to mesic areas such as the borders of bogs, marshes, springs, wet grasslands, and the like, with a thick cover of grasses, sedges, or shrubs. When populations are high, *S. cooperi* moves to drier habitats of matted grassy cover; this species is rare in some areas. Bog lemmings use runways built by other microtines and also construct their own. Piles of cut vegetation, principally grasses and sedges, are found along the runways. Nests, four to eight inches in diameter, are built of shredded vegetation along principal trails; nests are located underground or under thickly matted grasses or other cover on the surface, well above water level.

Food consists primarily of plant material—leafy parts of sedges and grasses, leaves and tender twigs of shrubs, fruit, rootlets, fungi, mosses, ferns, and bark. Bright green feces in runways signal the presence of bog lemmings. Home ranges generally are a tenth to half an acre. Little information has been published on population densities. Foxes, coyotes, wolves, weasels, raccoons, badgers, bobcats, and several kinds of snakes and owls are known predators. Fleas, lice, mites, ticks, cestodes, and trematodes are known parasites.

These rodents are active all year, but the breeding season normally is restricted to the warmer months—March to December. Sixteen gravid females from Indiana carried two to six fetuses (average slightly more than three). Gestation lasts 21–23 days and neonates weigh about 4 g. Average maximum longevity is about a year.

Selected References. Linzey (1983).

Zapus hudsonius
Meadow Jumping Mouse

Distribution. The meadow jumping mouse is found from coast to coast in boreal North America—from Alaska to Labrador. Southwardly, it extends to Arizona and New Mexico in the mountains, to northeastern Oklahoma, and to Alabama and Georgia in the east. It occurs throughout the seven north-central states.

Description. Distinguished from other mice of this region (except *Napaeozapus*) by elongate hind legs and feet, exceptionally long tail, and four upper and three lower cheekteeth. Pelage relatively coarse, with broad, dark brownish dorsal band; flanks yellowish brown; underparts white, sometimes with a yellowish suffusion; tail bicolored, dark brown above, yellowish white below. Total length, 190–240; tail, 110–150; hind foot, 28–34; ear, 12–16; weight averaging about 19 g, up to 35 or more before hibernation.

Natural History. This species lives in a variety of habitats, including grassy fields, meadows, thick vegetation along streams and the edges of ponds and marshes, and herbaceous cover bordering wooded areas. *Z. hudsonius* hibernates, usually from early to midautumn until April or May, longer than most mammals, in a nest of dried vegetation that is located in a burrow below the frost line. Mortality among hibernating individuals, particularly young of the year, is frequently high, probably because of inadequate fat reserves and unusually severe winters.

Jumping mice feed on both vegetable and animal materials. Seeds of grasses seemingly are preferred later in the growing season, as well as the fungus *Endogone*; insects, especially moth larvae and beetles, are important earlier and may make up half the diet; fruits also are eaten. *Z. hudsonius* dives and swims well. On land, individuals do not jump except when frightened or pursued, normally moving on all four feet.

Home ranges usually are less than an acre in extent, those of males the larger; but in one Minnesota study, ranges of males averaged 2.7 acres, females about 1.5. Densities of more than 10 mice per acre have been reported but usually are two to three per acre in good habitat, and may vary considerably from year to year. Females normally bear at least two litters each summer; two to eight fetuses have been reported, litters averaging four to five young.

Selected References. Whitaker (1972).

Napaeozapus insignis
Woodland Jumping Mouse

Distribution. This mouse occurs in southeastern and south-central Canada, from Labrador west to Manitoba, and in the adjacent northern United States, south in the Appalachians to northern Georgia. It occurs in northeastern Minnesota, the northern parts of Michigan and Wisconsin, and in eastern Ohio.

Description. General appearance much as in *Zapus.* Differs in having only three maxillary cheekteeth and tip of tail white. Recent studies suggest that all jumping mice are best assigned to the genus *Zapus.* Dorsum with broad, brownish to blackish stripe; flanks orangish; underparts white; tail distinctly bicolored, grayish brown above, white below, almost always white tipped. Total length, 210–250; tail, 120–155; hind foot, 28–33; ear, 15–18; weight, 17–26 g. Females average slightly larger than males.

Natural History. This jumping mouse lives in the cool, moist environments of woodlands, both coniferous and mixed, and forest edge, especially around logs, along grassy-banked streams, damp rocky areas, and the like. Only in successional and ecotonal situations does its range overlap that of *Z. hudsonius.* Activity is mostly nocturnal, but individuals can be observed abroad at any time. Home ranges vary from about one up to nine acres. Density estimates have ranged from less than one mouse per acre up to more than 20, with four to five probably average in good habitat. Because they hibernate about six months annually, some individuals may well live three to four years. Both kinds of jumping mice are preyed upon occasionally by snakes, raptors, and carnivores, but they probably do not provide a staple item for any predator.

Napaeozapus digs its own burrows or uses those of other small mammals. The nest, made of dry leaves and grasses, may be located in summer under brush piles or logs, or in a burrow; deeper burrows are used for hibernation. Foods consist primarily of seeds, small nuts, berries, roots, and other plant material; insects; and fungi. These mice swim well and also climb in low bushes. Parasites include protozoans, trematodes, and cestodes internally, botfly larvae, fleas, mites, and ticks externally.

Females usually bear two litters annually of two to seven young. Breeding peaks are in late spring and midsummer.

Selected References. Whitaker and Wrigley (1972); Wrigley (1972).

Erethizon dorsatum
Porcupine

Distribution. The porcupine ranges across boreal North America from Alaska to Labrador and southward to northern Mexico, the Lake States, and New England. Formerly, it occurred farther south in the eastern United States. In the north-central region, this species now is found only in Michigan, Minnesota, and Wisconsin; within historical times it ranged southward into the four southern states.

Description. Large rodent with heavy body, stout legs and claws, short tail, covered dorsally with underfur, long guard hairs, and quills; unlike any other mammal of region. Color variable, usually overall brownish to brownish black, paler ventrally. Total length, 600–900; tail, 160–220; hind foot, 75–110; ear, 28–40; weight, 5.5–12 kg or more.

Natural History. Coniferous forests are the primary habitat of porcupines, but they occur north of the tree line in the Arctic, in various scrub habitats on the Great Plains and in the Southwest, and in mixed and occasionally even deciduous woodlands. They are entirely vegetarian, eating a variety of woody, herbaceous, and other vegetation in the warm months and mostly inner bark of trees in winter. Sometimes they do serious damage to trees. These animals, which climb well, walk or run with an awkward gait on the ground.

Porcupines are active the year around and are mostly nocturnal. They are usually solitary, except for females with young, but several may den together, especially in winter. Dens are in caves, under rock ledges, stumps, or logs, in hollow trees or abandoned buildings, or other shelters. Reported densities range from two or three up to 15 individuals per square mile, depending on habitat. Home ranges are large; territories are not defended. Humans and the fisher are the principal predators, but many large carnivores and some large raptors also take them. Major parasites include fleas, lice, ticks, mites, round-worms, flatworms, and tongue worms. Known longevity exceeds 10 years.

Mating takes place in late autumn and winter. Courtship is elaborate, and there is much socialization. Gestation lasts 205–217 days. The single (occasion-ally twins) young is born in April, May, or June. Offspring are precocial, furred and with eyes open, weighing 300 g or more. Quills, which are soft at birth, harden within an hour.

Selected References. Woods (1973).

Order Carnivora

Carnivores

Recent carnivores have a broad distribution, occurring on all major land masses with the exception of Australia and Antarctica; even there, pinnipeds are found along the coasts, and the wild dog (dingo) was transported to Australia by early humans a few thousand years ago. Carnivores, especially domestic dogs and cats and the mongoose, have been introduced in modern times on many oceanic islands. As the ordinal name implies, these mammals typically eat flesh, but some species regularly take fruits, nuts, other vegetable matter, and invertebrates. Bears and procyonids are truly omnivorous. The order has a long and fairly good fossil history, which dates back to the early Paleocene.

Modern members of the Carnivora are represented by 10–12 families (including the aquatic pinnipeds), depending on the authority consulted, which contain about 100 genera and 270 species. They are found in a variety of boreal, temperate, and tropical habitats. Members of all terrestrial families have well-developed canines and, except for the African aardwolf, a special pair of shearing teeth (carnassials) that are formed by the fourth premolar in the upper dentition and the first lower molar. Carnassials are best developed in felids and least developed in bears and in raccoons and their allies.

Five families of carnivores are known from the north-central states. These include 13 genera and 22 species, some of which no longer occur in the region or their current distribution is severely limited, principally through the activities of humans. As with the rodents, it is convenient to provide a key to families, followed by a key to species in each family (Canidae, Mustelidae, and Felidae) of which more than one species is treated here.

Key to Families of Carnivores

1. Claws retractile, can be completely concealed in fur; molars 1/1;
    premolars 2/2 or 3/2 ....Felidae
1'. Claws not retractile to completely so, not concealed in fur;
    molars 1/2 or more; premolars never fewer than 3/3 2
2. Tail conspicuously ringed; molars 2/2..................Procyonidae
2'. Tail not ringed; molars 1/2 or 2/3 3
3. Size small to medium (*Gulo* largest); molars 1/2; premolars 4/4
    (*Gulo, Martes*), 4/3 (*Lutra*), or 3/3 ....Mustelidae
3'. Size medium to large (*Vulpes* smallest); molars 2/3;
    premolars always 4/4...4
4. Size large; feet plantigrade; large cheekteeth flattened,
    only slightly cuspidate ....Ursidae
4'. Size medium; feet digitigrade; large cheekteeth not flattened,
    noticeably cuspidate ....Canidae

Key to Canids

1. Total length more than 1,050; condylobasal length of skull more
    than 160; weight more than 9 kg 2
1'. Total length less than 1,050; condylobasal length of skull less
    than 155; weight less than 9 kg...............................4
2. Total length usually more than 1,400; length of first lower molar
    more than 25; condylobasal length more than 200 ....*Canis lupus*
2'. Total length less than 1,400; length of first lower molar less
    than 25; condylobasal length less than 200 3
3. Dorsal pelage usually brownish gray; orbits not rising abruptly
    above rostrum ....*Canis latrans*
3'. Dorsal pelage variable in color; orbits usually rising abruptly
    above rostrum................................*Canis familiaris*
4. Dorsal surface of skull more or less flattened from nasals to orbits;
    temporal ridges prominent......................................5
4'. Dorsal surface of skull rising abruptly at orbits; temporal ridges
    rarely prominent ....*Canis familiaris*
5. Dorsal pelage reddish; ears with black tips; condylobasal length
    usually more than 130; temporal ridges not lyre shaped.*Vulpes vulpes*
5'. Dorsal pelage grizzled grayish; ears lacking black tips;
    condylobasal length less than 130; temporal ridges lyre
    shaped ....*Urocyon cinereoargenteus*

Notes: Canis rufus and *Vulpes velox* no longer occur in the north-central region and thus are not included in this key. The domestic dog (*Canis familiaris*) is included because feral individuals are relatively common in some areas.

Key to Mustelids

1. Feet webbed; tail thickened at base and tapering toward tip; premolars 4/3 . . . . *Lutra canadensis*

1′. Feet not webbed; tail not thickened at base and not tapering toward tip; premolars 4/4 or 3/3 2

2. Length of hind foot 96 or more (rarely slightly less in *Taxidea taxus*); greatest length of skull 90 or more 3

2′. Length of hind foot 96 or less (rarely slightly more in *Martes americana*); greatest length of skull 85 or less 5

3. Dorsum yellowish gray, with white medial stripe from nose to neck or beyond; premolars 3/3 . . . .*Taxidea taxus*

3′. Dorsum brownish, lacking white stripe; premolars 4/4 4

4. Dorsum dark brown to blackish, with pale reddish stripes extending from shoulder to rump on each side; length of tail approximately 25 percent of total length; greatest length of skull more than 130 . . . .*Gulo gulo*

4′. Dorsum grizzled dark brown to blackish, accentuated by pale head, neck, and shoulders, lacking stripes on sides; length of tail approximately 40 percent of total length; greatest length of skull less than 130 . . . .*Martes pennanti*

5. Pelage black, with white stripes or spots on dorsum; palate extending posteriorly to level of last upper molar or only slightly beyond 6

5′. Pelage not black, lacking white stripes or spots on dorsum; palate extending posteriorly well beyond last upper molar 7

6. Dorsum black, with two white stripes of variable length that merge with a white spot on the head and neck; greatest length of skull more than 65 . . . .*Mephitis mephitis*

6′. Dorsum black, with four to six white stripes, broken into spots posteriorly; greatest length of skull less than 65 . . .*Spilogale putorius*

7. Length of hind foot more than 80 in males, more than 70 in females; premolars 4/4 . . . .*Martes americana*

7′. Length of hind foot less than 80 in males, less than 70 in females; premolars 3/3 8

8. Total length usually more than 475; greatest length of skull more than 55 ....*Mustela vison*

8′. Total length usually less than 450; greatest length of skull less than 55 9

9. Total length less than 230, usually less than 200; tail less than one-third length of body, lacking distinct black tip; greatest length of skull less than 37 in males (32 in females)...*Mustela nivalis*

9′. Total length more than 230; tail at least one-third length of body, with distinct black tip; greatest length of skull more than 37 in males (32 in females)..12

10. Length of tail usually more than 100, more than 44 percent of length of body; summer pelage of venter not extending to inner sides of hind legs; greatest length of skull usually more than 47 in males (42 in females) ....*Mustela frenata*

10′. Length of tail usually less than 100, less than 44 percent of length of body; summer pelage of venter extending to inner sides of hind legs; greatest length of skull usually less than 47 in males (42 in females)............................*Mustela erminea*

Key to Felids

1. Tail long, more than 500; weight more than 30 kg; zygomatic breadth more than 115 ....*Felis concolor*

1′. Tail short, less than 200; weight less than 25 kg; zygomatic breadth usually less than 100 2

2. Tail less than half length of hind foot, black at tip both above and below; two foramina at posterointernal base of bulla...*Felis lynx*

2′. Tail more than half length of hind foot, black on upper surface of tip, white below; single foramen at posterointernal base of bulla ....*Felis rufus*

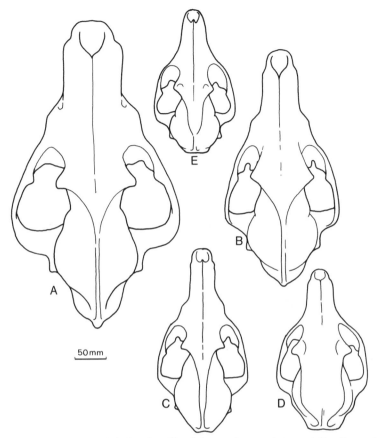

Figure 4. Dorsal view of skulls of canids of the north-central states (after Jones et al., 1983). A, *Canis lupus*; B, *C. latrans*; C, *Vulpes vulpes*; D, *Urocyon cinereoargenteus*; E, *Vulpes velox*.

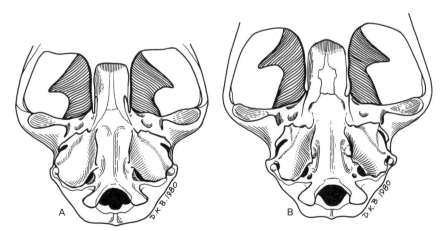

Figure 5. Ventral view of occipital region of skulls of (A) *Felis rufus* and (B) *F. lynx* (after Jones et al., 1983).

Canis latrans
Coyote

Distribution. The coyote is distributed from Alaska southeastward through Canada to New England, throughout most of the United States and Mexico, to Costa Rica. Typically an animal of open country, it has expanded its range within historical times. The species now is known all across the north-central states; it once occurred on Isle Royale but apparently is no longer present there.

Description. Smallest of New World wild *Canis*, but larger than any foxes. Dorsal color variable but generally grayish brown to grayish buff; venter paler. Total length, 1,050–1,350; tail, 290–390; hind foot, 180–210; ear, 95–120; weight, 9–20 kg. Males are larger and heavier than females.

Natural History. The coyote occupies a variety of habitats, even occasionally urban environments, and is one of the most successful carnivores in adapting to human presence. Mammalian flesh makes up about 90 percent of the varied diet – rodents, rabbits, deer, carrion, and occasionally livestock; ground-nesting birds, lizards, amphibians, and invertebrates also are eaten, as are berries and fruits. Large carnivores and humans are among the few enemies of *C. latrans*. It cannot directly compete physically with the larger gray wolf, but it may be able to compete in an ecological sense. In recent years, prime pelts have brought an average of about 50 dollars.

Coyotes are most active in the evening and at night, but they may be on the move at any time. Locomotion includes a walk, trot, and bound. Maximum running speed is about 40 miles per hour. They are frequently solitary but may hunt in family groups in autumn and winter. Densities vary considerably with habitat and human interference, but one animal per one to two square miles is probably about average. Longevity in the wild usually does not exceed 10 years, but animals have lived almost 20 in captivity. Like *C. lupus*, this species harbors a variety of internal and external parasites.

The one annual litter averages about six pups, which are born in spring after 63 days of gestation. Young are nursed by the female, which the male provisions, in a den under a rock, cutbank, or downed tree, or in a burrow. They are weaned in about a month and a half.

Selected References. Bekoff (1977).

Canis lupus
Gray Wolf

Distribution. The gray wolf once had an exceptionally broad distribution across the northern and temperate parts of both the Old and New Worlds. It occurs on Greenland and all across Canada to Alaska, and formerly was found southward through most of the United States to central Mexico. Extirpated in much of the southern part of its range in the Western Hemisphere, it now is found in our region only in the northern parts of Michigan, Minnesota, and Wisconsin.

Description. Largest of wild canids. Dorsum usually grizzled gray, but varying from white through brown to black; paler ventrally. Average measurements of males and females from Minnesota, respectively: total length, 1,545, 1,485; tail, 430, 410; hind foot, 270, 260; ear, 121, 115. Weight averages about 27 kg, but large males may weigh 65 or more.

Natural History. Wolves are social mammals, usually living in packs of two to eight family members in our region. Larger groups have been reported farther north. A dominant male and female head each pack and typically are the only pack members to breed. Communication includes howling and other vocalizations, visual displays, and scent marking with urine or feces. Wolves occupy, or once occupied, a wide variety of habitats. Prey in North America consists mostly of ungulates such as moose, deer, and caribou, but beavers and snowshoe hares may be important seasonally. Humans hunt wolves for sport, bounties, and their fur (a prime pelt may bring as much as 100 dollars). Few if any other mammals kill adult wolves.

Wolves travel considerably, mostly at night. Home ranges may be 50 square miles or larger in Minnesota. In studies on Isle Royale, densities varied from one individual per five to 10 square miles. These canids are good swimmers and do not hesitate to enter water. Each pack defends a well-defined territory, but does not have a permanent homesite except when pups are present. A mated pair evidently remains together permanently, remating only after one member dies. Breeding occurs in late February or March. After 63 days of gestation, a litter of four to 10 (average seven) pups is born in a burrow or other protected den.

Selected References. Mech (1974); Fritts and Mech (1981).

Canis rufus
Red Wolf

Distribution. This canid once occurred in the southeastern United States–from Texas eastward to Virginia and Florida. Its range apparently reached the southern part of the north-central region (not mapped).

Description. Medium-sized among American *Canis*, smaller than wolf, larger than coyote. Dorsal color usually reddish brown, but variable; more sparsely haired than other species. Total length, 1,350–1,650; weight, 20–40 kg. Males average larger than females.

Notes. This wolf has been nearly (possibly entirely) extirpated by humans and through hybridization with the coyote. If pure stocks still occur, they are in the coastal area of southeastern Texas and adjacent Louisiana. From our region, there is one specimen taken on the Wabash River, Indiana, and a questionable specimen from Hancock County, Illinois, both recorded many years ago.

Selected References. Paradiso and Nowak (1972); Young and Goldman (1944).

Vulpes velox
Swift Fox

Distribution. The swift fox formerly was distributed across the northern and central plains of North America, from southern Canada to the Texas Panhandle. It once may have occurred in western Minnesota and possibly adjacent northwestern Iowa (not mapped).

Description. Smallest fox of north-central region, only slightly larger than house cat. Dorsal pelage buffy gray; throat, chest, and venter pale buff to white; tail with black tip. Total length, 700–880; tail, 240–350; hind foot, 115–135; ear, 55–75; weight, 1.7–3 kg.

Notes. This little fox was extirpated over much of its range, probably as a result of indiscriminate carnivore poisoning, by the early 1900s. It has made a spectacular comeback in recent years, however, and now is common in some places. There are records within the past decade from the Dakotas and Nebraska, and *V. velox* may be found once again in our region.

Selected References. Egoscue (1979).

Canis rufus

Vulpes velox

Vulpes vulpes

Red Fox

Distribution. This fox ranges over most of boreal and temperate North America, south to the Gulf Coast, Texas, and California. It also has a broad distribution in the Old World. *V. vulpes* is found throughout the north-central states.

Description. Largest fox of region. Upper parts yellowish red to fulvous overall, darkest at midline; face, head, and nape yellowish to rusty red; underparts and tip of tail white; outer sides of ears, legs, and feet blackish. Total length, 900–1,060; tail, 320–390; hind foot, 135–175; ear, 70–90; weight, 3.5–7 kg.

Natural History. Meadows, wooded or grassy borders of streams and lakes, brushy fencerows, and similar habitats provide optimal foraging and denning areas for red foxes. Clearing of land for agricultural purposes apparently has benefited this fox, including range expansion. Home ranges vary with food availability, cover, and other factors, from about 160 to almost 1,500 acres. One home range typically, but not invariably, is occupied by a mated pair (with offspring in season) and abuts those of other such groups. The area is scent marked, and either males or females will harass intruders.

Foxes usually hunt alone. Their keen senses of hearing and smell are used to detect prey, mostly rabbits, rodents, birds, and carrion. However, like many canids, they are opportunistic feeders and also take lower vertebrates, invertebrates, and fruits and nuts in season.

Females bear a litter, averaging about five pups, in March or April. The offspring are raised in a den prepared by the mated pair. Occasionally, two females cohabit a den, or, conversely, pups of a single litter may be found in separate dens. Gestation lasts 51–53 days; neonates weigh about 100 g, have eyes closed, and are covered with a woolly pelage. Males provision females until the pups are weaned, at about 60 days, when both parents bring them food. Young disperse from the home area in autumn. Adults molt but once a year, as do other canids, in a gradual process from spring to autumn. A prime pelt has averaged about 50 dollars at auctions in recent years.

Selected References. Pils and Martin (1978); Samuel and Nelson (1982); Storm et al. (1976).

Urocyon cinereoargenteus
Gray Fox

Distribution. This species ranges from southeastern Canada through the eastern and central United States to northern South America; it also is found in the American Southwest, northward along the Pacific Coast to Oregon. It occurs throughout the seven-state region.

Description. Slightly smaller than red fox; braincase with lyre-shaped temporal ridges. Dorsum grizzled buffy gray, blackish middorsally; black, white, and rufous markings on head; parts of neck, flanks, and limbs cinnamon to rufous; underparts whitish; tail tipped with black. Total length, 880–1,040; tail, 280–370; hind foot, 125–145; ear, 70–80; weight, 3.5–6.5 kg.

Natural History. The gray fox is typically at home in wooded, brushy, and rocky habitats. Within the past century, it has expanded its range into some previously unoccupied areas and others from which it was earlier extirpated. Woodland-farmland borders and brushy edge situations, as well as abandoned fields, are favored in many areas. Dens, less conspicuous than those of the red fox, are used any time but most often during whelping season. Home ranges, calculated through radio-tracking, of two males and four females in southern Illinois averaged 336 and 254 acres, respectively. Density estimates range from about two to three per square mile in good habitat.

This fox is primarily crepuscular and nocturnal. The diet consists of small mammals and birds, carrion, and invertebrates, along with substantial amounts of fruits, berries, and corn. Individuals do not hesitate to climb into lower branches of trees in search of food. Hollow logs or trees, crevices in rocks, caves, piles of brush and wood, abandoned buildings, and underground burrows serve as den sites.

Gray foxes are parasitized by fleas, lice, mites, and ticks externally, but unlike most other canids are highly resistant to infection by mange mites. Cestodes, nematodes, trematodes, and acanthocephalans infest them internally. They also suffer from several diseases, including distemper and rabies, as do their relatives. Humans are their most important enemy, but larger carnivores and raptors take young. The fur is about half as valuable as that of the red fox. Reproductive features are much the same as *V. vulpes*. Litters consist of one to seven (average four) young.

Selected References. Fritzell and Haroldson (1982).

Ursus americanus
Black Bear

Distribution. This bear once occurred all across North America, from Labrador to Alaska and south through most of the United States to north-central Mexico. It ranged throughout the seven-state region, but now is limited, save for an occasional wanderer, to the northern parts of Michigan, Minnesota, and Wisconsin.

Description. Body size large; ears prominent and rounded; tail short; pelage long, glossy. Color unusually blackish throughout except for white blotch on throat and cinnamon brown muzzle; occasional brownish individuals are encountered. Males larger than females. Total length, 1,200–1,800; tail, 80–125; hind foot, 200–275; ear, 100–135; weight, 115–225 kg, large males up to 275 or so.

Natural History. Black bears generally are restricted to wooded habitats, both hardwood and coniferous, including swampy areas. They once occurred throughout the north-central states but were extirpated in the southern part before the end of the last century through the activities of humans. Bears are hunted for sport, meat, and their pelts, which have brought about 100 dollars in recent years.

These animals are solitary and primarily diurnal and crepuscular. Adult females defend summer territories, but adult males share large, overlapping home ranges. The usual gait is a plodding walk, but bears can run up to 30 miles per hour, climb trees easily, and swim well. They are omnivores, eating ants, berries, fruits, nuts, honey, carrion, fish, birds and eggs, small mammals, and invertebrates. They have few natural enemies except humans, although large carnivores occasionally take cubs or even adults in exposed dens.

Although their body temperatures remain relatively high, bears spend from October or November until March or April in deep sleep in a den beneath roots of a tree, in a rock cavity, under boulders, and the like. A thick layer of fat sustains them. During this entire period, they do not urinate or defecate. They breed in early summer, but embryos do not implant until autumn. One to five (usually two or three) small young are born in late winter to the dormant female. Cubs accompany their mother when she leaves the winter den. Maximum longevity may be 20 years or more.

Selected References. Erickson et al. (1964); Pelton (1982).

Procyon lotor

Raccoon

Distribution. This species occurs from southern Canada southward through the United States (except for the arid interior basins of the Southwest) and Mexico to Panama. It is found throughout the north-central states.

Description. Solidly built, medium-sized carnivore, with blackish mask on face and bushy tail with alternating black and pale rings. Dorsum grayish black to brownish gray, somewhat grizzled in appearance; ears prominent, rounded, white edged; underparts grayer than back. Total length, 700–950; tail, 220–260; hind foot, 110–125; ear, 50–60; weight, 6.5–13 kg but occasionally up to 20 or more.

Natural History. Few carnivores are as readily recognizable to the general public as are raccoons. These common and ubiquitous animals are mostly nocturnal. They walk with a kind of lumbering gait, because of the semi-elongate hind legs, but can run reasonably rapidly and climb exceedingly well. Essentially solitary by nature, raccoons will gather at a concentrated food source and at denning sites in winter. They do not hibernate but may remain inactive in periods of especially cold or inclement weather.

Dens are usually in hollow trees or in ground burrows abandoned by another mammal, but they also may be in rock crevices, caves, and outbuildings. Hardwood forests, riparian woodlands, scattered woodlots, and even marshlands are favored habitats, as are wooded suburban areas. These are omnivores, and they eat a variety of foods such as berries, fruit, nuts, corn, seeds, invertebrates (especially crayfish and crabs when available), turtles and their eggs, toads, young muskrats, and waterfowl. Humans are the most important enemy of the raccoon (the flesh is eaten and pelts have averaged about 25 dollars the past few years), but larger carnivores and raptors take a few. Disease is an important cause of mortality. A variety of ectoparasites and endoparasites has been recorded.

Breeding extends from midwinter to early summer, but most matings occur in February and March. Females bear a single litter annually, averaging three to four (up to seven) young, after a gestation period of 63–65 days. Thus, most litters are born in April and May, but sometimes as late as August. Known longevity in the wild exceeds 12 years (17 in captivity). Adults molt but once a year, in spring.

Selected References. Lotze and Anderson (1979).

Martes americana
Marten

Distribution. This mustelid once was found from the Lake States and New England northward in the boreal forests of Canada to Alaska and in the forested mountains of the western United States. In our region, it occurred as far south as Ohio and northern Illinois, but it now is limited to the northern parts of Michigan, Minnesota, and Wisconsin, having been reintroduced in some areas.

Description. Weasel-like and partly arboreal. Dorsum rich yellowish brown to dark brown overall, head paler, ears white tipped; venter same color as upper parts except for cream-colored to yellowish splotches on throat and chest; legs and bushy tail dark brown to blackish. Total length, 600–660; tail, 180–220; hind foot, 80–95; ear, 35–48; weight, 0.5–1.5 kg. Foregoing measurements of males, females average 10–15 percent smaller.

Natural History. The marten is at home in mature stands of coniferous forest but occurs also in mixed deciduous-coniferous woodlands. It is a valuable furbearer, and overtrapping combined with destruction of habitat drove it to extinction, or nearly so, in this region. However, the species has returned to northern Minnesota by natural means and has been reintroduced in northern Wisconsin and Michigan's Upper Peninsula. Now under complete protection, it is locally common in northern Minnesota, and it is hoped that it again will become a common inhabitant of our northern forests.

Martens are mostly, but not entirely, noctural and are generally solitary. They forage both on the ground and in trees. Opportunistic feeders, these mustelids take small to medium-sized mammals such as mice, voles, chipmunks, squirrels, and hares, as well as birds, some insects, and occasionally fruit and berries. They have few natural enemies except humans. In a Minnesota study, home ranges of males varied from about four to eight square miles, those of females being smaller.

Mating occurs in midsummer, but, as in many mustelids, implantation of fertilized eggs is delayed until late winter or early spring. A litter of two to six (average three to four) young is born in a den in a hollow log or stump, rock pile, or crevice. The offspring leave the nest when about three months old.

Selected References. Mech and Rogers (1977); Strickland et al. (1982).

Photo by D. Randall

Martes pennanti
Fisher

Distribution. The fisher once occurred across southern Canada, from eastern Quebec to southern Yukon, and southward in the United States to Kentucky and North Carolina in the east and to California and Utah in the west. It was found in all north-central states but today is limited to the northern part.

Description. Largest of weasel-like mustelids. Upper parts dark grayish brown to blackish brown, fur thick, luxuriant, glossy, but somewhat coarse on males; head, ears, and nape paler; venter same color as dorsum except for irregular spots of white; tail long and bushy. Total length, 920–1,050; tail, 340–400; hind foot, 110–125; ear, 45–55; weight, 2.5–5.5 kg. Foregoing measurements for males; females average smaller.

Natural History. This animal occurs in coniferous, mixed, and hardwood forests. Unlike the marten, it is quite successful in deciduous woodlands and also survives in cutover areas and second growth with continuous canopy. Fishers once occurred much farther south in eastern North America than at present. Because of the hunting for its valuable pelt, along with destruction of its favored habitats, the species became extinct in the north-central states save for small populations in northeastern Minnesota. Through protection and restocking, it now occurs over much of the northern part of the region.

Fishers are generally solitary and tend to travel substantial distances within their home ranges; one tracked in Ontario covered 40 miles in three days. In studies in Ontario and New York, densities ranged from one to four animals per square mile. Most activity is at night, but *M. pennanti* may be partly diurnal in winter. Dens are in tree holes, hollow logs, crevices, rock piles, and the like.

Fishers eat mostly animal food. Porcupines, snowshoe hares, tree squirrels, and voles are most prevalent in the diet, but other small mammals, birds, carrion, lower vertebrates, fruits, nuts, and berries also are consumed. The name is a misnomer, because fish are rarely sought; evidently it results from the fisher's resemblance to the European polecat, which was referred to as *fitch, fizhe,* and similar names. Mating takes place in early spring, shortly after birth of the litter, which usually consists of two to three (up to five) young.

Selected References. Powell (1981, 1982).

Mustela erminea
Ermine

Distribution. The ermine ranges all across the northern part of the Western Hemisphere, north to Greenland and southward in the United States to Iowa, Pennsylvania, and Maryland in the east and the mountains of New Mexico in the west. It also occurs in the Old World. In the north-central region, *M. erminea* is found in the three northern states, in northern Iowa, and in northeastern Ohio.

Description. Middle-sized among midwestern members of genus *Mustela*. Dorsum uniformly dark brown in summer; relatively short tail brown with black tip; underparts white, sometimes tinged with pale yellowish, color extending down inside of legs to feet and toes; pelage white in winter except black tip of tail. Total length, 240–330; tail, 60–95; hind foot, 30–45; ear, 15–20; weight, 60–150 g. Males larger than females.

Natural History. In the southern part of its range, this weasel is found in open country adjacent to woodlands or shrubby areas; along the wooded borders of streams, lakes, and marshes; in rocky outcroppings; along brushy fencerows; and in successional habitats. It rarely occurs in deep woods. Nests usually are in hollow trees, rock piles, or burrows.

These are generally solitary animals, adult males and females maintaining discrete home ranges, which may be 60 acres for the former and 30 for females. Courtship and breeding occur in early summer. Uterine implantation of embryos is delayed until late winter or early spring, after which the active period of gestation lasts about four weeks. A litter of four to 13 young (usually four to eight) is born in April or May. Neonates are blind, covered with a fine coat of white hair, and weigh about 2 g.

Ermines prey primarily on small mammals and birds; invertebrates also are eaten. In winter, they forage extensively under the snow. Raptors and larger carnivores prey on these animals, and their white winter pelage has a modest value on the fur market. Ectoparasites include fleas, lice, mites, and ticks. Internally they are parasitized by trematodes, nematodes, cestodes, and acanthocephalans. As in many other mustelids, nasal roundworms may cause severe lesions and even disfigure the skull. Maximum longevity in nature is about seven years.

Selected References. King (1983).

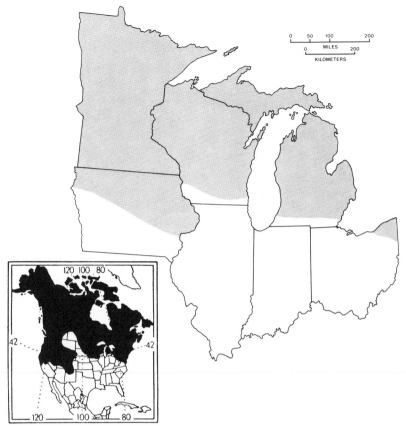

Photo by James F. Parnell

Mustela frenata
Long-tailed Weasel

Distribution. Unlike the ermine and least weasel, *M. frenata* is exclusively American in distribution. It occurs over a broad area from southern Canada southward into northern South America. It is found throughout the seven-state region.

Description. Largest weasel of region but smaller than mink. Upper parts brown in summer, much like *M. erminea;* tail brown (except for black tip); venter white to yellowish, color not extending to inside of legs; pelage white in winter save for black-tipped tail. Total length, 350–430; tail, 110–140; hind foot, 35–50; ear, 15–22; weight, 170–240 g. Foregoing measurements are for males; females average considerably smaller.

Natural History. Long-tailed weasels occupy a variety of habitats but are most common in open brushy areas, woodland borders, overgrown fencerows, and the like, frequently in the vicinity of water. Like other mustelids, they hunt at any time. A long, cylindrical body, although energetically expensive, allows them to follow prey into small burrows. Small mammals, from mice and voles to rabbits, typically make up 90 percent or more of the diet. Interaction between the three weasels that occur in this region is not well known and is deserving of study.

Weasels rarely dig burrows, but they frequently occupy those abandoned by other small mammals. Nests also may be beneath rocks, in crevices or hollow logs, under brush piles and haystacks, and in similar retreats. Most foraging takes place on the ground, but weasels climb readily and can pursue prey in trees. Adults are solitary except in the mating season, which is in summer. Implantation of blastocysts is delayed, so the "gestation period" may be as long as 11 months (actually only about 27 days after implantation). Four to nine (usually six to eight) young are born in April or May. Little is known of mortality and longevity in *M. frenata.*

Densities and spatial distribution vary with habitat and season. In a study on open land in Iowa, one weasel per 40 acres was estimated, but in a similar study in Michigan the ratio was one per 300 acres. Home ranges seem to vary from 30 or 40 acres up to 180 or more.

Selected References. Hall (1951); Jones et al. (1983); Svendsen (1982).

Mustela nivalis
Least Weasel

Distribution. This circumboreal species occurs across North America from Alaska to Labrador. It ranges southward to Kansas and the north-central states, and in the Appalachians to North Carolina and Tennessee. In our region, the species is found in all but southern Illinois and Indiana.

Description. Smallest of weasels. Upper parts in summer chocolate brown to umber; venter white, sometimes with isolated brown patches; tail brown, lacking black tip (at most a few isolated black hairs); winter pelage white. Like other weasels, molting animals in spring and autumn are "piebald." Total length, 190–215 (males), 170–185 (females); tail, 25–45; hind foot, 20–28; ear, 10–15; weight, 30–65 g.

Natural History. Least weasels have been recorded from many habitats but seem to prefer meadows, grasslands, marshy and shrubby areas, and other more or less open places, especially in the southern part of the range. Voles and mice make up most of the diet, but insects and smaller ground-nesting birds also are taken. It has been estimated that these animals consume a third to a half of their own body weight daily, and they thus are an important component in the food chain. *M. nivalis* is preyed upon by raptors and larger carnivores. It is too small to be valuable as a furbearer.

Nests are located in abandoned rodent burrows or under ground cover such as corn shocks and haystacks. Like other weasels, individuals may be active at any time. Adults are solitary except during breeding periods. Home ranges may overlap, and they vary up to about 60 acres for males, smaller for females. Populations seemingly fluctuate with availability of small rodents. Fleas, lice, mites, and ticks parasitize this weasel externally; nematodes and cestodes are known endoparasites.

Unlike their larger relatives, females do not have delayed implantation; they may produce two or more litters annually, of one to six young, after 35 days of gestation. Neonates are naked, blind, and weigh about 1.5 g. They begin to eat solid food by three weeks of age and reach maturity at 12–14 weeks, when they disperse. Females may breed later in the year of birth.

Selected References. Erlinge (1974, 1975); Hall (1951); Heidt (1970); Heidt et al. (1968).

Photo by James F. Parnell

Mustela vison
Mink

Distribution. This species is distributed over much of boreal North America, southward throughout the eastern United States and in the west to California, New Mexico, and Texas. It is found in all the north-central states. The mink has a close relative in Eurasia and also has been introduced there.

Description. Relatively large weasel-like mammal. Color uniformly dark brown except for white blotches on chin, throat, and sometimes chest and belly; pelage long and glossy. Total length, 570–680; tail, 185–210; hind foot, 60–75; ear, 20–27; weight, 1–1.7 kg. Foregoing measurements for males; females average about 10 percent smaller.

Natural History. The mink is equally at home on land and in the water. Only heavily wooded upland habitats are avoided, but areas around lakes, ponds, impoundments, streams, rivers, and marshes are preferred. As in other mustelids, anal scent glands are well developed, emitting a strong, musty odor.

The food habits of the mink reflect its varied life style. Muskrats (especially young), voles, mice, and cottontails are staple items, but birds, fish, crayfish and other invertebrates, frogs, snakes, squirrels, shrews, and even some plant material also are eaten. In contrast to weasels, mink rarely cache food for future use. They are solitary animals except during the breeding season. Dens generally are located near water. They may be fashioned by the animal itself under roots of a tree or a fallen log, but more often are abandoned burrows of other mammals or unused muskrat houses. Home ranges tend to be somewhat linear because they follow shorelines; those of females range from 20 to 50 acres, whereas ranges of males are much larger.

Mink have few enemies other than humans. Although pelt prices fluctuate, they have averaged between 25 and 50 dollars each in recent years. Because of the market for the fur and because they adapt readily to captivity, many mink are raised on fur farms.

Breeding takes place in middle to late winter. Gestation begins after a relatively short period of delayed implantation, and a litter of one to 10 (usually four or five) young is born in April or May.

Selected References. Enders (1952); Errington (1943, 1954); Linscombe et al. (1982).

Photo by W.D. Zehr

Gulo gulo
Wolverine

Distribution. This unique mammal once occurred all across boreal North America and Eurasia. In the New World, it was found southward to northern New England, the Lake States, the northern Great Plains, and in the western mountains. Aside from an occasional wanderer, it evidently is now absent from the north-central region, except possibly for a few in extreme northern Minnesota (not mapped).

Description. Largest of mustelids; legs stocky and powerful, feet large, claws strong. Overall color dark yellowish brown to blackish brown; pale reddish to pale brownish stripe extending from behind shoulder to rump, and on side of head from eye to ear; pale-colored patches on throat, chest, and venter; legs, feet, and most of tail blackish. Total length, 950–1,070; tail, 200–260; hind foot, 175–200; ear, 45–55; weight, 11–16 kg. Females average smaller than the above measurements of males, as in most mustelids.

Natural History. The wolverine, although primarily a denizen of the boreal forest, occurs on tundra well north of the timberline and once was found southward into mixed and deciduous forests and even on the northern plains. It has long been extirpated from most of the southeastern part of its former range. Aside from a few reports of sightings, some open to question, the last undoubted record of this species from Minnesota was a specimen taken in Itasca County in 1899, and *G. gulo* is reported to have lived in Michigan's Huron Mountains until about 1903. A specimen was taken in Tama County, Iowa, in 1960, but it is uncertain whether this was an accidental wanderer or reached the state by unnatural means. Two possibly questionable records from Indiana are dated 1840 and 1852.

These animals are primarily nocturnal but may be active by day as well. They range over broad areas, up to 100 square miles or more, in search of food. The diet consists of many kinds of mammals, large and small, carrion, ground-nesting birds and their eggs, fish, larvae of wasps and bees and possibly other invertebrate material, and even roots and berries. Females bear a litter averaging three or four young in February or March.

Selected References. Birney (1974); Mumford (1969); Wilson (1982).

Taxidea taxus
Badger

Distribution. The badger is found in western North America from Canada to central Mexico. Eastwardly, the range extends throughout the plains region to the Lake States. In the seven north-central states, this species occurs in all but parts of southern Illinois and Indiana and eastern Ohio; it has expanded its distribution eastward within historical times.

Description. Stocky, large, muscular mustelid with short, powerful legs and short tail. Foreclaws long and curved; hind claws shovel-like. Dorsal pelage shaggy, grizzled grayish to brownish, with medial white stripe on head and upper back; black "badge" on face and at bases of ears; venter buff to yellowish white. Total length, 690–780; tail, 110–150; hind foot, 95–125; ear, 45–60; weight, 5–12 kg.

*Natural History.*The badger is active both day and night and is an excellent digger, using its large claws to dig out prey species and to excavate its own burrows, of which there may be several. At high altitudes and latitudes, badgers may be torpid in winter, but they do not truly hibernate. They are essentially solitary animals as adults.

Food includes a variety of small vertebrates, especially rodents; carrion, fish, snakes, insects, small birds, and invertebrates also are eaten, but apparently no vegetable matter. Food sometimes is cached. Population structure and home ranges are not well known for *T. taxus*. In summer, the home range may be as much as two to three square miles, but it is smaller in colder months. Badgers are parasitized by cestodes, nematodes, and trematodes internally and fleas, lice, ticks, and mites externally. They have been reported to contract both rabies and tularemia. Occasionally they are preyed upon by eagles and large carnivores, but humans are their greatest enemy. The fur is of modest value.

Mating takes place in summer and early autumn, but implantation of blastocysts does not occur until middle to late winter. The single annual litter, consisting of one to five young, is born in March or April. Young females may breed in their first year, but males do not become sexually mature until about 14 months old. Longevity in nature is unknown, but captives have lived as long as 15 years.

Selected References. Lindzey (1982); Long (1973).

Photo by D. Randall

Spilogale putorius
Eastern Spotted Skunk

Distribution. This skunk occurs on the Great Plains, from North Dakota to Texas and adjacent northeastern Mexico, and in the southeastern United States. In the north-central region it is found in Iowa, most of Minnesota, and western Wisconsin. It once occurred also in southern Indiana and possibly adjacent Illinois. A closely related species occupies western North America.

Description. Smaller of two skunks in region, weasel-like. Black overall, with four (usually) to six white to yellowish white stripes on back, breaking into blotches posteriorly, and white patch on forehead; long, bushy tail may be tipped with white. Total length, 470–540; tail, 175–230; hind foot, 45–50; ear, 25–30; weight, 350–600 g. Males average somewhat larger than females.

Natural History. Spotted skunks are solitary except during the breeding season and occasionally in the coldest part of winter, when several may occupy a communal den. They are omnivores, shifting their diet seasonally. Small mammals, up to the size of rabbits, are important prey species; but insects are eaten in great numbers in the warm months, and lower vertebrates, fruits, berries, and corn and other grains are consumed. These skunks climb well and thus also take birds and their eggs, sometimes poultry. As with its larger relative, the conspicuous black-and-white color "advertises" to potential attackers the danger of a double spray of musk from the anal glands.

Spotted skunks are primarily inhabitants of open lands, finding sufficient cover in fencerows, riparian growth, and brushy areas, but they frequently are uncommon. Opening of land for agricultural purposes led to a northeastward movement in our region in the past century. Home ranges average about one-fourth a square mile and contain two or three dens, which may be under outbuildings, haystacks, woodpiles, scrap heaps, or other shelter, in abandoned burrows of other mammals, or in rock crevices or even hollow logs. Promiscuous males wander over several square miles in the spring breeding season.

Only a single litter is produced in this region—in May or June—consisting of four to nine (average five) young. Unlike its western counterpart, there is little or no delayed implantation; gestation lasts 50–65 days.

Selected References. Crabb (1941, 1948); Van Gelder (1959).

Mephitis mephitis
Striped Skunk

Distribution. The striped skunk ranges from central Canada southward through most of the United States to northern Mexico. It is found throughout the seven-state region.

Description. Larger, more robust, and less weasel-like than *S. putorius.* Color black except for narrow white stripe on forehead and two broad white stripes extending posteriorly along upper flanks to rump from white patch on nape; usually also some white hairs in bushy tail; color variable and some individuals almost entirely black. Total length, 620–790; tail, 200–280; hind foot, 75–85; ear, 25–35; weight, 2.5–5 kg. Foregoing measurements for males; females average slightly smaller.

Natural History. Probably no carnivore in the north-central region is more widely recognized by humans than the striped skunk, whether by direct observation, depiction in cartoons, or through their malodorous presence. The odor is somewhat less offensive than that emitted by spotted skunks.

This skunk is the most common carnivore in many places. It occupies a variety of habitats–almost anywhere adequate shelter is available–although deep woods and marshy areas generally are avoided. Woodland edge and brushy situations are favored. Dens usually are within a few hundred yards of water and are in natural cavities, under outbuildings, or in burrows dug by the animal or abandoned by other mammals such as woodchucks and badgers. Like the spotted skunk, *M. mephitis* is omnivorous, the diet varying with local availability of food. Small mammals and birds, insects and other invertebrates, carrion, eggs, berries and fruits, frogs, and lizards all are eaten. These animals are mostly solitary as adults and, although primarily nocturnal, may be active by day. Home ranges vary from about 40 acres in some females up to 1,000 acres or more and overlap broadly.

Enemies include large raptors, larger carnivores, and humans. Thousands are killed each year on roadways and by farm machinery. Prime pelts have averaged little more than two dollars each in recent years. Skunks generally are heavily parasitized, both externally and internally, and are susceptible to many diseases, including distemper and rabies. Mating occurs in late winter, and a litter of four to 11 (average six or seven) young is born in spring.

Selected References. Wade-Smith and Verts (1982).

Photo by N.L. Olson

Lutra canadensis
River Otter

Distribution. The otter once enjoyed a wide distribution, from Alaska to Labrador in the north southward throughout the United States, excepting parts of the arid Southwest. It was found in suitable habitat in all north-central states but has been extirpated in many areas, apparently no longer occurring in Indiana or Ohio and only sporadically along major river systems in Illinois and Iowa. Stable populations are mostly limited to the northern parts of Michigan, Minnesota, and Wisconsin.

Description. Large, semiaquatic mustelid, feet webbed, muscular tail thick at base and tapering to tip; conspicuous whiskers. Upper parts rich dark brown; venter pale grayish brown; muzzle and throat silvery gray. Total length, 900–1,300; tail, 320–500; hind foot, 110–135; ear, 15–25; weight, 5–14 kg. Females average smaller than males.

Natural History. Otters are active the year around and, although normally crepuscular, can be observed at any time. On land they move with a cumbersome lope, but they move more rapidly on ice by leaping and then sliding for 25 feet or more. These animals are excellent swimmers, relying primarily on a sinuous movement of the body and tail, although occasionally paddling with the hind feet. They can remain underwater for up to two minutes and dive to depths of 45 feet.

This carnivore eats primarily crayfish, turtles, frogs, fish, and sometimes young muskrats and beavers. Insects and earthworms may be taken on occasion. They are sociable animals and frequently occur as pairs or in family groups. They den under roots or logs or in abandoned burrows of other mammals, some distance from water or with burrow openings at or under water level, and also in abandoned muskrat and beaver lodges. Their distribution is narrowly limited to aquatic habitats. Efforts to clean the country's polluted waterways may lead to the return of this species to areas from which it has been extirpated. It is regarded as an endangered mammal in some places but is trapped for its fur, worth up to 100 dollars a pelt, in others. After prolonged delayed implantation, females give birth to a litter of two or three (up to six) young in March or April.

Selected References. Toweill and Tabor (1982); van Zyll de Jong (1972).

Felis concolor
Mountain Lion

Distribution. The mountain lion formerly had the broadest distribution of any New World mammal except humans – occurring from the southern Yukon southward to Argentina. It once occurred throughout the north-central states but, except for an occasional wandering individual, probably was extirpated there long ago. The most recent report from Indiana was in 1851, for example, and the species probably was extinct in Wisconsin by 1920 or earlier. Unsubstantiated sightings from northern Minnesota and recent reports from adjacent Manitoba and North Dakota, however, may signal the return of small numbers of this large felid to those regions (not mapped).

Description. Largest of temperate and boreal American cats. Upper parts typically buff to grayish brown, darkest middorsally; venter and legs paler; throat and chest whitish; tip of tail and muzzle stripes black; young with dark brown or blackish blotches. Total length, 1,500–2,500; tail, 550–850; hind foot, 220–290; ear, 75–100; weight, 35–90 kg. Males average larger than females.

Natural History. As indicated by its broad distribution, *F. concolor* thrives in a variety of habitats, today mostly in sparsely populated areas and those remote from the activities of humans. Deer and other large ungulates, including at times domestic stock, make up the bulk of the diet of this "top carnivore," but a variety of small and medium-sized mammals – from mice to beavers – also are preyed upon. Wild turkey, grouse, and other large birds are taken when available and, surprisingly, berries and other vegetation on occasion. It takes about a deer a week, or its equivalent, to sustain an adult lion.

Mountain lions are solitary, except for females with young. Home ranges are large, and temporary retreats thus are utilized on a day-to-day basis. Ranges of adult males may be exclusive.

This species is polygamous, but, because of the territorial spacing patterns, females may mate year after year with the same male. Females bear a litter of one to six (average about three) young at any time of year but mostly in the warm months. Longevity in captivity can be 20 years or more, probably about 12 in the wild.

Selected References. Anderson (1983); Currier (1983); Dixon (1982); Wrigley and Nero (1982).

Felis lynx
Lynx

Distribution. The lynx occurs across boreal America, from Alaska to Labrador, and once was found southward to New England, Indiana, Nebraska, and Utah. It has been mostly extirpated in the southeastern part of its former range, except for occasional wanderers (one was taken as far south as Shelby County, Iowa, in 1963, for example), and now is mostly limited in the seven-state region to the northern parts of Michigan, Minnesota, and Wisconsin.

Description. A relatively large, short-tailed cat with long, pointed tufts on ears; legs long, feet large with well-furred pads. Distinguished from bobcat (*F. rufus*) by generally larger size, more grayish pelage, longer ear tufts, and more extensive black tip on tail. Total length, 850–1,050; tail, 100–125; hind foot, 200–250; ear, 70–80; weight, 7–18 kg. There still is controversy as to whether this species and the bobcat represent a genus (*Lynx*) distinct from *Felis* and as to whether the New World population represents a different species (*canadensis*) from lynx in the Old World.

Natural History. This cat is primarily a denizen of forested environments, especially boreal evergreen woodlands. It once occurred throughout much of the north-central region, but its numbers were substantially reduced in some areas; it was extirpated from many others by about the turn of the last century. Natural immigration has resulted in rejuvenated populations in the northern part of the region.

The lynx is a solitary hunter and relies on stealth and ambush to capture prey. The snowshoe hare is a staple food item, and populations of this lagomorph cycle in density, with nine to 10 years between peaks. Populations of lynx lag a year or two behind those of hares. In those years when hare populations are low, reproduction in lynx is curtailed and individuals may wander far to the south of their normal range in search of food.

The lynx breeds in February or March. Gestation lasts 63 days; litters (one to six kittens, usually two or three) are born in April or May. They acquire adult pelage when about nine months old; there is one molt annually, in spring, thereafter.

Selected References. Brand et al. (1976); McCord and Cardoza (1982); Tumlison (1987).

Felis rufus
Bobcat

Distribution. This cat is found from southern Canada southward throughout the United States to central Mexico. It occurs, or once occurred, within the entire north-central region. Currently, it is most common northwardly; but recent records are available from other areas, and it is to be looked for in all seven states.

Description. Smallest of native north-central cats. Upper parts overall reddish brown to grayish brown, characterized by irregular dark spotting (as in *F. lynx*), especially toward midline; venter (whitish) and legs also spotted; tail tipped with black only dorsally. Total length, 800–1,000; tail, 130–180; hind foot, 160–190; ear, 60–80; weight, 5–13 kg.

Natural History. Unlike the lynx, the bobcat does not seem to have cyclic populations, or at least they are not so pronounced, probably because it does not depend on one primary food source that also varies cyclically. Bobcats prey primarily on small mammals – mice, voles, squirrels, and rabbits – but sometimes feed on young deer, a variety of birds, carrion, small carnivores, moles and shrews, and even a few invertebrates. Larger carnivores such as mountain lions and wolves sometimes catch bobcats, especially young, and humans hunt and trap this species for its fur. Like the lynx, select pelts have averaged 100 dollars or more in value at auction in recent years.

Bobcats are mostly crepuscular and nocturnal. Home ranges of males vary considerably with habitat and season but probably fall typically in the range of five to 10 square miles; those of females average smaller. Movements of two to 10 miles in a single night have been reported. Ectoparasites reported from this species include ticks, fleas, and mites; acanthocephalans, cestodes, nematodes, and trematodes are known internally.

Courtship activities take place in midwinter, with most mating in February and March. The gestation period is about 62 days; thus, most litters (one to four young) are born in April or May. Young are weaned at two months of age but remain with the female until the next breeding season. One captive bobcat lived 32 years, but 12–14 years probably represents maximum longevity in the wild.

Selected References. McCord and Cardoza (1982); Young (1958).

Order Artiodactyla

Artiodactyls

Seven species of artiodactyls, or even-toed ungulates, occur (or once occurred) in the north-central states; in addition, *Cervus nippon* was introduced from the Old World. Of the seven, only one species of deer (*Odocoileus virginianus*) is at all common and widespread at the present time; four species (bison, pronghorn, caribou, and wapiti) were extirpated from the region years ago. Bison and wapiti have been reintroduced in captivity or semicaptivity, or, in the case of the latter species, as free-living herds in Michigan and Minnesota. Recent sightings of caribou and pronghorn in Minnesota suggest that these two species may be reinvading selected areas in that state.

The order Artiodactyla has an extensive fossil record dating back to the early Eocene. It contains nine modern families, three of which (Antilocapridae, Bovidae, Cervidae) are (or were) native to the seven north-central states. The order encompasses about 80 Recent genera and 185 Recent species, and artiodactyls occur natively on all continents except Australia (where they have been introduced) and Antarctica.

Key to Artiodactyls

1. Horned (both sexes); if horn sheath shed, bony core permanent 2
1'. Antlered (males only except *Rangifer*); antlers without bony core
   and shed annually (Cervidae) 3
2. Horns with one prong (prong lacking in many females), tip
   somewhat recurved, sheath shed annually; white and brown or
   black markings on throat (Antilocapridae) . . . .*Antilocapra americana*

279

2'.   Horns unbranched, not shed; tips not recurved; no distinctive
markings on throat (Bovidae) . . . . *Bison bison*

3.   Antlers palmate, at least in part 4

3'.   Antlers not palmate 5

4.   Antlers palmate on most of main beam; greatest length of skull
more than 500 . . . . *Alces alces*

4'.   Antlers palmate distally on both main beam and one or more tines;
greatest length of skull less than 500 . . . . *Rangifer tarandus*

5.   Upper canine teeth present; underparts brownish, same color as
dorsum, or dorsum spotted 6

5'.   Upper canine teeth absent; underparts distinctly paler than
dorsum, which is not spotted 7

6.   Dorsum spotted, underparts whitish to grayish; condylobasal
length less than 300 . . . . *Cervus nippon*

6'.   Dorsum unspotted, underparts brownish; condylobasal length
more than 300 . . . . *Cervus elaphus*

7.   Hindquarters mostly white; tail large and white below, often held
high while running; antlers with single main beam that gives rise
to series of simple tines . . . . *Odocoileus virginianus*

7'.   Hindquarters mostly grayish; tail smaller and tipped with black, held
down while running; antlers with main beam forked, forming two
secondary branches, each of which bears tines . . *Odocoileus hemionus*

Figure 6. White-tailed deer (left) and mule deer illustrating differences between antlers, ears, and tails (reprinted from Nebraskaland Magazine, published by Nebraska Game and Parks Comm.).

Cervus elaphus
Wapiti

Distribution. The wapiti, or American elk, formerly ranged over much of the United States and southern Canada. It was found throughout the seven-state region until extirpated by humans (not mapped).

Description. Large cervid with dark mane that hangs to brisket. Pelage reddish brown in summer, grayish brown with dark brown head, neck, and legs in winter; rump yellowish to yellowish brown. Males larger than females and with heavy antlers. Total length, 2,150–2,700; tail, 120–160; hind foot, 580–700; ear, 130–300; weight, 225–450 kg.

Notes. Wapiti occur today in the north-central states only in confinement except for a small herd that was reintroduced near Grygla, Minnesota, and another in the northern part of Michigan's Lower Peninsula. The original animals came mostly from Wyoming.

Selected References. Murie (1951); Peek (1982).

Rangifer tarandus
Caribou

Distribution. This circumboreal species once occurred all across northern North America, from Alaska through much of Canada and northward to Greenland, barely reaching the United States including the northern part of the seven-state region (not mapped).

Description. Both sexes antlered, antlers palmate distally on main beam and one or more tines, one palmate brow tine modified as shovel-like structure extending over face. Pelage grayish brown to grayish white, with white rump patch. Total length, 1,600–2,300; tail, 100–150; hind foot, 500–650; ear, 110–150; weight usually 90–175 kg, to 275 in large males.

Notes. Caribou inhabited northern parts of Minnesota, Michigan, and Wisconsin, but the last record, until recently, was about 1937 in northern Minnesota. In the winter of 1980–81, however, there were several sightings and other sign of caribou in Cook County, Minnesota; perhaps *R. tarandus* is returning to the extreme northern part of the region.

Selected References. Banfield (1962); Bergerud (1978); Mech and Nelson (1982); Miller (1982).

Cervus elaphus

Photo courtesy of U.S. Fish and Wildlife Service

Rangifer tarandus

Odocoileus hemionus
Mule Deer

Distribution. The mule deer (termed black-tailed deer in some areas) is a native of western North America, ranging from southeastern Alaska and Canada southward through the plains and mountains to northern Mexico. This species is known from much of Minnesota and Iowa, but most of the sporadic records probably relate to wandering individuals, mostly males. There is no current evidence of breeding populations in either state.

Description. About the size of white-tailed deer, with long ears and small, black-tipped tail. Dorsum reddish brown after molt to summer pelage, grayish brown in winter; rump patch grayish white, venter whitish. Antlers of bucks divided into equal-sided branches. Total length, 1,400–1,800; tail, 160–200; hind foot, 410–520; ear, 180–220; weight usually 45–90 kg, but up to more than 175 in large males.

Natural History. The mule deer is more an animal of open country than its white-tailed relative, resting by day in brushy or wooded areas if available. Activity is mostly crepuscular and nocturnal. The diet consists of a variety of plant species; in a study in Nebraska, it was made up of about 40 percent agricultural crops, 30 percent browse, and 30 percent grasses, forbs, and sedges.

These deer tend to remain in an area of a few square miles if good food, water, and cover are available but may travel 100 miles or more when necessary in search of better habitat. Typically they run with a stiff-legged gait, with tail held down, and they cannot jump as high as can white-tails. *O. hemionus* is an important game animal over much of its range. It is host to a variety of internal parasites and also to fleas, lice, and ticks externally. A number of maladies such as epizootic hemorrhagic disease, bluetongue, foot-and-mouth disease, and brucellosis are known to affect the species, and infectious or parasitic diseases, along with malnutrition and starvation, are major causes of mortality.

Mule deer breed from October to December. Gestation generally lasts 200–208 days. One to three precocial fawns (usually twins) are born in spring. Known longevity in the wild is 20 years.

Selected References. Anderson and Wallmo (1984); Wallmo (1981).

Odocoileus virginianus
White-tailed Deer

Distribution. The broad distribution of this cervid extends from Canada southward through most of the United States (absent only in the Southwest), Mexico, Central America, and into South America. It ranges across all the north-central states, but apparently has occupied some of the northernmost areas there within the past century.

Description. Medium-sized cervid. Dorsum reddish tan to pale brownish in summer, grizzled brownish gray in winter; underparts white; tail relatively large, brownish with black tip and fringed with white above, white below. Differs from mule deer in: ear smaller; tail larger, fringed with white above, pure white below, held high and frequently waved from side to side while running; antlers (males) with main beam having upright, unbranched tines; runs with a graceful lope, not a bounce. Total length, 1,550–2,125; tail, 250–350; hind foot, 475–525; ear, 140–230; weight, 40–135 kg, exceptionally large males to 175.

Natural History. This deer is one of the most conspicuous large mammals in the region and is a popular game species. Unlike the mule deer, it is not an animal of open or semiopen country, preferring wooded areas or forest edge for daytime retreats. During periods of crepuscular and nocturnal activity, individuals venture from woodland cover into adjacent agricultural plantings, clearings, and meadows.

White-tails may be solitary or found in small groups that usually comprise a doe, her female yearlings, and fawns. Food consists mostly of browse in winter, but grasses, forbs, fruits, and foliage of shrubs and small trees are eaten in summer. *O. virginianus* is preyed upon by large carnivores and hunted by humans; starvation and disease also are important controls. A nematode brainworm that parasitizes deer but has little adverse effect on them has a serious effect on caribou, moose, and wapiti.

Rutting takes place in autumn, and most females are bred in November and December. Young are born after about 200 days of gestation. Yearling does usually have but one offspring; adults normally have two but triplets and even quadruplets are known. Longevity is about 15 years in the wild, 20 or so in captivity.

Selected References. Hesselton and Hesselton (1982); Jenkins and Bartlett (1959); Taylor (1956); Woolf and Harder (1979).

Alces alces
Moose

Distribution. The moose is an Holarctic species, once inhabiting most of the boreal forests of both Eurasia and North America. In the north-central states, it formerly ranged over much of Michigan, Minnesota, and Wisconsin. Today, partly through reintroductions, this species is found on Isle Royale and Michigan's Upper Peninsula, in adjacent northernmost Wisconsin, and in northern (especially northeastern) Minnesota. Occasional individuals wander southward, and there are recent reports of moose in southern Minnesota, northeastern South Dakota, and even Iowa.

Description. Largest of North American cervids. Antlers of males large and palmate; prominent dewlap suspended from throat; nose enlarged; legs long, hooves large, dewclaws well developed. Overall color blackish brown, paler in winter. Total length, 2,000–2,800; tail, 80–120; hind foot, 730–830; ear, 250–265; weight to more than 450 kg, usually 320–375. Males average larger than females.

Natural History. The North American distribution of moose is closely associated with boreal forests where early successional stages of shrubby growth and young fir and spruce trees provide optimum habitat. Swamps, lakeshores, and marshes adjacent to subclimax woody vegetation are preferred in summer. These animals swim well. They may be active at any time but are most often abroad in the twilight of early morning and evening, bedding down at other times. They tend to be solitary except in the rutting season and for females with young.

Moose browse on a variety of herbaceous plants, including aquatic vegetation in summer. They are reported to eat 20–30 kg of food a day. In earlier times, mountain lions and gray wolves probably were the principal predators on this large cervid; the present relationship between wolves and moose on Isle Royale has been studied in detail over the past several decades. Humans and a meningeal roundworm, which normally infests deer but does little harm to them, are the most important current controls on mainland populations.

Rutting occurs in September and early October. After a gestation period of about 240 days, one or two calves, rarely triplets, are born in May or June. The unspotted offspring weigh 10–16 kg. Longevity may be 20 years or more.

Selected References. Coady (1982); Franzmann (1981); Peek et al. (1976).

Antilocapra americana
Pronghorn

Distribution. This unique ungulate once occurred throughout much of the North American grasslands, from the Prairie Provinces of Canada southward to central Mexico. By the early 1900s it was endangered, but through protection and wise management the pronghorn now is found over much of its former range (not mapped).

Description. Smallest artiodactyl in region, about one meter tall at shoulder. Pelage tan-colored above, whitish below, white and brown or blackish bands across throat; sheath of horns (both sexes) shed annually. Total length, 1,200–1,500; tail, 80–140; hind foot, 380–440; ear, 135–160; weight averaging 40 kg in females, 50 in males.

Notes. In historical times, the pronghorn occurred in western Iowa and presumably adjacent Minnesota. There have been sightings in southwestern Minnesota in the past 15 years or so, the most recent of a small herd that wintered in Lac Qui Parle County in 1978. These animals are thought to be the result of stocking operations in the nearby Sisseton Hills of South Dakota.

Selected References. Kitchen and O'Gara (1982); O'Gara (1978).

Bison bison
Bison

Distribution. The bison once enjoyed a broad distribution in North America—from the Atlantic Coast westward through the central United States into much of the mountainous West, northward at least to central and western Canada, and southward to northernmost Mexico. It occurred in all seven north-central states, northward to southern Michigan, central Wisconsin, and northwestern Minnesota (not mapped).

Description. Large bovid with massive forequarters and large head. Horns (sheaths not shed) present in both sexes. Pelage yellowish brown to blackish, longer on front half of body than rear. Total length, 2,000–3,800; tail, 450–800; hind foot, 460–660; ear, 120–150; weight up to 500 kg in females, 900 in males.

Notes. The bison was extirpated long ago by humans in the north-central region and now occurs there only in captivity.

Selected References. Meagher (1986); Reynolds et al. (1982); Roe (1970).

Antilocapra americana

Bison bison

INTRODUCED MAMMALS
AND SPECIES OF
POSSIBLE OCCURRENCE

Introduced Mammals
and Species of
Possible Occurrence

In addition to the 99 species of native mammals that occur, or once occurred in Recent times, in the north-central region, five species introduced from outside North America are present in the wild state and are listed here. Introduced stocks of several other Old World taxa failed to survive in their new surroundings and are not included. Reintroductions of mammals previously extirpated from the region, such as the wapiti, are mentioned in the appropriate accounts in the foregoing text. Furthermore, we do not provide accounts here of introduced North American mammals not originally native to the seven states because we are unaware of any surviving populations – the kangaroo rat along the shore of Lake Erie in Ohio and the prairie dog in western Iowa, for example.

Following the accounts of the five non-native mammals is a listing of nine native species not yet recorded from the north-central states but that may be found there or once may have occurred in the region.

Introduced Mammals

Lepus capensis (Lagomorpha, Leporidae), European or Cape hare. This hare was introduced in southeastern Ontario as early as 1912, even earlier in the northeastern United States. The species has spread westward from Ontario into both the Upper Peninsula and Lower Peninsula of Michigan, and it is also to be looked for in extreme northern Wisconsin.

These hares are much larger (total 600 or more, hind foot 135 or more) than snowshoe hares, *L. americanus*, the only other species of the genus occurring in the same geographic area. They also have a more massive skull and do not molt to a white coat in winter.

Another leporid, the domestic rabbit, *Oryctolagus cuniculus*, has been in-

Photo by Glenn Wells

Lepus capensis

troduced in the north-central states, especially in Indiana, but apparently has not become established. It is also widely raised in captivity in North America, and individuals occasionally escape confinement. Many of the domestic strains bear little resemblance to native rabbits, but one in essentially wild-type pelage could be mistaken for a large *Sylvilagus*. From the latter, *Oryctolagus* differs, aside from being larger, in having a strongly flared posterior projection of the supraorbital process that is free of the braincase.

Mus musculus (Rodentia, Muridae), house mouse. This common inhabitant of human environs was first introduced to the New World by early immigrants from Eurasia and now occurs throughout much of temperate and tropical America. Feral populations occasionally are well removed from the influence of humans. The house mouse occurs throughout the region but is uncommon in remote areas of the northern part.

Mus, especially young individuals, may be confused initially with native mice of the genera *Reithrodontomys* and *Peromyscus*. It differs from these native species as follows: ears and tail nearly naked, the tail conspicuously scaled; venter grayish or occasionally dark buff, not white; molars with three longitudinal rows of tubercles; distinct notch, best seen in lateral view, on the

Mus musculus

occlusal surface of the upper incisors. It differs further from *Reithrodontomys* in that it lacks grooves on the upper incisors.

Rattus norvegicus (Rodentia, Muridae), Norway rat. This species occurs widely in the north-central states but is almost entirely limited to urban areas, around farmsteads, and the like. Feral populations are rare. About the size of the eastern woodrat (*Neotoma floridana*), this murid differs from it as follows: tail scaly, scantily haired; underparts usually some color other than white; skull with well-developed temporal ridges; crowns of molars cuspidate and more or less squared, not elongate and semiprismatic as in *Neotoma*.

The Norway rat, a native of Eurasia, first was introduced into North America at East Coast ports about the time of the American Revolution.

Myocastor coypus (Rodentia, Myocastoridae), nutria. Wild-taken individuals of this large, semiaquatic rodent are on record from several north-central states, although it is uncertain whether there currently are any established populations there. If so, these likely will be found along major river systems in the southern part of the region. The species occurs widely along the Gulf and Atlantic coasts and northward some distance in major drainage ba-

Rattus norvegicus

sins; it is also known from several western states. *M. coypus* was introduced into the United States from South America as a furbearing mammal, first in California in 1899.

In general, the nutria is reminiscent of a strange "cross" between a muskrat and beaver, from which it can be distinguished on the basis of characters in the key to families of Rodentia.

Cervus nippon (Artiodactyla, Cervidae), sika deer. Wild populations of this native of the Orient now occur in several areas in the United States, including a small part of southern Wisconsin. *C. nippon* is treated in the key to artiodactyls in text.

Myocastor coypus

Species of Past or Present Possible Occurrence

Nine species of Recent mammals occur (or, in the case of the grizzly bear, once occurred) near enough to the borders of the north-central states that they one day may be found there. These are listed below along with an indication of where they might be found and how they can be distinguished from relatives already on record from the seven-state region.

Sorex dispar (Insectivora, Soricidae), long-tailed shrew. This species is known from western Pennsylvania and possibly may be found in adjacent Ohio. It can be distinguished from *S. fumeus*, which occurs in the same region, in that the third upper unicuspid is equal to or slightly smaller than the fourth (third larger in *fumeus*) and the fifth unicuspid is relatively large. From *Sorex cinereus*, the long-tailed shrew differs in averaging larger (total length to 139, hind foot to 16), in that a postmandibular foramen usually is present and well developed, and in structure of the upper unicuspids. See Kirkland (1981).

Plecotus townsendii (Chiroptera, Vespertilionidae), Townsend's big-eared bat. This bat occurs in Kentucky and West Virginia and may range northward to the extreme southern part of the north-central region. See the text account

Photo by James F. Parnell

Cervus nippon

of *P. rafinesquii* for differences between the two species. See Barbour and Davis (1969).

Lepus californicus (Lagomorpha, Leporidae), black-tailed jackrabbit. Known from eastern Nebraska and northwestern Missouri, this hare one day may be found in at least southwestern Iowa. It differs from the white-tailed jackrabbit, the only species of *Lepus* occurring in the southwestern part of our region, in being smaller, having the dorsal aspect of the tail black rather than white with a thin black stripe, and in several cranial and dental features. Furthermore, molt in autumn does not result in a more or less white winter coat as in *L. townsendii*. See Bowles (1975).

Perognathus fasciatus (Rodentia, Heteromyidae), olive-backed pocket mouse. This mouse occurs in eastern North Dakota and possibly will be found in the grasslands of western Minnesota. It resembles *P. flavescens*, differing from it in having dark olivaceous dorsal pelage, in that the auditory bullae rarely meet anteriorly, and in that the lower premolar is the same size as (or only slightly smaller than) the first lower molar instead of distinctly smaller as in *P. flavescens*. See Williams and Genoways (1979).

Ursus arctos

Chaetodipus hispidus (Rodentia, Heteromyidae), hispid pocket mouse. This species has been taken in the floodplain of the Missouri River in southeastern Nebraska. It is possible that it could cross that river into adjacent Iowa, although the Missouri probably is an effective barrier to eastward movement. *C. hispidus* differs from other pocket mice of the plains region in being much larger (total length to 240) and in having coarser pelage. See Jones (1964).

Reithrodontomys montanus (Rodentia, Cricetidae), plains harvest mouse. This small mouse is known from eastern Nebraska and Kansas. The Missouri River probably serves as a barrier to eastward dispersal, but it is possible that the species could reach western Iowa. From the only other harvest mouse in that area (*R. megalotis*), it differs in being smaller both externally and cranially and in having a narrow, dark stripe on the dorsum of the tail. See Bowles (1975).

Zapus princeps (Rodentia, Zapodidae), western jumping mouse. The western jumping mouse is known to occur in northeastern North Dakota, not far west of the Minnesota border, and is to be looked for in the extreme western part of that state. From *Z. hudsonius*, it differs in averaging slightly larger, being paler, somewhat drabber in color, and having the edge of the ear bordered by white hairs. See Jones et al. (1983).

Alopex lagopus (Carnivora, Canidae), arctic fox. There are several extralimital records of this fox in southern Ontario, and it is possible that individuals occasionally wander as far south as the extreme northern part of the north-central region (there is a recent, unconfirmed newspaper account of one taken in Wisconsin). Small size and pale color (grayish white in summer, white in winter) immediately separate it from other foxes. See Banfield (1974).

Ursus arctos (Carnivora, Ursidae), grizzly bear. This large carnivore does not now occur in the north-central states and perhaps never did. There is, however, a questionable record from the Sandhill River, Polk County, northwestern Minnesota, dating from 1807. *U. arctos* is known certainly to have occurred in adjacent North Dakota. See Hall (1984) and Swanson et al. (1945).

GLOSSARY

Glossary

This list of terms, modified from Jones et al. (1983, 1985), includes those frequently used in descriptions or discussions of mammals and should prove useful to students. Not all of the entries have been used in the foregoing text. Some that appear on one or more of the three figures in the glossary are not otherwise defined. Where a term listed has two or more meanings in the English language, only the one applying to mammalian biology is given.

abdomen. Ventral part of body, lying between thorax (rib cage) and pelvis.

acanthocephalan. Spiny-headed worm of parasitic phylum Acanthocephala.

aestivation. Torpidity in summer.

agouti hair. Hair with alternate pale and dark bands of color.

albinism. Lacking external pigmentation; albino (may be only partial).

allopatric. Pertaining to two or more populations that occupy disjunct or nonoverlapping geographic areas.

altricial. Pertaining to young that are blind, frequently naked, and entirely dependent on parental care at birth.

alveolus. Socket in jawbone that receives root(s) of tooth.

angular process. Posterior projection of dentary ventral to condyloid (articular) process; evident but not labeled on figure.

annulation. Circular or ringlike formation as in dermal scales on tail of a mammal or in dentine of a tooth.

anterior. Pertaining to or toward front end.

antler. Branched (usually), bony head ornament found on cervids, covered with skin (velvet) during growth; shed annually.

arboreal. Pertaining to activity in trees.

articular condyle. Surface of condyloid (articular) process (fig. 8), articulating lower jaw with skull.

auditory bulla. Bony capsule enclosing middle ear; when formed by tympanic bone, termed **tympanic bulla** (see fig. 9).

auditory meatus. Opening leading from external ear to eardrum (see fig. 8).

baculum. Sesmoid bone (os penis) in penis of males of certain mammalian groups.

basal. Pertaining to base.

baubellum. See **os clitoridis**.

beam. Main trunk of antler.

bez tine. First tine above brow tine of antler.

bifid. Divided into two nearly equal lobes.

bifurcate. Divided into two branches.

bipedal. Pertaining to locomotion on two legs.

blastocyst. In embryonic development of mammals, a ball of cells produced by repeated division (cleavage) of fertilized egg; stage of implantation in uterine wall.

boreal. Northern, of high latitudes.

braincase. Posterior portion of skull; part that encloses and protects brain.

breech birth. Birth in which posterior part of body emerges first.

brisket. Breast or lower part of chest.

brow tine. First tine above base of antler.

buccal. Pertaining to cheek.

bunodont. Low-crowned, rectangular grinding teeth, typical of omnivores.

calcar. Spur of cartilage or bone that projects medially from ankle of many species of bats and helps support uropatagium.

canine. One of four basic kinds of mammalian teeth; anteriormost tooth in maxilla (and counterpart in dentary), frequently elongate, unicuspid, and single-rooted; never more than one per quadrant (see figs. 7–8). Also a term pertaining to dogs or to Canidae.

carnassials. Pair of large, bladelike teeth (last upper premolar and first lower molar) that occlude with scissorlike action; possessed by most modern members of order Carnivora.

carnivore. Animal that consumes meat as primary component of diet.

carpal. Any one of group of bones in wrist region, distal to radius and ulna and proximal to metacarpals.

caudal. Pertaining to tail or toward tail (caudad).

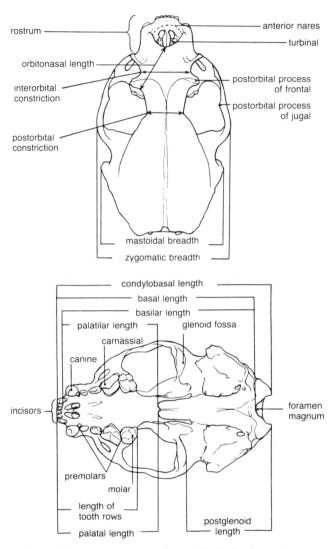

Figure 7. Dorsal and ventral views of skull of a river otter, showing cranial features and measurements (after Hall, 1955).

cavernicolous. Living in caves (or mines).

centimeter (cm). Unit of linear measure in metric system equal to 10 mm; 2.54 cm equal one inch.

cestode. Tapeworm of parasitic class Cestoda, phylum Platyhelminthes.

cheekteeth. Collectively, postcanine teeth (premolars and molars).

cingulum. Enamel shelf bordering margin(s) of a tooth (cingulid used for those of teeth in lower jaw).

circumboreal. Around the boreal (northern) parts of the world.

claw. Sheath of keratin on digits; usually long, curved, and sharply pointed.

cline. Gradual change in morphological character through a series of interbreeding populations; character gradient.

condylobasal length. See figure 7.

coprophagy. Feeding upon feces.

coronoid process. Projection of posterior portion of dentary dorsal to mandibular condyle (see fig. 8).

cosmopolitan. Common to all the world; not local or limited, but widely distributed.

cranial breadth. Measurement of cranium taken across its broadest point perpendicular to long axis of skull; frequently used for insectivores.

crepuscular. Pertaining to periods of dusk and dawn (twilight); active by twilight.

Cretaceous. See **geologic time**.

cursorial. Pertaining to running; running locomotion.

cusp. Point, projection, or bump on crown of a tooth.

cuspidate. Presence of cusp or cusps on a tooth.

deciduous dentition. Juvenile or milk teeth, those that appear first in lifetime of a mammal, consisting (if complete) of incisors, canines, and premolars; generally replaced by adult (permanent) dentition.

delayed implantation. Postponement of embedding of blastocyst (embryo) in uterine epithelium for several days, weeks, or months; typical of some carnivores.

dental formula. Convenient way of designating number and arrangement of mammalian teeth: (for example, $i\,3/3$, $c\,1/1$, $p\,4/4$, $m\,3/3$); letters indicate incisors, canines, premolars, and molars, respectively; numbers before slashes (or above line) indicate number of teeth on one side of upper jaw, whereas those following (or below) line indicate number on one side of lower jaw.

dentary. One of pair of bones that constitute entire lower jaw (mandible) of mammals.

dentine. Hard, generally acellular material between pulp and enamel of tooth; sometimes exposed on surface of crown.

dentition. Teeth of mammal considered collectively.

dewclaw. Vestigial digit on foot.

dewlap. Pendulous fold of skin under neck.

diastema. Space between adjacent teeth; for example, space between incisors and cheekteeth in species lacking canines.

dichromatism. Having two distinct color phases.

digit. Finger or toe.

digitigrade. Pertaining to walking on digits, with wrist and heel bones held off ground.

distal. Away from base or point of attachment, or from any named reference point (as opposed to proximal).

distichous. Arranged alternately in two vertical rows on opposite sides of an axis, as in hairs on tail of some rodents.

diurnal. Pertaining to daylight hours; active by day.

dorsal. Pertaining to back or upper surface (dorsum).

ectoparasite. Parasite living on, and feeding from, external surface of an animal (for example, fleas, lice, ticks, mites).

enamel. Hard outer layer of tooth consisting of calcareous compounds and small amount of organic matrix.

endemic. Native to a particular region and occurring nowhere else.

endoparasite. Parasite living within host (for example, flatworms, tapeworms).

Eocene. See **geologic time**.

epiphysis. Secondary growth center near end of long bone.

estrous cycle. Recurring growth and development of uterine endometrium, culminating in time when female is receptive to male.

estrus. Stage of reproductive receptivity of female for male; "heat."

excrescence. Dermal projection, as on face and ears of bats.

extirpation. Extinction, usually referring to a specified geographic area.

familial name. Name applying to a group of organisms of family rank among animals, ending in *-idae* (names of subfamilies end in *-inae*).

feces. Excrement.

fecundity. Rate of producing offspring; fertility.

femur. Single bone of upper (proximal) part of each hind (pelvic) limb.

fenestrate. Having openings.

feral. Domestic animal that has reverted to wild state.

fetal membranes. Tissue layers that surround, or attach to, the growing mammalian embryo (chorion, amnion, allantois).

fetus. Embryo in later stages of development (still in uterus).

fibula. Smaller of two bones in lower part of hind (pelvic) limb.

flank. Sides of animal between ribs and hips.

flatworm. See **trematode**.

foramen. Any opening, orifice, or perforation, especially through bone.

foramen magnum. Large opening at posterior of skull through which spinal cord emerges from braincase (see figs. 7, 9).

fossa. Pit or depression in bone; frequently site of bone articulation or muscle attachment.

fossorial. Pertaining to life under surface of ground.

frontal bone. See figure 9.

fusiform. Compact, tapered; pertaining to body form with shortened projections and no abrupt constrictions.

geologic time. Mammals arose in the *Mesozoic* era, which began some 230 million years ago. Periods of the Mesozoic (from oldest to youngest) are: *Triassic*; *Jurassic*, which began about 180 million years ago; and *Cretaceous*, which began about 135 million years ago. The following *Cenozoic* era, termed the *Age of Mammals*, was the time of evolution and radiation of major modern groups. The Cenozoic is divided into two periods, *Tertiary* (beginning about 65 million years ago and continuing until two million years ago) and *Quaternary* (two million years ago to present). Subdivisions of the Tertiary (termed *epochs*) are (oldest to youngest): *Paleocene*; *Eocene*, which began about 58 million years ago; *Oligocene*, which began about 36 million years ago; *Miocene*, which began about 25 million years ago; and *Pliocene*, which began about 12 million years ago. The Quaternary has only two epochs, *Pleistocene* (two million years ago to 10,000 years ago) and *Holocene* or *Recent* (10,000 years before the present until now).

gestation period. Period of embryonic development during which developing zygote is in uterus; period between fertilization and parturition.

gram (g). Unit of weight in metric system; there are 28.5 g in an ounce.

granivorous. Subsisting on diet of grains and seeds from cereal grasses.

gravid. Pregnant.

greatest length of skull. Measurement encompassing overall length of skull, including teeth that may project anterior to premaxilla; frequently recorded instead of condylobasal length in some kinds of mammals.

guano. Excrement of bats or birds; sometimes sold commercially as fertilizer.

guard hairs. Outer coat of coarse protective hairs found in most mammals.

hallux. First (most medial) digit of hind foot (pes).

hamular process. Hooklike projection, such as hamular process of pterygoid bone.

hectare. Unit of land area in metric system equal to 10,000 square meters and 2.47 acres.

heifer. A bovid that has not produced a calf and is less than three years old.

herbivore. Animal that consumes plant material as primary component of diet.

hibernaculum. Shelter in which animal hibernates.

hibernation. Torpidity in winter.

holarctic. Parts of both New World and Old World together lying north of tropics.

home range. Area in which an animal lives, containing all necessities of life; generally is not entirely defended and, therefore, can overlap with those of other individuals.

horn. Structure projecting from head of mammal and generally used for offense, defense, or social interaction; members of family Bovidae have horns formed by permanent hollow keratin sheaths growing over bony cores (see also **pronghorn**).

humerus. Single bone in upper (proximal) portion of each front (pectoral) limb.

hypsodont. Pertaining to a particularly high-crowned tooth; such teeth have shallow roots.

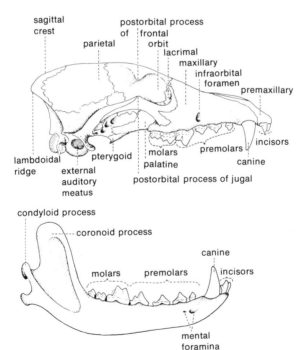

Figure 8. Lateral views of skull and lower jaw of a coyote, showing cranial and mandibular features (after Beckoff, 1977).

imbricate. Overlapping, as shingles of a roof.

implantation. Process by which blastocyst (embryo) embeds in uterine lining.

incisive foramen. See figure 9.

incisor. One of four basic kinds of teeth in mammals, usually chisel shaped; anterior-most of teeth; always rooted in premaxilla in upper jaw (see figs. 7–8).

infraorbital canal. Canal through zygomatic process of maxilla, from anterior wall of orbit to side of rostrum (see fig. 8).

infraorbital foramen. Foramen through zygomatic process of maxilla (see fig. 8 and above).

inguinal. Pertaining to region of groin.

insectivorous. Preying on insects.

interfemoral membrane. See **uropatagium**.

interorbital. Referring to region of skull between eye sockets.

interparietal. Unpaired bone on dorsal part of braincase between parietals and just anterior to supraoccipital (see fig. 9).

interspecific. Between or among species (interspecific competition, for example).

intraspecific. Within a species (intraspecific variation, for example).

jugal bone. Bone connecting maxillary and squamosal bones to form midpart of zygomatic arch (see fig. 9).

juvenile pelage. Pelage characteristic of juvenile (young) mammals.

karyotype. Morphological description of chromosomes of cell, including size, shape, position of centromere, and number.

keel. Ridge that provides expanded surface for attachment.

keratin. Tough, fibrous protein especially abundant in epidermis and epidermal derivatives.

kilogram (kg). Unit of weight in metric system (frequently shortened to "kilo") equal to 1,000 g or 2.2 lb.

kilometer (km). Unit of linear measure in metric system equal to 1,000 m, slightly more than six-tenths of a mile.

labial. Pertaining to lips; for example, labial side of a tooth is side nearer lips (as opposed to lingual side, which is nearer tongue).

lacrimal ridge. Ridge on lacrimal bone (see fig. 9).

lactating. Secreting milk.

lateral. Located away from midline; at or near sides.

lingual. Pertaining to tongue; lingual side of a tooth is side nearer tongue.

live trap. Any one of several kinds of traps designed to catch mammals alive.

loph. Ridge on occlusal surface of tooth formed by elongation and fusion of cusps.

malar process. Projection of maxillary that makes contact with jugal bone and forms base of zygomatic arch.

mammae. Milk-producing glands unique to mammals; growth and activity governed by hormones of ovary, uterus, and pituitary; present in both sexes but degenerate in males.

mandible. Lower jaw; in mammals composed of single pair of bones, the dentaries.

marsupium. External pouch formed by fold of skin in abdominal wall and supported by epipubic bones; found in most marsupials and some monotremes; encloses mammary glands and serves as incubation chamber.

masticate. To chew.

mastoid. Bone bounded by squamosal, exoccipital, and tympanic bones.

mastoid process. Exposed portion of petromastoid bone; situated anterior or lateral to auditory bulla (evident but not labeled in ventral view, fig. 9).

maturational molt. Molt from juvenile or subadult pelage.

maxilla. Either of pair of relatively large bones that form major portion of side and ventral part of rostrum; contribute to hard palate, form anterior root of zygomatic arch, and bear all upper teeth except incisors; also termed **maxillary** (see figs. 8–9).

maxillary toothrow. That part of toothrow in cranium of a mammal seated in maxilla; length includes all postincisor teeth and generally is taken parallel to long axis of skull (measurement shown in fig. 7 is of total upper toothrow).

medial. Pertaining to middle, as of a bone or other structure.

melanism. Unusual darkening of coloration owing to deposition of abnormally large amounts of melanins in integument.

mesic. Pertaining to habitats or areas with available water or moisture; moderately moist or humid.

Mesozoic. See **geologic time**.

metabolic water. Water formed biochemically as end product of carbohydrate metabolism in body of animal.

metacarpals. Bones of forefoot (hand) exclusive of phalanges.

metatarsals. Bones of hind foot exclusive of phalanges.

meter (m). Unit of linear measure in metric system equal to 100 cm and 39.37 inches.

milk dentition. See **deciduous dentition**.

millimeter (mm). Unit of linear measure in metric system; 25.4 mm equal one inch.

Miocene. See **geologic time**.

mist net. Net of fine mesh used to capture birds and bats; usually 2 m high and ranging from six to 30 m long.

molar. One of four basic kinds of mammalian teeth; any cheektooth situated posterior to premolars and having no deciduous precursor; normally not exceeding three per quadrant, four in some marsupials (see figs. 7–8).

molariform. Pertaining to teeth the form of which is molarlike.

molt. Process by which hair is shed and replaced.

monestrous. Having a single estrous cycle per year.

monotypic. Pertaining to taxon that contains only one immediately subordinate taxon; for example, genus that contains only one species.

musk gland. One of several kinds of glands in mammals with secretions that have a musky odor.

muzzle. Projecting snout.

nail. Flat, keratinized, translucent, epidermal growth protecting upper portion of tips of digits in some mammals; a modified claw.

nape. Back of neck.

nares. Openings of nose.

natal. Pertaining to birth.

nematode. Roundworm of parasitic or free-living phylum Nematoda.

neonate. Newborn.

nictitating membrane. Thin membrane at inner angle of eye in some species (such as cats), which can be drawn over surface of eyeball; a "third" eyelid.

nocturnal. Pertaining to night (hours without daylight); active by night.

nomadic. Wandering.

nominal species. Named species (sometimes implies species in name only).

occipital bone. Bone surrounding foramen magnum and bearing occipital condyles (see occiput on fig. 9); formed from four embryonic elements – a ventral basioccipital, a dorsal supraoccipital, and two lateral exoccipitals.

occiput. General term for posterior portion of skull (see fig. 9).

occlusal. Pertaining to contact surfaces of upper (cranial) and lower (mandibular) teeth.

Oligocene. See **geologic time.**

omnivorous. Pertaining to animals that eat both animal and vegetable food.

orbit. Bony socket in skull in which eyeball is situated (see fig. 8).

ordinal name. Name applying to an order of organisms.

os clitoridis. Small sesamoid bone present in clitoris of females of some mammalian species; homologous to baculum in males.

ossify. To become bony or hardened and bonelike.

palate. Bony plate formed by palatine bones and palatal branches of maxillae and premaxillae (see figs. 8–9).

Paleocene. See **geologic time.**

palmate. Pertaining to presence of webbing between digits or to flattening of tines of antler.

papilla. Any blunt, rounded, or nipple-shaped projection.

parapatric. Pertaining to two or more populations that occupy locally contiguous geographic areas in which they are ecologically isolated.

parietal. Either of pair of bones contributing to roof of cranium posterior to frontals and anterior to occipital (see figs. 8–9).

parturition. Process by which fetus of therian mammals separates from uterine wall of mother and is born; birth.

patagium. Web of skin; in bats, the wing membrane.

patronym. Scientific name based on name of a person or persons.

pectoral. Pertaining to chest.

pectoral girdle. Shoulder girdle, composed in most mammals of clavicle and scapula, or scapula alone.

pelage. Collectively, all the hairs on a mammal.

pelvic girdle. Hip girdle, composed of ischium, ilium, and pubis.

penicillate. Ending in tuft of fine hairs.

phalangeal epiphyses. Growth centers just proximal to articular surfaces of phalanges; fusion of epiphyses to shafts of phalanges used as a means of determining age in bats.

phalanges. Bones of fingers and toes, distal to metacarpals and metatarsals.

pigment. Minute granules that impart color to an organism; such granules are usually metabolic wastes and may be shades of black, brown, red, or yellow.

pinna. Externally projecting part of ear.

placenta. Composite structure formed by maternal and fetal tissues across which gases, nutrients, and wastes are exchanged.

placental scar. Scar that remains on uterine wall after deciduate placenta detaches at parturition.

plantar pad (tubercle). Cutaneous pad or tubercle on sole of foot.

plantigrade. Foot structure in which phalanges and metatarsals or metacarpals touch ground; basic structure of ambulatory (walking) locomotion.

Pleistocene. See **geologic time.**

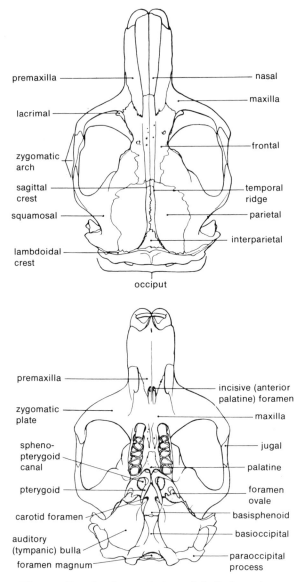

Figure 9. Dorsal and ventral views of skull of a pocket gopher (*Thomomys*), showing cranial features (after Hall, 1955).

Pliocene. See **geologic time**.

pollex. Thumb; first (most medial) digit on hand (manus).

polyestrous. Having more than one estrous cycle each year.

polygamous. Pertaining to sexual behavior when individual of one sex breeds with two or more individuals of the opposite sex.

polygynous. Male breeding with several females.

postauricular. Pertaining to behind the ear.

posterior. Pertaining to or toward rear end.

postorbital process. Projection of frontal bone that marks posterior margin of orbit (see figs. 7–8).

postpartum estrus. Ability of female to become receptive to male directly after giving birth.

precocial. Pertaining to young that are born at relatively advanced stage, capable of moving about shortly after birth and usually of some feeding without parental assistance.

prehensile. Adapted for grasping by curling or wrapping around.

premaxilla. One of paired bones at anterior end of rostrum (see figs. 8–9); also termed **premaxillary**.

premolar. One of four basic kinds of teeth in mammals; situated anterior to molars and posterior to canines; only cheekteeth usually present in both permanent and milk dentitions; normally not exceeding four per quadrant, three in marsupials (see figs. 7–8).

progeny. Offspring.

pronghorn. Modified horn (in both sexes of Antilocapridae) that grows over permanent bony cores and is shed annually; each is slightly curved, with one anterolateral prong in males and some females.

proximal. Situated toward or near a point of reference or attachment (as opposed to distal).

pterygoid. Either of paired bones in ventral wall of braincase, posterior to palatines (see figs. 8–9).

pubic symphysis. Midventral plane of contact between two halves of pelvic girdle.

quadrupedal. Pertaining to use of all four limbs for locomotion.

rabies. A viral disease of central nervous system, transmitted by infected canids, skunks, bats, and some other mammals to each other and also to humans, usually in saliva transmitted through biting.

race. Informal term for **subspecies** (which see).

radius. Medial of two bones in lower part of front (pectoral) limb.

ramus. Horizontal portion of dentary, that part in which teeth are rooted.

range. Geographic area inhabited by a particular taxon.

Recent. See **geologic time**.

recurved. Curved downward and backward.

reentrant angle. Inward infolding of enamel layer on side, front, or back of cheektooth.

refugium. Geographic area to which species retreats in time of stress, such as glacial episode.

retractile. Capable of being drawn back or in (as retractile claws of felids).

riparian. Referring to floodplains or valleys of watercourses.

root. Portion of tooth that lies below gum line and fills alveolus.

rooted tooth. Tooth with definitive growth; not evergrowing.

rootless tooth. Tooth that is evergrowing, having continuously open root canal.

rostrum. Facial region of skull anterior to plane drawn through anterior margin of orbits (see fig. 7).

roundworm. See **nematode**.

rugose. Wrinkled.

rumen. First "stomach" of ruminant mammals; modification of esophagus.

ruminant. Any of the Artiodactyla (including all those occurring in the north-central states) that possess a rumen; cud chewing.

runway. Worn or otherwise detectable pathway caused by repeated usage.

rutting season. Season of sexual activity when mating occurs; particularly applied to deer and other artiodactyls.

sagittal crest. Medial dorsal ridge on braincase, often formed by coalescence of temporal ridges.

saltatory. Adapted for leaping; usually with elongate and unusually well-developed hind legs.

saxicolous. Living among rocks.

scansorial. Pertaining to arboreal animals that climb by means of sharp, curved claws.

scapula. Shoulder blade.

scent glands. Sweat or sebaceous glands, or combination of these two, modified for production of odoriferous secretions.

scrotum. Pouch of skin in which testes are contained outside the abdominal cavity; permanently present in some species, seasonally present in some, and lacking in others.

scute. Thin plate or scale.

sebaceous glands. Epidermal glands that secrete fatty substance and usually open into hair follicle.

septum. A dividing wall, such as one formed by membrane or thin bone.

sexual dimorphism. Difference in sexual or other (secondary sexual, such as size) features between males and females of species.

snap trap. Kill trap that usually consists of wooden base with wire bail, spring, and trigger mechanism; designed primarily to catch rodents and insectivores.

snout. Nose; muzzle.

species. Group of naturally or potentially interbreeding populations reproductively isolated (or mostly so) from other such groups.

spiny-headed worm. See **acanthocephalan.**

squamosal. Either of pair of bones contributing to side of cranium (see fig. 9) and forming posterior part of zygomatic arch.

subspecies. Relatively uniform and genetically distinctive population of a species that represents a separately or recently evolved lineage, with its own evolutionary tendencies, definite geographic range, and actual or potential zone of intergradation (interbreeding) with another such group or groups.

superciliary. Pertaining to eyebrow.

supraorbital process. Projection of frontal bone on superior rim of orbit, as in hares and rabbits.

sweat gland. Tubular epidermal gland that extends into dermis and secretes sweat or perspiration and also various scents.

sympatric. Pertaining to two or more populations that occupy overlapping geographic areas.

symphysis. Relatively immovable articulation between bones.

tapeworm. See **cestode.**

tarsal. Any one of group of bones in ankle region, distal to fibula and proximal to metatarsals.

taxon. Any group (in this case, of mammals) distinctive from other groups at same taxonomic level.

teat. Protuberance of mammary gland in which numerous small ducts empty into common collecting structure that in turn opens to exterior through one or a few pores.

temperate. As a climatic term, referring to middle latitudes, those between boreal and tropical regions.

temporal ridges. Pair of ridges atop braincase of many mammals; usually originating on frontal bones near postorbital processes and converging posteriorly to form mid-dorsal sagittal crest (see fig. 9).

territory. Portion of home range that individual defends against members of same (and sometimes different) species.

tibia. Larger of two bones in lower part of hind (pelvic) limb.

tine. Spike on an antler.

torpor. Dormancy; body temperature approximates that of surroundings; rate of respiration and heartbeat ordinarily much slower than in active animal.

tragus. Fleshy projection from lower medial margin or ear of most microchiropteran bats.

trematode. Flatworm of parasitic class Trematoda, phylum Platyhelminthes.

tricolored. Having three colors.

trifid. Divided into three nearly equal lobes.

trifurcate. Having three branches.

tularemia. Bacterial disease contracted by humans through bite of tick harbored principally by hares and rabbits, but also by rodents and birds; may also be transmitted by direct contact with infected animal.

tympanic bulla. See **auditory bulla** and figure 9.

tympanum. Eardrum; thin membranous structure that receives external vibrations from air and transmits them to middle ear ossicles.

type specimen. Specimen (holotype) on which a species or subspecies name is based.

ulna. Outermost of two bones in lower part of front (pectoral) limb.

underfur. Short hairs of mammal that serve primarily as insulation.

ungulate. Hoofed mammals of extant orders Perissodactyla and Artiodactyla; term has no formal taxonomic status, but refers to broad group of herbivorous mammals.

unguligrade. Foot structure in which only the unguis (hoof) is in contact with ground.

unicuspid. Single-cusped tooth in shrews posterior to large, anteriormost tooth (an incisor) and anterior to fourth premolar in upper jaw and first true molar in lower jaw.

uropatagium. Web of skin between hind legs of bats, frequently enclosing tail; interfemoral membrane.

valvular. Capable of being closed, like a valve.

ventral. Pertaining to under or lower surface (venter).

vernacular name. Common (as opposed to scientific) name.

vernal. Seasonal term pertaining to spring.

vibrissae. Long, stiff hairs that serve primarily as tactile receptors.

volant. Able to fly.

vomer. Unpaired bone that forms septum between nasal passages.

vulva. External genitalia of female.

wool. Underhair with angora growth; serves primarily for insulation.

xeric. Pertaining to dry habitats or areas.

zygomatic arch. Arch of bone enclosing orbit and temporal fossa formed by jugal bone and parts of maxilla (malar process) and squamosal.

zygomatic breadth. See figure 7.

zygomatic plate. Bony plate, part of zygomatic process of maxilla, forming anterior face of zygomatic arch (see fig. 9).

REFERENCES

References

Allen, D. L. 1943. Michigan fox squirrel management. Game Div. Publ., Michigan Dept. Conserv., 100:1–404.

——. 1979. Wolves of Minong. . . . Houghton Mifflin Co., Boston, xxv + 499 pp.

Allen, J. M. 1952. Gray and fox squirrel management in Indiana. Indiana Dept. Conserv., Pittman-Robertson Bull., 1:1–112.

Andersen, D. C. 1978. Observations on reproduction, growth, and behavior of the northern pocket gopher (*Thomomys talpoides*). J. Mamm., 59:418–422.

Anderson, A. E. 1983. A critical review of literature on puma (*Felis concolor*). Spec. Rept. Colorado Div. Wildlife, 54:1–91.

Anderson, A. E., and O. C. Wallmo. 1984. Odocoileus hemionus. Mamm. Species, 219:1–9.

Anderson, E. 1984. Who's who in the Pleistocene: a mammalian bestiary. Pp. 40–89, *in* Quaternary extinctions: a prehistoric revolution (P.S. Martin and A. G. Klein, eds.). Univ. Arizona Press, x + 892 pp.

Anderson, S., and J. K. Jones, Jr. (eds.). 1984. Orders and families of Recent mammals of the world. John Wiley and Sons, New York, xiv + 686 pp.

Baird, D. D., R. M. Timm, and G. E. Nordquist. 1983. Reproduction in the arctic shrew, *Sorex arcticus*. J. Mamm., 64:298–301.

Baker, R. H. 1983. Michigan mammals. Michigan State Univ. Press, East Lansing, xxi + 642 pp.

Baker, V. R. 1983. Late-Pleistocene fluvial systems. Pp. 115–129, *in* Late-Quaternary environments of the United States: the late Pleistocene (H. E. Wright, Jr., and S. C. Porter, eds.). Univ. Minnesota Press, Minneapolis, 1:xiv + 1–407.

Banfield, A. W. F. 1962. A revison of the reindeer and caribou, genus *Rangifer*. Bull. Natl. Mus. Canada, 177:vi + 1–137.

——. 1974. The mammals of Canada. Univ. Toronto Press, Toronto, xxv + 438 pp.

Barbour, R. W., and W. H. Davis. 1969. Bats of America. Univ. Press Kentucky, Lexington, 286 pp.

——. 1974. Mammals of Kentucky. Univ. Kentucky Press, Lexington, xii + 322 pp.

Bear, G. H., and R. M. Hansen. 1966. Food habits, growth and reproduction of white-tailed jackrabbits in southern Colorado. Tech. Bull. Agric. Exp. Sta., Colorado State Univ., 90:viii + 1–59.

Beer, J. R. 1961. Hibernation in *Perognathus flavenscens*. J. Mamm., 42:103.

Bekoff, M. 1977. Canis latrans. Mamm. Species, 79:1–9.

325

Bergerud, A. T. 1978. Caribou. Pp. 83–101, *in* Big game of North America (J. L. Schmidt and D. L. Gilbert, eds.). Stackpole Books, Harrisburg, Pennsylvania, xv + 494 pp.

Birney, E. C. 1974. Twentieth century records of wolverine in Minnesota. Loon, 46:78–81.

Bittner, S. L., and O. J. Rongstad. 1982. Snowshoe hare and allies. Pp. 146–163, *in* Wild mammals of North America . . . (J. A. Chapman and G. A. Feldhamer, eds.). Johns Hopkins Univ. Press, Baltimore, xiii + 1147 pp.

Blair, W. F. 1940. A study of prairie deer-mouse populations in southern Michigan. Amer. Midland Nat., 24:273–305.

Bowles, J. B. 1975. Distribution and biogeography of mammals of Iowa. Spec. Publ. Mus., Texas Tech Univ., 9:1–184.

Brady, N. C. 1984. The nature and properties of soils. Ninth ed., Macmillan Publ. Co., New York, xvii + 750 pp.

Brand, C. J., L. B. Keith, and C. A. Fischer. 1976. Lynx responses to changing snowshoe hare densities in central Alberta. J. Wildlife Mgmt., 40:416–428.

Bryson, R. A., and F. K. Hare. 1974. Climates of North America. Pp. 1–47, *in* Climates of North America. World Surv. Climatology, Elsevier Sci. Publ. Co., New York, 11:x + 1–420.

Buckner, C. H. 1964. Metabolism and feeding behavior of three species of shrews. Canadian J. Zool., 42:259–279.

——. 1966. Populations and ecological relationships of shrews in tamarack bogs of southeastern Manitoba. J. Mamm., 47:181–194.

Burnett, C. D. 1983. Geographic and secondary sexual variation in the morphology of *Eptesicus fuscus*. Ann. Carnegie Mus., 52:139–162.

Burns, J. C., J. R. Choate, and E. G. Zimmermann. 1985. Systematic relationships of pocket gophers (genus *Geomys*) on the central Great Plains. J. Mamm., 66:102–118.

Burt, W. H. 1957. Mammals of the Great Lakes region. Univ. Michigan Press, Ann Arbor, xv + 246 pp.

Cameron, G. N., and S. R. Spencer. 1981. Sigmodon hispidus. Mamm. Species, 158:1–9.

Chapman, J. A., and G. A. Feldhamer. 1981. Sylvilagus aquaticus. Mamm. Species, 151:1–4.

Chapman, J. A., J. G. Hockman, and W. R. Edwards. 1982. Cottontails. Pp. 83–123, *in* Wild mammals of North America . . . (J. A. Chapman and G. A. Feldhamer, eds.). Johns Hopkins Univ. Press, Baltimore, xiii + 1147 pp.

Chapman, J. A., J. G. Hockman, and M. M. Ojeda C. 1980. Sylvilagus floridanus. Mamm. Species, 136:1–8.

Choate, J. R., and S. L. Williams. 1978. Biogeographic interpretation of variation within and among populations of the prairie vole, Microtus ochrogaster. Occas. Papers Mus., Texas Tech Univ., 49:1–25.

Coady, J. W. 1982. Moose. Pp. 902–922, *in* Wild mammals of North America . . . (J. A. Chapman and G. A. Feldhamer, eds.). Johns Hopkins Univ. Press, Baltimore, xiii + 1147 pp.

Colton, G. W. 1970. The Appalachian Basin—its depositional sequences and their geologic relationships. Pp. 5–47, *in* Studies of Appalachian geology: central and southern (G. W. Fisher, F. J. Pettijohn, J. C. Reed, Jr., and K. N. Weaver, eds.). John Wiley and Sons, New York, xx + 460 pp.

Conaway, C. H. 1952. Life history of the water shrew (Sorex palustris navigator). Amer. Midland Nat., 48:219–248.

Court, A. 1974. The climate of the conterminous United States. Pp. 193–343, *in* Climates of North America. World Surv. Climatology, Elsevier Sci. Publ. Co., New York, 11:x + 1–420.

Crabb, W. D. 1941. Food habits of the prairie spotted skunk in southeastern Iowa. J. Mamm., 22:349–364.

———. 1948. The ecology and management of the prairie spotted skunk in Iowa. Ecol. Monogr., 18:201–232.

Currier, M. J. P. 1983. Felis concolor. Mamm. Species, 200:1–7.

Curtis, J. T. 1959. The vegetation of Wisconsin. Univ. Wisconsin Press, Madison, xii + 657 pp.

Dapson, R. W. 1968. Reproduction and age structure in a population of short-tailed shrews, *Blarina brevicauda*. J. Mamm., 49:205–214.

Davis, M. B. 1983. Holocene vegetational history of the eastern United States. Pp. 166–181, *in* Late-Quaternary environments of the United States: the Holocene (H. E. Wright, Jr., ed.). Univ. Minnesota Press, Minneapolis, 2:xviii + 277.

Dawson, M. R., and L. Krishtalka. 1984. Fossil history of the families of Recent mammals. Pp. 11–57, *in* Orders and families of Recent mammals of the world (S. Anderson and J. K. Jones, Jr., eds.). John Wiley and Sons, New York, xiv + 686 pp.

de Vos, A. 1964. Range changes of mammals in the Great Lakes region. Amer. Midland Nat., 71:210–231.

de Vos, A., and D.I. Gillespie. 1960. A study of woodchucks on an Ontario farm. Canadian Field-Nat., 74:130–145.

Diersing, V. E. 1980. Systematics and evolution of the pygmy shrews (subgenus *Microsorex*) of North America. J. Mamm., 61:76–101.

Diersing, V. E., and D. F. Hoffmeister. 1981. Distribution and systematics of the masked shrew (*Sorex cinereus*) in Illinois. Nat. Hist. Misc., Chicago Acad. Sci., 213:1–11.

Dixon, K. R. 1982. Mountain lion. Pp. 711–727, *in* Wild mammals of North America . . . (J. A. Chapman and G. A. Feldhamer, eds.). Johns Hopkins Univ. Press, Baltimore, xiii + 1147 pp.

Dolan, P. G., and D. C. Carter. 1977. Glaucomys volans. Mamm. Species, 78:1–6.

Doutt, J. K., C. A. Heppenstall, and J. E. Guilday. 1966. Mammals of Pennsylvania. Pennsylvania Game Comm., Harrisburg, 273 pp.

Downhower, J. F., and E. R. Hall. 1966. The pocket gopher in Kansas. Misc. Publ. Mus. Nat. Hist., Univ. Kansas, 44:1–32.

Dunaway, P. B. 1968. Life history and populational aspects of the eastern harvest mouse. Amer. Midland Nat., 79:48–67.

Easterla, D. A. 1973. Ecology of the 18 species of Chiroptera at Big Bend National Park, Texas. Northwest Missouri St. Univ. Stud., 34(2–3):1–165.

Egoscue, H. J. 1979. Vulpes velox. Mamm. Species, 122:1–5.

Eisenberg, J. F. 1981. The mammalian radiations: an analysis of trends in evolution, adaptation, and behavior. Univ. Chicago Press, Chicago, xx + 610 pp.

Ellis, L. S., V. E. Diersing, and D. F. Hoffmeister. 1978. Taxonomic status of short-tailed shrews (*Blarina*) in Illinois. J. Mamm., 59:305–311.

Enders, R. K. 1952. Reproduction in the mink (*Mustela vison*). Proc. Amer. Philos. Soc., 96:691–755.

Engstrom, M. D., and J. R. Choate. 1979. Systematics of the northern grasshopper mouse (*Onychomys leucogaster*) on the central Great Plains. J. Mamm., 60:723–739.

Erickson, A. W., J. Nellor, and G. A. Petrides. 1964. The black bear in Michigan. Res. Bull. Agric. Exp. Sta., Michigan State Univ., 4:1–102.

Erlinge, S. 1974. Distribution, territoriality, and numbers of the weasel *Mustela nivalis* in relation to prey abundance. Oikos, 25:308–314.

——. 1975. Feeding habits of the weasel *Mustela nivalis* in relation to prey abundance. Oikos, 26:378–384.

Errington, P. L. 1943. An analysis of mink predation upon muskrats in northcentral United States. Res. Bull Agric. Exp. Sta., Iowa State Coll., 320:797–924.

——. 1954. The special responsiveness of minks to epizootics in muskrat populations. Ecol. Monogr., 24:377–393.

Feldmann, R. M., A. H. Coogan, and R. A. Heimlich. 1977. Southern Great Lakes. Kendall/Hunt Publ. Co., Dubuque, Iowa, xiv + 241 pp.

Fenton, M. B., and R. M. R. Barclay. 1980. Myotis lucifugus. Mamm. Species, 142:1–8.

Fitch, J. H., and K. A. Shump, Jr. 1979. Myotis keenii. Mamm. Species, 121:1–3.

Follmer, L. R. 1983. Sangamon and Wisconsin pedogenesis in the midwestern United States. Pp. 138–144, *in* Late-Quaternary environments of the United States: the late Pleistocene (H. E. Wright, Jr., and S. C. Porter, eds.). Univ. Minnesota Press, Minneapolis, 1:xiv + 1–407.

Forbes, R. B. 1966. Studies of the biology of Minnesotan chipmunks. Amer. Midland Nat., 76:290–308.

Forsyth, D. J. 1976. A field study of growth and development of nestling masked shrews (*Sorex cinereus*). J. Mamm., 57:708–721.

Foster, J. B. 1961. Life history of the phenacomys vole. J. Mamm., 42:181–198.

Foster, J. B., and R. L. Peterson. 1961. Age variation in Phenacomys. J. Mamm., 42:44–53.

Franzmann, A. W. 1981. Alces alces. Mamm. Species, 154:1–7.

French. T. W. 1980*a*. Sorex longirostris. Mamm. Species, 143:1–3.

——. 1980*b*. Natural history of the southeastern shrew, Sorex longirostris Bachman. Amer. Midland Nat., 104:13–31.

——. 1982. Ectoparasites of the southeastern shrew, *Sorex longirostris*, and the masked shrew, *S. cinereus*, in Virgo County, Indiana USA. J. Med. Entomol., 19:628–630.

Fritts, S. H., and L. D. Mech. 1981. Dynamics, movements, and feeding ecology of a newly protected wolf population in northwestern Minnesota. Wildlife Monogr., 80:1–79.

Fritzell, E. K., and K. J. Haroldson. 1982. Urocyon cinereoargenteus. Mamm. Species, 189:1–8.

Frye, J. C., H. B. Willman, and R. F. Black. 1965. Outline of glacial geology of Illinois and Wisconsin. Pp. 43–61, *in* The Quaternary of the United States (H. E. Wright, Jr., and D. G. Frey, eds.). Princeton Univ. Press, Princeton, New Jersey, x + 922 pp.

Fujita, M. S., and T. H. Kunz. 1984. Pipistrellus subflavus. Mamm. Species, 228:1–6.

Gaines, M. S., and R. K. Rose. 1976. Population dynamics of *Microtus ochrogaster* in eastern Kansas. Ecology, 57:1145–1161.

Gardner, A. L. 1973. The systematics of the genus Didelphis (Marsupialia: Didelphidae) in North and Middle America. Spec. Publ. Mus., Texas Tech Univ., 4:1–81.

——. 1982. Virginia opossum. Pp. 3–36, *in* Wild mammals of North America . . . (J. A. Chapman and G. A. Feldhamer, eds.). Johns Hopkins Univ. Press, Baltimore, xiii + 1147 pp.

George, S. B., J. R. Choate, and H. H. Genoways. 1981. Distribution and taxonomic status of *Blarina hylophaga* Elliot (Insectivora: Soricidae). Ann. Carnegie Mus., 50:493–513.

——. 1986. Blarina brevicauda. Mamm. Species, 261: 1–9.

George, S. B., H. H. Genoways, J. R. Choate, and R. J. Baker. 1982. Karyotypic relationships within the short-tailed shrews, genus *Blarina*. J. Mamm., 63:639–645.

Gingerich, P. D. 1984. Pleistocene extinctions in the context of origination and extinction equilibria in Cenozoic mammals. Pp. 211–222, *in* Quaternary extinctions: a prehistoric revolution (P. S. Martin and R. G. Klein, eds.). Univ. Arizona Press, Tucson, x + 892 pp.

Goehring, H. H. 1972. Twenty-year study of *Eptesicus fuscus* in Minnesota. J. Mamm., 53:201–207.

Goldthwait, R. P., A. Preimanais, J. L. Forsyth, P. F. Karrow, and G. W. White. 1965. Pleistocene deposits of the Erie lobe. Pp. 85–97, *in* The Quaternary of the United States (H. E. Wright, Jr., and D. G. Frey, eds.). Princeton Univ. Press, Princeton, New Jersey, x + 922 pp.

Gottschang, J. L. 1981. A guide to the mammals of Ohio. Ohio State Univ. Press, Columbus, xi + 176 pp.

Graham, R. W. 1976. Late Wisconsin mammalian faunas and environmental gradients of the eastern United States. Paleobiology, 2:343–350.

——. 1979. Paleoclimates and late Pleistocene faunal provinces in North America. Pp. 49–69, *in* Pre-Llano cultures of the Americas: paradoxes and possibilities (R. L. Humphrey and D. Stanford, eds.). The Anthropological Soc. Washington, ix + 150 pp.

Graham, R. W., and E. L. Lundelius, Jr. 1984. Coevolutionary disequilibrium and Pleistocene extinctions. Pp. 223–249, *in* Quaternary extinctions: a prehistoric revolution (P. S. Martin and R. G. Klein, eds.). Univ. Arizona Press, Tucson, x + 892 pp.

Grizzell, R. A. 1955. A study of the southern woodchuck, Marmota monax monax. Amer. Midland Nat., 53:257–293.

Guilday, J. E. 1984. Pleistocene extinction and environmental change: case study of the Appalachians. Pp. 250–258, *in* Quaternary extinctions: a prehistoric revolution (P. S. Martin and R. G. Klein, eds.). Univ. Arizona Press, Tucson, x + 892 pp.

Guthire, R. D. 1984. Mosaics, alleochemics, and nutrients: an ecological theory of late Pleistocene megafaunal extinctions. Pp. 259–298, *in* Quaternary extinctions: a prehistoric revolution (P. S. Martin and R. G. Klein, eds.). Univ. Arizona Press, Tucson, x + 892 pp.

Hall, E. R. 1951. American weasels. Univ. Kansas Publ., Mus. Nat. Hist., 4:1–466.

——. 1955. Handbook of mammals of Kansas. Misc. Publ. Mus. Nat. Hist., Univ. Kansas, 7:1–303.

——. 1981. The mammals of North America. Second ed., John Wiley and Sons, New York, 1:xv + 1–600 + *90* and 2:vi + 601–1181 + *90*.

——. 1984. Geographic variation among brown and grizzly bears (*Ursus arctos*) in North America. Spec. Publ. Mus. Nat. Hist., Univ. Kansas, 13:ii + 1–16.

Hallett, J. G. 1978. Parascalops breweri. Mamm. Species, 98:1–4.

Hamilton, W. J., Jr. 1934. The life history of the rufescent woodchuck. Ann. Carnegie Mus., 23:85–178.

Hamilton, W. J., Jr., and J. O. Whitaker, Jr. 1979. Mammals of the eastern United States. Cornell Univ. Press, Ithaca, New York, 346 pp.

Hazard, E. B. 1982. The mammals of Minnesota. Univ. Minnesota Press, Minneapolis, xii + 280 pp.

Heaney, L. R., and R. M. Timm. 1983. Relationships of pocket gophers of the genus *Geomys* from the central and northern Great Plains. Misc. Publ. Mus. Nat. Hist., Univ. Kansas, 74:1–59.

Heidt, G. A. 1970. The least weasel *Mustela nivalis* Linnaeus. Developmental biology in comparison with other North American *Mustela*. Publ. Mus. Michigan State Univ., Biol. Ser., 4:227–282.

Heidt, G. A., M. K. Petersen, and G. L. Kirkland, Jr. 1968. Mating behavior and development of least weasels (*Mustela nivalis*) in capitivity. J. Mamm., 49:413–419.

Hesselton, W. T., and R. M. Hesselton. 1982. White-tailed deer. Pp. 878–901, *in* Wild mammals of North America . . . (J. A. Chapman and G. A. Feldhamer, eds.). Johns Hopkins Univ. Press, Baltimore, xiii + 1147 pp.

Hibbard, C. W., D. E. Ray, D. E. Savage, D. W. Taylor, and J. E. Guilday. 1965. Quaternary mammals of North America. Pp. 509–525, *in* The Quaternary of the United States (H. E. Wright, Jr., and D. G. Frey, eds.). Princeton Univ. Press, Princeton, New Jersey, x + 922 pp.

Hibbard, E. A., and J. R. Beer. 1960. The plains pocket mouse in Minnesota. Flicker, 32:89–94.

Hoffmann, R. S., and J. K. Jones, Jr. 1970. Influence of late-glacial and post-glacial events on the distribution of Recent mammals of the Northern Great Plains. Pp. 355–396, *in* Pleistocene and Recent environments of the Central Great Plains (W. Dort, Jr., and J. K. Jones, Jr., eds.). Univ. Kansas Press, Lawrence, x + 433 pp.

Hoffmeister, D. F., and C. O. Mohr. 1957. Fieldbook of Illinois mammals. Manual Illinois Nat. Hist. Surv., 4:xi + 1–233.

Honacki, J. H., K. E. Kinman, and J. W. Koeppl (eds.). 1982. Mammal species of the world: a taxonomic and geographic reference. Allen Press, Lawrence, Kansas, x + 694 pp.

Hooper, E. T. 1942. An effect on the *Peromyscus maniculatus* rassenkreis of land utilization in Michigan. J. Mamm., 23:193–196.

Hough, J. L. 1958. Geology of the Great Lakes. Univ. Illinois Press, Urbana, xviii + 313 pp.

Humphrey, S. R., A. R. Richter, and J. B. Cope. 1977. Summer habitat and ecology of the endangered Indiana bat, *Myotis sodalis*. J. Mamm., 58:334–346.

Hutchinson, G. E. 1965. The ecological theater and the evolutionary play. Yale Univ. Press, New Haven, Connecticut, xiv + 139 pp.

Iverson, S. L., and B. N. Turner. 1972. Natural history of a Manitoba population of Franklin's ground squirrels. Canadian Field-Nat., 86:145–149.

Jackson, H. H. T. 1928. A taxonomic review of the American long-tailed shrews (genus *Sorex* and *Microsorex*). N. Amer. Fauna, 51:vi + 1–238.

———. 1961. Mammals of Wisconsin. Univ. Wisconsin Press, Madison, xiii + 504 pp.

James, T. R., and R. W. Seabloom. 1969*a*. Reproductive biology of the white-tailed jack rabbit in North Dakota. J. Wildlife Mgmt., 33:558–568.

———. 1969*b*. Aspects of growth in the white-tailed jackrabbit. Proc. North Dakota Acad. Sci., 23:7–14.

Jameson, E. W., Jr. 1947. Natural history of the prairie vole (mammalian genus *Microtus*). Univ. Kansas Publ., Mus. Nat. Hist., 1:125–151.

Jenkins, D. H., and I. H. Bartlett. 1959. Michigan whitetails. Michigan Dept. Conserv., Game Div., 80 pp.

Jenkins, S. H., and P. E. Busher. 1979. Castor canadensis. Mamm. Species, 120:1–8.

Jones, C. 1977. Plecotus rafinesquii. Mamm. Species, 69:1–4.

Jones, C., and J. Pagels. 1968. Notes on a population of *Pipistrellus subflavus* in southern Louisiana. J. Mamm., 49:134–139.

Jones, C. A., J. R. Choate, and H. H. Genoways. 1984. Phylogeny and paleobiogeography of short-tailed shrews (genus *Blarina*). Pp. 56–148, *in* Contributions in Quaternary vertebrate paleontology . . . (H. H. Genoways and M. R. Dawson, eds.). Spec. Publ. Carnegie Mus. Nat. Hist., 8:v + 1–538.

Jones, J. K., Jr. 1964. Distribution and taxonomy of mammals of Nebraska. Univ. Kansas Publ., Mus. Nat. Hist., 16:1–356.

Jones, J. K., Jr., D. M. Armstrong, and J. R. Choate. 1985. Guide to mammals of the plains states. Univ. Nebraska Press, Lincoln, xx + 371 pp.

Jones, J. K., Jr., D. M. Armstrong, R. S. Hoffmann, and C. Jones. 1983. Mammals of the northern Great Plains. Univ. Nebraska Press, Lincoln, xii + 379 pp.

Jones, J. K., Jr., D. C. Carter, H. H. Genoways, R. S. Hoffmann, D. W. Rice, and C. Jones. 1986. Revised checklist of North American mammals north of Mexico, 1986. Occas. Papers Mus., Texas Tech Univ., 107:1–22.

Judson, S., K. S. Deffeyes, and B. Hargraves. 1976. Physical geology. Prentice-Hall, Englewood Cliffs, New Jersey, xiii + 560 pp.

Kaye, S. V. 1961a. Movements of harvest mice tagged with gold-198. J. Mamm., 42:323–337.

——. 1961b. Laboratory life history of the eastern harvest mouse. Amer. Midland Nat., 66:439–451.

Keith, L. B., and L. A. Windberg. 1978. A demographic analysis of the snowshoe hare cycle. Wildlife Monogr., 58:1–70.

King, C. M. 1983. Mustela erminea. Mamm. Species, 195:1–8.

King, J. A. 1958. Maternal behavior and behavioral development in two subspecies of *Peromyscus maniculatus*. J. Mamm., 39:177–190.

—— (ed.). 1968. Biology of Peromyscus (Rodentia). Spec. Publ. Amer. Soc. Mamm., 2:xiii + 1–593.

Kirkland, G. L., Jr. 1977. The rock vole, *Microtus chrotorrhinus* (Miller) (Mammalia: Rodentia) in West Virginia. Ann. Carnegie Mus., 46:45–53.

——. 1981. Sorex dispar and Sorex gaspensis. Mamm. Species, 155:1–4.

Kirkland, G. L., Jr., and F. J. Jannett, Jr. 1982. Microtus chrotorrhinus. Mamm. Species, 180:1–5.

Kitchen, D. W., and B. W. O'Gara. 1982. Pronghorn. Pp. 960–971, *in* Wild mammals of North America . . . (J. A. Chapman and G. A. Feldhamer, eds.). Johns Hopkins Univ. Press, Baltimore, xiii + 1147 pp.

Klein, H. G. 1960. Ecological relationships of *Peromyscus leucopus noveboracensis* and *Peromyscus maniculatus gracilis* in central New York. Ecol. Monogr., 30:387–407.

Knox, J. C. 1983. Responses of river systems to Holocene climates. Pp. 26–41, *in* Late-Quaternary environments of the United States: the Holocene (H. E. Wright, Jr., ed.). Univ. Minnesota Press, Minneapolis, 2:xviii + 1–277.

Komarek, E. V., Sr. 1968. Lightning and lightning fires as ecological forces. Proc. Tall Timbers Fire Ecol. Conf., 8:169–197.

Küchler, A. W. 1964. Manual to accompany the map potential natural vegetation of the conterminous United States. Spec. Publ. Amer. Geogr. Soc., 36:vi + 1–40 + *116* + map.

Kunz, T. H. 1982. Lasionycteris noctivagans. Mamm. Species, 172:1–5.

Kurtén, B. 1972. The age of mammals. Columbia Univ. Press, New York, 250 pp.

Kurtén, B., and E. Anderson. 1980. Pleistocene mammals of North America. Columbia Univ. Press, New York, xviii + 442 pp.

Lackey, J. A., D. G. Huckaby, and B. G. Ormiston, 1985. Peromyscus leucopus. Mamm. Species, 247:1–10.

Lampe, R. P., J. B. Bowles, and R. Spengler. 1982. First state record of Richardson's ground squirrel in Iowa. Prairie Nat., 13:94–96.

LaVal, R. K. 1970. Intraspecific relationships of bats of the species *Myotis austroriparius*. J. Mamm., 51:542–552.

Layne, J. N. 1954. The biology of the red squirrel, *Tamiasciurus hudsonicus loquax* (Bangs) in central New York. Ecol. Monogr., 24:227–267.

——. 1959. Growth and development of the eastern harvest mouse, *Reithrodontomys humulis*. Bull. Florida State Mus., 4:61–82.

Lillegraven, J. A., Z. Kielan-Jaworowska, and W. A. Clemens (eds.). 1979. Mesozoic mammals: the first two-thirds of mammalian history. Univ. California Press, Berkeley, x + 311 pp.

Lindsey, A. A., W. B. Crankshaw, and S. A. Qadir. 1965. Soil relations and distribution map of the vegetation of presettlement Indiana. Bot. Gazette, 126:155–163.

Lindzey, F. G. 1982. Badger. Pp. 653–663, in Wild mammals of North America . . . (J. A. Chapman and G. A. Feldhamer, eds.). Johns Hopkins Univ. Press, Baltimore, xiii + 1147 pp.

Linscombe, G. L., N. Kinler, and R. J. Aulerich. 1982. Mink. Pp. 629–643, in Wild mammals of North America . . . (J. A. Chapman and G. A. Feldhamer, eds.). Johns Hopkins Univ. Press, Baltimore, xiii + 1147 pp.

Linzey, A. V. 1983. Synaptomys cooperi. Mamm. Species, 210:1–5.

Linzey, D. W., and R. L. Packard. 1977. Ochrotomys nuttalli. Mamm. Species, 75:1–6.

Long, C. A. 1973. Taxidea taxus. Mamm. Species, 26:1–4.

———. 1974. Microsorex hoyi and Microsorex thompsoni. Mamm. Species, 33:1–4.

Longley, W. H. 1963. Minnesota gray and fox squirrels. Amer. Midland Nat., 69:82–98.

Lotze, J. H., and S. Anderson. 1979. Procyon lotor. Mamm. Species, 119:1–8.

Lowery, G. H., Jr. 1974. The mammals of Louisiana and its adjacent waters. Louisiana State Univ. Press, Baton Rouge, xxii + 565 pp.

Lundelius, E. L., Jr., et al. 1983. Terrestrial vertebrate faunas. Pp. 311–353, in Late-Quaternary environments of the United States: the late Pleistocene (H. E. Wright, Jr., and S. C. Porter, eds.). Univ. Minnesota Press, Minneapolis, 1:xiv + 1–407.

Manville, R. H. 1949. A study of small mammal populations in southern Michigan. Misc. Publ. Mus. Zool., Univ. Michigan, 73:1–93.

Marshall, L. G. 1984. Monotremes and marsupials. Pp. 59–115, in Orders and families of Recent mammals of the world (S. Anderson and J. K. Jones, Jr., eds.). John Wiley and Sons, New York, xii + 686 pp.

Martin, P. S., and R. G. Klein (eds.). 1984. Quaternary extinctions: a prehistoric revolution. Univ. Arizona Press, x + 892 pp.

McCarty, R. 1978. Onychomys leucogaster. Mamm. Species, 87:1–6.

McCord, C. M., and J. E. Cardoza. 1982. Bobcat and lynx. Pp. 728–766, in Wild mammals of North America . . . (J. A. Chapman and G. A. Feldhamer, eds.). Johns Hopkins Univ. Press, Baltimore, xiii + 1147 pp.

McManus, J. J. 1974. Didelphis virginiana. Mamm. Species, 40:1–6.

Meagher, M. 1986. Bison bison. Mamm. Species, 266:1–8.

Mech, L. D. 1974. Canis lupus. Mamm. Species, 37:1–6.

Mech, L. D., and M. E. Nelson. 1982. Reoccurrence of caribou in Minnesota. Amer. Midland Nat., 108:206–208.

Mech, L. D., and L. L. Rogers. 1977. Status, distribution and movements of martens in northeastern Minnesota. Res. Paper Northcentral Forest Exp. Sta., U.S. Dept. Agric., NC-143:1–7.

Meckel, L. D. 1970. Paleozoic alluvial deposition in the central Appalachians: a summary. Pp. 49–67, in Studies of Appalachian geology: central and southern (G. W. Fisher, F. J. Pettijohn, J. C. Reed, Jr., and K. N. Weaver, eds.). John Wiley and Sons, New York, xx + 460 pp.

Merritt, J. F. 1981. Clethrionomys gapperi. Mamm. Species, 146:1–9.

Metzgar, L. H. 1973. Home range shape and activity in Peromyscus leucopus. J. Mamm., 54:383–390.

Michener, G. R., and J. W. Koeppel, 1985. Spermophilus richardsonii, Mamm. Species, 243:1–8.

Mickelson, D. M., L. Clayton, D. S. Fullerton, and H. W. Borns, Jr. 1983. The late Wisconsin glacial record of the Laurentide ice sheet in the United States. Pp. 3–37, *in* Late-Quaternary environments of the United States: the late Pleistocene (H. E. Wright, Jr., and S. C. Porter, eds.). Univ. Minnesota Press, Minneapolis, 1:xiv + 1–407.

Miller, F. L. 1982. Caribou. Pp. 923–959, *in* Wild mammals of North America . . . (J. A. Chapman and G. A. Feldhamer, eds.). Johns Hopkins Univ. Press, Baltimore, xiii + 1147 pp.

Mohr, C. E. 1933. Pennsylvania bats of the genus Myotis. Proc. Pennsylvania Acad. Sci., 7:39–43.

——. 1936. Notes on the least bat, *Myotis subulatus leibii*. Proc. Pennsylvania Acad. Sci., 10:62–65.

Moncrief, N. D., J. R. Choate, and H. H. Genoways. 1982. Morphometric and geographic relationships of short-tailed shrews (genus *Blarina*) in Kansas, Iowa, and Missouri. Ann. Carnegie Mus., 51:157–180.

Moore, J. C. 1957. The natural history of the fox squirrel, *Sciurus niger shermani*. Bull. Amer. Mus. Nat. Hist., 113:1–72.

Mumford, R. E. 1969. Distribution of the mammals of Indiana. Monogr. Indiana Acad. Sci., 1:vii + 1–114.

Mumford, R. E., and J. O. Whitaker, Jr. 1982. Mammals of Indiana. Indiana Univ. Press, Bloomington, xvii + 537 pp.

Murie, J. O. 1973. Population characteristics and phenology of a Franklin ground squirrel (Spermophilus franklinii) colony in Alberta, Canada. Amer. Midland Nat., 90:334–340.

Murie, J. O., and G. R. Michener (eds.). 1984. The biology of ground-dwelling squirrels. Univ. Nebraska Press, Lincoln, xvi + 459 pp.

Murie, O. J. 1951. The elk of North America. Stackpole Books, Harrisburg, Pennsylvania, and Wildlife Mgmt. Inst., Washington, D.C., (10) + 376 pp.

Noble, A. G. 1975. Ohio's physical landscape. Bull. Ohio Div. Geol. Surv., 65:27–53.

Noble, A. G., and A. J. Korsok (eds.). 1975. Ohio–an American heartland. Bull. Ohio Div. Geol. Surv., 65:xiv + 1–230.

Nowak, R. M., and J. L. Paradiso. 1983. Walker's mammals of the world . . . Johns Hopkins Univ. Press, Baltimore, 1:xliv + 1–568 and 2:x + 569–1362.

O'Gara, B. W. 1978. Antilocapra americana. Mamm. Species, 90:1–7.

Ojakangas, B. W., and C. L. Matsch. 1982. Minnesota's geology. Univ. Minnesota Press, Minneapolis, x + 255 pp.

Owen, J. G. 1984. Sorex fumeus. Mamm. Species, 215:1–8.

Packard, R. L. 1956. The tree squirrels of Kansas. Misc. Publ. Mus. Nat. Hist., Univ. Kansas, 11:1–67.

——. 1969. Taxonomic review of the golden mouse, Ochrotomys nuttallii. Misc. Publ. Mus. Nat. Hist., Univ. Kansas, 51:373–406.

Paradiso, J. L., and R. M. Nowak. 1972. Canis rufus. Mamm. Species, 22:1–4.

Pearson, O. P. 1944. Reproduction in the shrew (*Blarina brevicauda* Say). Amer. J. Anat. 75:39–93.

——. 1945. Longevity of the short-tailed shrew. Amer. Midland Nat., 34:531–546.

Peek, J. M. 1982. Elk. Pp. 851–861, *in* Wild mammals of North America . . . (J. A. Chapman and G. A. Feldhamer, eds.). Johns Hopkins Univ. Press, Baltimore, xiii + 1147 pp.

Peek, J. M., D. L. Urich, and R. J. Mackie. 1976. Moose habitat selection and relationships to forest management in northeastern Minnesota. Wildlife Monogr., 48:1–65.

Pelton, M. R. 1982. Black bear. Pp. 504–514, *in* Wild mammals of North America . . . (J. A. Chapman and G. A. Feldhamer, eds.). Johns Hopkins Univ. Press, Baltimore, xiii + 1147 pp.

Petersen, K. E., and T. L. Yates. 1980. Condylura cristata. Mamm. Species, 129:1-4.

Peterson, R. L. 1966. The mammals of eastern Canada. Oxford Univ. Press, Toronto, xxxii + 465 pp.

Pewe, T. L. 1983. The periglacial environment in North America during Wisconsin time. Pp. 157-189, in Late-Quaternary environments of the United States: the late Pleistocene (H. E. Wright, Jr., and S. C. Porter, eds.). Univ. Minnesota Press, Minneapolis, 1:xiv + 1-407.

Pils, C. M., and M. A. Martin. 1978. Population dynamics, predator-prey relationships and management of the red fox in Wisconsin. Tech. Bull. Wisconsin Dept. Nat. Res., 105:1-56.

Platt, W. J. 1976. The social organization and territoriality of short-tailed shrew (*Blarina brevicauda*) populations in old-field habitats. Anim. Behav., 24:305-318.

Powell, R. A. 1981. Martes pennanti. Mamm. Species, 156:1-6.

——. 1982. The fisher: life history, ecology, and behavior. Univ. Minnesota Press, Minneapolis, xvi + 219 pp.

Reich, L. M. 1981. Microtus pennsylvanicus. Mamm. Species, 159:1-8.

Reichard, T. A. 1976. Spring food habits and feeding behavior of fox squirrels and red squirrels. Amer. Midland Nat., 92:443-450.

Reid, V. H. 1973. Population biology of the northern pocket gopher. Bull. Agric. Exp. Sta., Colorado State Univ., 554-S:21-41.

Reynolds, H. W., R. D. Glaholt, and A. W. L. Hawley. 1982. Bison. Pp. 972-1007, in Wild mammals of North America . . . (J. A. Chapman and G. A. Feldhamer, eds.). Johns Hopkins Univ. Press, Baltimore, xiii + 1147 pp.

Risser, P. G., E. C. Birney, H. D. Blocker, S. W. May, W. J. Parton, and J. A. Wiens. 1981. The true prairie ecosystem. Hutchinson Ross Publ. Co., Stroudsburg, Pennsylvania, US/IBP Synthesis Ser., 16:xiv + 1-557.

Roe, F. G. 1970. The North American buffalo, a critical study of the species in its wild state. Univ. Toronto Press, xi + 991 pp.

Ruhe, R. V. 1969. Quaternary landscapes in Iowa. Iowa State Univ. Press, Ames, xii + 255 pp.

——. 1983a. Depositional environment of late Wisconsin loess in the midcontinental United States. Pp. 130-137, in Late-Quaternary environments of the United States: the late Pleistocene (H. E. Wright, Jr., and S. C. Porter, eds.). Univ. Minnesota Press, Minneapolis, 1:xiv + 1-407.

——. 1983b. Aspects of Holocene pedology in the United States. Pp. 12-25 in Late-Quaternary environments of the United States: the Holocene (H. E. Wright, Jr., ed.). Univ. Minnesota Press, Minneapolis, 2:xviii + 1-277.

Samuel, D. E., and B. B. Nelson. 1982. Foxes. Pp. 475-490, in Wild mammals of North America . . . (J. A. Chapman and G. A. Feldhamer, eds.). Johns Hopkins Univ. Press, Baltimore, xiii + 1147 pp.

Schmidly, D. J. 1983. Texas mammals east of the Balcones Fault Zone. Texas A & M Univ. Press, College Station, xviii + 400 pp.

Schwartz, C. W., and E. R. Schwartz. 1981. The wild mammals of Missouri. Univ. Missouri Press and Missouri Dept. Conserv., rev. ed., viii + 356 pp.

Semken, H. A., Jr. 1983. Holocene mammalian biogeography and climatic change in the eastern and central United States. Pp. 182-207, in Late-Quaternary environments of the United States: the Holocene (H. E. Wright, Jr., ed.). Univ. Minnesota Press, Minneapolis, 2:xviii + 1-277.

Sheppard, D. H. 1968. Seasonal changes in body and adrenal weights of chipmunks (*Eutamias*). J. Mamm., 49:463–474.

——. 1972. Home ranges of chipmunks (*Eutamias*) in Alberta. J. Mamm., 53:379–380.

Shump, K. A., Jr., and A. U. Shump. 1982a. Lasiurus borealis. Mamm. Species, 183:1–6.

——. 1982b. Lasiurus cinereus. Mamm. Species, 185:1–5.

Sly, G. R. 1976. Small mammal succession on strip-mined land in Virgo County, Indiana. Amer. Midland Nat., 95:257–267.

Smith, C. C. 1968. The adaptive nature of social organization in the genus of tree squirrels *Tamiasciurus*. Ecol. Monogr., 38:31–63.

——. 1970. The coevolution of pine squirrels (*Tamiasciurus*) and conifers. Ecol. Monogr., 40:349–371.

——. 1978. Structure and function of the vocalizations of tree squirrels (*Tamiasciurus*). J. Mamm., 59:793–808.

Smith, P. W. 1957. An analysis of post-Wisconsin biogeography of the prairie peninsula region based on distributional phenomena among terrestrial vertebrate populations. Ecology, 38:205–218.

Smolen, M. J. 1981. Microtus pinetorum. Mamm. Species, 147:1–7.

Snyder, D. P. 1982. Tamias striatus. Mamm. Species, 168:1–8.

Sorenson, M. W. 1962. Some aspects of water shrew behavior. Amer. Midland Nat., 68:445–462.

Sowls, L. K. 1948. The Franklin ground squirrel, *Citellus franklinii* (Sabine), and its relationship to nesting ducks. J. Mamm., 29:113–137.

Stoltman, J. B., and D. A. Baerreis. 1983. The evolution of human ecosystems in the eastern United States. Pp. 252–268, *in* Late-Quaternary environments of the United States: the Holocene (H. E. Wright, Jr., ed.). Univ. Minnesota Press, Minneapolis, 2:xviii + 1–277.

Storm, G. L., et al. 1976. Morphology, reproduction, dispersal, and mortality of midwestern red fox populations. Wildlife Monogr., 49:1–82.

Streubel, D. P., and J. P. Fitzgerald. 1978. Spermophilus spilosoma. Mamm. Species, 101:1–4.

Strickland, M. A., C. W. Douglas, M. Novak, and N. P. Hunzinger. 1982. Marten. Pp 599–612, *in* Wild mammals of North America . . . (J. A. Chapman and G. A. Feldhamer, eds.). Johns Hopkins Univ. Press, Baltimore, xiii + 1147 pp.

Svendsen, G. E. 1982. Weasels. Pp. 613–628, *in* Wild mammals of North America . . . (J. A. Chapman and G. A. Feldhamer, eds.). Johns Hopkins Univ. Press, Baltimore, xiii + 1147 pp.

Swanson, G., T. Surber, and T. S. Roberts. 1945. The mammals of Minnesota. Tech. Bull. Minnesota Dept. Conserv., 2:1–108.

Taylor, W. P. (ed.). 1956. The deer of North America. . . . Stackpole Books, Harrisburg, Pennsylvania, and Wildlife Mgmt. Inst., Washington, D. C., xvii + 922 pp.

Thomas, J. A., and E. C. Birney. 1979. Parental care and mating system of the prairie vole, *Microtus ochrogaster*. Behav. Ecol. Sociobiol., 5:171–186.

Thomson, C. E. 1982. Myotis sodalis. Mamm. Species, 163:1–5.

Timm, R. M. 1975. Distribution, natural history, and parasites of mammals of Cook County, Minnesota. Occas. Papers Bell Mus. Nat. Hist., Univ. Minnesota, 14:1–56.

Timm, R. M., L. R. Heaney, and D. D. Baird. 1977. Natural History of rock voles (*Microtus chrotorrhinus*) in Minnesota. Canadian Field-Nat., 91:177–181.

Toweill, D. E., and J. E. Tabor. 1982. River otter. Pp. 688–703, *in* Wild mammals of North America . . . (J. A. Chapman and G. A. Feldhamer, eds.). Johns Hopkins Univ. Press, Baltimore, xiii + 1147 pp.

Transeau, E. N. 1935. The prairie peninsula. Ecology, 16:423–437.

Tryon, C. A., Jr. 1947. The biology of the pocket gopher (*Thomomys talpoides*) in Montana. Tech. Bull. Agric. Exp. Sta., Montana State Coll., 448:1–30.

Tumlison, R. 1987. Felis lynx. Mamm. Species, 269:1–8.

Turner, B. N., S. L. Iverson, and K. L. Severson. 1976. Postnatal growth and development of captive Franklin's ground squirrels (Spermophilus franklinii). Amer. Midland Nat., 95:93–102.

Tuttle, M. D. 1975. Population ecology of the gray bat (*Myotis grisescens*): factors influencing early growth and development. Occas. Papers Mus. Nat. Hist., Univ. Kansas, 36:1–24.

——. 1976a. Population ecology of the gray bat (*Myotis grisescens*): philopatry, timing and patterns of movement, weight loss during migration, and seasonal adaptive strategies. Occas. Papers Mus. Nat. Hist., Univ. Kansas, 54:1–38.

——. 1976b. Population ecology of the gray bat (*Myotis grisescens*): factors influencing growth and survival of newly volant young. Ecology, 57:587–595.

——. 1979. Status, causes of decline, and management of endangered gray bats. J. Wildlife Mgmt., 43:1–17.

Tuttle, M. D., and D. E. Stevenson. 1977. An analysis of migration as a mortality factor in the gray bat based on public recoveries of banded bats. Amer. Midland Nat., 97:235–240.

Uhlig, H. G. 1955. The gray squirrel, its life history, ecology and population characteristics in West Virginia. West Virginia Conserv. Comm., P.-R. Proj. Rept., 31-R:1–175.

Van Gelder, R. G. 1959. A taxonomic revision of the spotted skunks (genus *Spilogale*). Bull Amer. Mus. Nat. Hist., 117:229–392.

van Zyll de Jong, C. G. 1972. A systematic review of the Nearctic and Neotropical river otters (genus *Lutra*, Mustelidae, Carnivora). Life Sci. Contrib., Royal Ontario Mus., 80:1–104.

——. 1976. A comparison between woodland and tundra forms of the common shrew (*Sorex cinereus*). Canadian J. Zool., 54:963–973.

——. 1979. Distribution and systematic relationships of long-eared *Myotis* in western Canada. Canadian J. Zool., 57:987–994.

——. 1980. Systematic relationships of woodland and prairie forms of the common shrew, *Sorex cinereus cinereus*, Kerr and *S. c. haydeni* Baird, in the Canadian prairie provinces. J. Mamm., 61:66–75.

——. 1983. Handbook of Canadian mammals. 1. Marsupials and insectivores. Natl. Mus. Canada, Ottawa, 210 pp.

——. 1985. Handbook of Canadian mammals. 2. Bats. Natl. Mus. Canada, Ottawa, 212 pp.

Vaughan, T. A. 1962. Reproduction in the plains pocket gopher in Colorado. J. Mamm., 41:1–13.

——. 1986. Mammalogy. Third ed., Saunders College Publ., Philadelphia, vii + 576 pp.

Wade-Smith, J., and B. J. Verts. 1982. Mephitis mephitis. Mamm. Species, 173:1–7.

Wallmo, O. C. (ed.). 1981. Mule and black-tailed deer of North America. Wildlife Mgmt. Inst. and Univ. Nebraska Press, Lincoln, xvii + 605 pp.

Watkins, L. C. 1972. Nycticeius humeralis. Mamm. Species, 23:1–4.

Watkins, L. C., and K. A. Shump, Jr. 1981. Behavior of the evening bat Nycticeius humeralis at a nursery roost. Amer. Midland Nat., 105:258–268.

Watts, W. A. 1983. Vegetational history of the eastern United States 25,000 to 10,000 years ago. Pp. 294–310, *in* Late-Quaternary environments of the United States: the late Pleistocene (H. E. Wright, Jr., and S. C. Porter, eds.). Univ. Minnesota Press, Minneapolis, 1:xiv + 1–407.

Wayne, W. J., and J. H. Zumberge. 1965. Pleistocene geology of Indiana and Michigan. Pp.

63–84, *in* The Quaternary of the United States (H. E. Wright, Jr., and D. G. Frey, eds.). Princeton Univ. Press, Princeton, New Jersey, x + 922 pp.

Webb, S. D. 1984. Ten million years of mammal extinctions in North America. Pp. 189–210, *in* Quaternary extinctions: a prehistoric revolution (P. S. Martin and R. G. Klein, eds.). Univ. Arizona Press, x + 892 pp.

Webb, T., III, E. J. Cushing, and H. E. Wright, Jr. 1983. Holocene changes in the vegetation of the midwest. Pp. 142–165, *in* Late-Quaternary environments of the United States: the Holocene (H. E. Wright, Jr., ed.). Univ. Minnesota Press, Minneapolis, 2:xviii + 1–277.

Webster, W. D., and J. K. Jones, Jr. 1982. Reithrodontomys megalotis. Mamm. Species, 167:1–5.

Weigl, P. D. 1978. Resource overlap, interspecific interactions, and the distribution of the flying squirrels, Glaucomys volans and G. sabrinus. Amer. Midland Nat., 100:83–96.

Wells-Gosling, N., and L. R. Heaney. 1984. Glaucomys sabrinus. Mamm. Species, 229:1–8.

West, F. H. 1983. The antiquity of man in America. Pp. 364–382, *in* Late-Quaternary environments of the United States: the late Pleistocene (H. E. Wright, Jr., and S. C. Porter, eds.). Univ. Minnesota Press, Minneapolis, 1:xiv + 1–407.

Whitaker, J. O., Jr. 1972. Zapus hudsonius. Mamm. Species, 11:1–7.

——. 1974. Cryptotis parva. Mamm. Species, 43:1–8.

Whitaker, J. O., Jr., and R. E. Wrigley. 1972. Napaeozapus insignis. Mamm. Species, 14:1–6.

Wiley, R. W. 1980. Neotoma floridana. Mamm. Species, 139:1–7.

Williams, D. F. 1978. Karyological affinities of the species groups of silky pocket mice (Rodentia, Heteromyidae). J. Mamm., 59:599–612.

Williams, D. F., and H. H. Genoways. 1979. A systematic review of the olive-backed pocket mouse, *Perognathus fasciatus* (Rodentia, Heteromyidae). Ann. Carnegie Mus. Nat. Hist., 48:73–102.

Willner, G. R., G. A. Feldhamer, E. E. Zucker, and J. A. Chapman. 1980. Ondatra zibethicus. Mamm. Species, 141:1–8.

Wilson, D. E. 1982. Wolverine. Pp. 644–652, *in* Wild mammals of North America . . . (J. A. Chapman and G. A. Feldhamer, eds.). Johns Hopkins Univ. Press, Baltimore, xiii + 1147 pp.

Wolfe, J. L. 1982. Oryzomys palustris. Mamm. Species, 176:1–5.

Wolfe, J. L., and A. V. Linzey. 1977. Peromyscus gossypinus. Mamm. Species, 70:1–5.

Woods, C. A. 1973. Erethizon dorsatum. Mamm. Species, 29:1–6.

Woolf, A., and J. D. Harder. 1979. Population dynamics of a captive white-tailed deer herd with emphasis on reproduction and mortality. Wildlife Monogr., 67:1–53.

Wright, H. E., Jr., and R. V. Ruhe. 1965. Glaciation of Minnesota and Iowa. Pp. 29–41, *in* The Quaternary of the United States (H. E. Wright, Jr., and D. G. Frey, eds.). Princeton Univ. Press, Princeton, New Jersey, x + 922 pp.

Wrigley, R. E. 1972. Systematics and biology of the woodland jumping mouse, *Napaeozapus insignis*. Illinois Biol. Monogr., 47:1–117.

Wrigley, R. E., and R. W. Nero. 1982. Manitoba's big cat. Manitoba Mus. Man Nat. Winnipeg, 68 pp.

Wrigley, R. E., J. E. DuBois, and H. W. R. Copland. 1979. Habitat, abundance, and distribution of six species of shrews in Manitoba. J. Mamm., 60:505–520.

Yates, T. L., and D. J. Schmidly. 1978. Scalopus aquaticus. Mamm. Species, 105:1–4.

Young, S. P. 1958. The bobcat of North America, its history, life habits, economic status, and control, with list of currently recognized subspecies. Stackpole Books, Harrisburg, Pennsylvania, and Wildlife Mgmt. Inst., Washington, D.C., xi + 193 pp.

Young, S. P., and E. A. Goldman. 1944. The wolves of North America. Amer. Wildlife Inst., Washington, D.C., xx + 636 pp.

Youngman, P. H. 1975. Mammals of the Yukon Territory. Publ. Zool. Natl. Mus. Canada, 10:1-191.

INDEX TO SCIENTIFIC AND
VERNACULAR NAMES

Index to Scientific
and Vernacular Names

J. Knox Jones, Jr., is Horn Professor of Biological Sciences and Museum Science and Curator in The Museum of Texas Tech University. *Guide to Mammals of the Plains States* and *Mammals of the Northern Great Plains* are two of his recently published works.

Elmer C. Birney is Professor of Ecology and Behavioral Biology at the University of Minnesota and Curator of Mammals at the University's Bell Museum of Natural History.